SECRETS OF UECHI RYU KARATE
and the
MYSTERIES OF OKINAWA

by

ALAN DOLLAR

上地流空手道

SECRETS OF UECHI RYU KARATE

and the

MYSTERIES OF OKINAWA

by

ALAN DOLLAR

2nd printing 2001

Printed in the United States of America
Library of Congress Catalog Number: 96-96179

ISBN: 0-9651671-1-9

Cherokee Publishing
Antioch, California

DEDICATION

I **DEDICATE THIS EFFORT** to the two people who have particularly influenced my life: my first Uechi ryu Sensei, Master Seiyu Shinjo and my remarkably supportive wife, Alice Marie Dollar, teacher of life.

ACKNOWLEDGMENT

I would like to acknowledge and thank the following people for their enormous help in translating the Japanese and Okinawan texts consulted for this book:

Tsutomu Shikiya
Yoshiaki Izena
Seisho Tanahara
Kiyohide Shinjo
Satoshi Kinjo
Tsucasa Higa
Shinyu Gushi
Ryusen Tomoyose
Junko Igei
Misako Haraguchi
Emiko Maeda

My deepest thanks go to editors Robert Davidson and Alice Dollar and especially, computer wizard Chris Fannuchi.

Finally, thank you Sensei Shinjo for driving me all over Japan, Okinawa and Ie-jima Island in pursuit of research.

DISCLAIMER

This book contains depictions and descriptions of karate techniques and related moves. It is not intended to teach karate. It is written as a historical and technical reference.

Anyone who desires karate training should first seek the advice of a physician. Then seek instruction in a qualified, reputable school of martial arts.

The author takes no responsibility for any injury or damage that may occur by anyone using the contents of this book in a negative or harmful way, either to themselves or others.

The author recognizes there may be errors, to some degree, due to the difficulty of researching Okinawa's past and variant current opinions about its history.

No disrespect to anyone, past or present, is intended by any portion of this publication. The purpose of this presentation is to perpetuate the history, culture and karate of the unique and magnificent Okinawan people.

FOREWORD

I am thankful to be one of the first people to read this superlative publication. With painstaking effort Alan Dollar has organized a wealth of information on Uechi Ryu Karate Do for the benefit of those who study Okinawan Karate. He has separated fact from fiction and truly identifies the essence of this historical style.

Sensei Dollar is just the person to create this work. His early years of karate study began in 1974 while serving with the U.S. Marines in Okinawa. He is one of the only Americans who completed his kyu (colored belt) ranks while living in Okinawa. Alan lived in Okinawa twice and returned for all black belt tests and more. He has developed enormous respect for the culture and relentlessly pursues his training the hard way; Okinawan style.

After leaving Okinawa, Sensei Dollar has diligently shared what he learned there and has touched the lives of literally thousands of devoted Karateka. He has organized traditional tournaments of the highest standard since 1983, provides training seminars with many of Okinawa's top Uechi Ryu Masters, and consistently operates a successful traditional dojo with a membership of four hundred students. How many karate students, instructors, or masters can say the same?

I respect Sensei Alan Dollar for what he has achieved for himself, for what he has shared with his students and friends and now for what he has created to document the Uechi Ryu karate style for future generations. He is quick to acknowledge the Okinawan teachers and people for perpetuating true Okinawan Karate Do through hard training, humility and quiet determination. He has always remembered the importance of being a respectful student.

I am honored to write the forward to this impressive book. Chapters about all Okinawan karate and kobudo styles and the history and culture of the people are something for all of us who study traditional martial arts have been searching for. It should motivate us to study our style with greater depth, understanding and appreciation.

Ric Martin
Okinawan Karate World Champion

Contents

HISTORICAL

I **WHAT IS KARATE THE EVOLUTION and CHRONOLOGY of OKINAWAN FIGHTING ARTS 1**
CHINA'S INFLUENCE ON OKINAWAN KARATE 5
OKINAWA TE 9
MASTERS OF OKINAWAN KARATE 10
SHURI TE MASTERS LINEAGE... 12
SHURI TE 13
NAHA TE MASTERS LINEAGE 22
NAHA TE 23
CHOJUN MIYAGI'S SENIOR STUDENTS 28
UECHI RYU MASTERS LINEAGE 30
UECHI RYU KARATE DO 31
TOMARI TE MASTERS LINEAGE 34
TOMARI TE 34
RYUEI RYU KARATE 36
TRADITIONAL OKINAWAN KARATE DO KATAS................ 37
OKINAWAN KARATE IS INTRODUCED TO JAPAN 39
KARATE BECOMES INTERNATIONAL 43

II **UECHI FAMILY KARATE HISTORY 47**
ADVENTURES IN CHINA 57
KANBUN UECHI RETURNS TO OKINAWA 67
THE WAKAYAMA PERIOD 69
PANGAINOON GOES PUBLIC 75
THE TEBIRA DOJO BECOMES A FORMAL ORGANIZATION 78
PANGAINOON SPREADS TO OSAKA AND OKINAWA 79
KANBUN UECHI LEAVES JAPAN 87
CONDITIONS ON OKINAWA AFTER THE WAR 87
THE CREST OF THE UECHI RYU KARATE-DO ASSOCIATION . 90
THE STRONG FIST GROUP OF SEIYU SHINJO............... 107

III SHINJO FAMILY KARATE HISTORY 115
WAKAYAMA PERIOD 120
RETURN TO OKINAWA AND IE-JIMA ISLAND 124
THE KADENA ERA OF UECHI RYU KARATE 129
TOURNAMENT HISTORY 131
SHINYU GUSHI 157
TSUTOMU NAKAHODO 158
SEIKI IREI 164
MINORU MIYAGI 168
YOSHITSUNE SENAGA 170
STRUCTURE OF THE UECHI RYU KENYUKAI ASSOCIATION
SEIYU SHINJO (1929-1981) 171
TAKEMEI TAKAYASU 172
SEIKO TOYAMA 175
CHOTOKU KYAN— A KADENA VILLAGE KARATE MASTER 180

IV KOBUDO OKINAWAN WEAPONS 189
ROKUSHAKUBO 193
TENBIN 194
SAI 195
NUNCHAKU 199
TONFA 203
EKU 205
TEKKO 208
KAMA 210
SURUCHIN 211
TINBE 212
SHINKEN TAIRA 213
KATSUKIHO MINOWA 214
MASAKAZU KINJO 215
SHINPO MATAYOSHI 216
YOSHITSUNE SENAGA 217
TAKASHI KINJO 218
SHINYU GUSHI 219
TETSUHIRO HOKAMA 220

V THE HISTORY AND CULTURE OF RYUKYU 225
RYUKYU ARCHIPELAGO 227
INTRODUCTION TO OKINAWA 228

THE ORIGINS OF THE RYUKYU ISLANDS 228
THE SHUNTEN DYNASTY 231
THE THREE KINGDOM PERIOD 232
CHINA AND OKINAWA ESTABLISH TRADE RELATIONS . 235
THE FOUNDING OF KUME MURA 237
THE SHO DYNASTY 238
THE WEST INFILTRATES OKINAWA 242
THE SATSUMA INVASION 244
THE MEIJI ERA 248
WORLD WAR II COMES TO OKINAWA 252
POST WAR OKINAWA 255
OKINAWA TODAY 258
OKINAWAN CULTURAL UNIQUENESS 258

TECHNICAL

VI IRON BODY CONDITIONING AND TAMESHIWARI — TAI GITAE 269
STRENGTH TRAINING IN CHINA 271
KOTE KITAE— FOREARM CONDITIONING 274
TRADITIONAL STRENGTH and CONDITIONING DEVICES 278
MAKIWARA 282
TAMESHIWARI 287

VII BLOCKING TECHNIQUES— UKE WAZA 297
BLOCK TECHNIQUE CHART 301
CIRCULAR MOTION BLOCKS 303
TWISTING FOREARM BLOCKS 306
JODAN UKE 307
SNAPPING FOREARM BLOCK 308
WRIST SNAP 310
RE-DIRECTING THE ATTACK 312
SUKUI - SCOOP, HOOK or LIFT BLOCKS 314
BLOCKING AN ATTACK BEFORE IT REACHES MAXIMUM POWER 319

VIII THRUST AND STRIKE TECHNIQUES— TSUKI WAZA..... 323
STRIKE TECHNIQUE CHART 327
HEISHU— CLOSED HAND 328
KAISHU— OPEN HAND 339

IX KICKING TECHNIQUES— KERI WAZA 349
KICK TECHNIQUE CHART 353
SOKUSEN 354
SOKUTO 360
KAKATO 368
HAISOKU 370
HIZA ATE 372

X THE KATAS OF UECHI RYU KARATE DO 375
WHAT IS A KATA? 377
KATA AS MOVING MEDITATION 378
TRAINING STRUCTURE OF UECHI RYU KARATE 379
PHILOSOPHY & ORGANIZATION of UECHI RYU KARATE 381
THE KATAS OF PANGAINOON 383
SANCHIN KATA 383
SEISAN KATA 398
SANSEIRYU KATA 414
REMAINING KATAS OF UECHI RYU 432
INSTRUCTIONAL SYSTEM of UECHI RYU KARATE 435

XI THE PATH OF AN AIMLESS WANDERER 443
DIRECTIONLESS AND UNEXPLOITED YOUTH 445
KARATE TRAINING IN OKINAWA 449
HAWAII TOUR OF DUTY AND A RETURN TO OKINAWA .. 456
RETURNING TO AMERICA 464
FORTIFYING THE COMMITMENT TO KARATE 476

APPENDIX 515
INDEX...516
PUBLICATIONS CONSULTED 521
PHOTOGRAPH AND ILLUSTRATION CREDITS 522

INTRODUCTION

This is the most complete and factual work ever presented, in English, about the history and technology of Uechi Ryu Karate Do.

Information presented has been personally gathered for over twenty years. A major source of that collection is first hand information from five Okinawan people who spent daily time with Kanbun Uechi for the last ten to twenty years of his life.

I have been fortunate enough to receive instruction from four students of Kanbun Uechi, namely Seiko Toyoma, Seiryo Shinjo, Kanei Uechi and Seiyu Shinjo. Additionally the wives of Seiyu Shinjo (Yoshi Shinjo) and Seiryo Shinjo (Tsuru Shinjo) have offered a wellspring of information about the men of Uechi ryu karate.

The book is rounded out with a presentation of the history and lineage of Okinawan karate and kobudo styles and body conditioning.

Finally, this book contains an informative historical and cultural explanation of Okinawa and its people. There is no more complete presentation of Okinawan life and karate than can be found between these covers.

All Japanese and Okinawan names will be written in the American family name system, first then last name. This is a departure from the Japanese name-order of placing the family name first and personal name second.

Okinawan and Japanese names have not always been standardized. A person of the past may have a different name as an adult than he did as a child. They may also have been given a posthumous name or one of official rank.

Okinawan, Japanese and Chinese interpretations of the same kanji character vary greatly. This sometimes offers a multitude of meanings for the same character. The most commonly accepted terminology will be used throughout this book.

All *italicized* foreign words are alphabetically listed in the Index, with page number, for easy reference. Less important foreign words and those listed in the Table of Contents are not *italicized.*

A margin of error must be allowed for dates. Historical dates of Okinawa are subject to dispute. Changing from the past lunar calendar to the current solar calendar and equating that with the Christian era has created many discrepancies. The Okinawan people, who in the past kept no dated records, eventually kept records in the Chinese then Japanese dating systems.

I hope you enjoy your journey through these pages!

WHAT IS KARATE

空手 唐手

THE EVOLUTION
and
CHRONOLOGY
of
OKINAWAN FIGHTING ARTS

鉄心

On a quiet village trail on the tiny island of Okinawa, a farmer is confronted by knife-wielding bandits. In a flurry of motion the farmer uses agile footwork and powerful hand motions to dispatch the thugs. As the farmer continues along his path he reflects how glad he is that no one else was present to witness his immoderate display of physical violence.

Halfway around the world a small drinking establishment in an American suburb is about to explode into chaos. Two men who have had too much to drink are past the stage of verbal abuse and have risen to their feet in the posture of charging bulls. One of the men assumes a karate stance and begins making Bruce Lee noises. "Kick his butt!" a bystander yells. The fight is over quickly. The intoxicated yuppie was no match for the rather clumsy but effective karate techniques of his opponent. "Wow, that karate stuff is bad!" comments a bystander. "Did you see him kick that guy's teeth in?" The victor walks away muttering something about how the guy got what he deserved.

Karate is basically a method of defending yourself without weapons, using the hands, feet and other body parts as weapons. It differs from other forms of self defense such as judo, jujutsu or sumo in that it employs open hand and fist strikes, as well as kicks. In order to completely understand the historical and cultural importance of this phenomenon it is necessary to read Chapters II, III and V.

Karate did not originally develop as a military art to be used on the battlefield. It was never a sport, confined by rules, but developed as a no holds barred system to protect your life and defeat your opponent without discrimination, at all costs and by any means.

Gichin Funakoshi's axiom *Karate ni sente nashi* (There is no first attack in karate), contains the essence of karate practice as an art form. Unlike sport or mutual combat, karate practice is much more than refined fighting ability. Karate is always defensive and endeavors to develop a stronger mind and character in its practitioners. The ultimate goal of karate is attaining harmony in spirit, body and technique. This balance of mind and body is called *Hito no michi.*

Achieving this level of growth increases health and vigor in addition to developing self defense. The discipline required for karate development teaches *Hei jo shin*, the presence of mind to be prepared to confront obstacles at any time. The obstacle may not be an aggressor. Challenges such as work related stress, raising your children, or worrying about how to pay your bills, require the same mental fortitude developed in karate practice.

The perception of karate by the modern world is vastly different than the honored position martial arts held in ancient Asian societies. While most karate training was conducted in secret, practitioners of karate were known and revered in local villages. These were men of nobility who used their karate strength and wisdom to help those around them.

Stories are told about past karate masters fighting each other to prove which style was better. These contests occurred between willing and highly trained combatants who often agreed to refrain from using the more damaging techniques of their style. Occasionally this mutual combat did result in the death of one of the fighters. Using karate skills against innocent members of the community however, was unheard of.

Karate training begins and ends with a bow. This is to exemplify courtesy. Without courtesy the deadly art of karate becomes harmful to society.

Okinawa's history as a society without weapons allowed them to develop an attitude of peace and harmony unparalleled in the world. The tiny country that developed one of the most effective fighting arts in the world is also a model for world peace.

Traditional Okinawan karate has developed, not as a method of competing against another or to possess the ability to break wood or bricks, but as a source of personal and internal growth leading to understanding oneself and those around you. The future survival of traditional martial arts in the Western world depends on recognizing the moral responsibility accompanying the physical ability of karate.

Karate, as it is known today unquestionably evolved from the fighting systems of Okinawa. It is believed that the *Ryukyu Islands* (ancient Okinawa, Chapter V) possessed its own crude fighting system as early as the sixth century. These loosely developed self defense styles were called *ti* or *te* (pronounced *dee*) meaning "hand". Martial arts techniques from these early systems are seen today in the movements of ancient Okinawan dances, *hono odori*.

Extensive shipping trade with Arabs, Malays, Indonesians and many other Asian countries, most notably China, lasted several centuries. The cultural exchange that resulted influenced Okinawa *te*. The numerous ships calling upon Naha Port meant a steady supply of sailors temporarily residing in Okinawa. Loneliness, boredom and intoxication often led to rousing exchanges of fighting techniques and the interchange of marital arts ideas.

Other countries of Asia and throughout the ancient world developed basic forms of self defense based on the size of people, the terrain in which they lived and the types of attacks they would face.

Outside Okinawa systematized weapons use developed more strongly than empty handed defense. Weapons use developed mainly along military lines. Most countries historically experienced war far more than Okinawa.

Okinawa's history as a culture deprived of weapons creates a rich environment for the development of empty hand defensive arts.

Documentation of ancient karate practice is virtually nonexistent. Martial arts were traditionally taught in private and very secretly, usually only to family members and selected students who were sworn to secrecy. Written accounts of karate were viewed as treason. To avoid punishment or death to the entire family, techniques and systems were handed down only by word of mouth.

The ban on martial arts practice was lifted in 1868 when Okinawa became a state *prefecture* of Japan. Records from 1868 until 1945 were destroyed during the Battle of Okinawa during World War II.

CHINA'S INFLUENCE ON OKINAWAN KARATE

中国

Cultural interchange with China greatly influenced Okinawa, including government, education and indigenous fighting arts.

Martial arts in China have more than one historical source of origin. One source attributes China's fighting arts to India. There is strong evidence of other cultural interchange between India and China dating back as far as 2500 B. C. It is believed a monk from India named *Bodhidharma* traveled through Tibet to the Shoalin Temple in the Songshan Mountains. He brought an organized system of body moves designed to strategically outmaneuver an attacker and save oneself from harm.

The method of learning and becoming proficient with this system was to repeat the moves many times in many directions. The opponent had to be imagined as the moves were performed. This intense focusing of energy coupled with demanding daily physical practice led to excellent health and awareness, even into old age. He stressed breathing exercises and meditation in conjunction with his self defense system. This derivative of Buddhism called *ch'uan* is believed to be the forerunner of *Shaolin Chuan fa*, (Shaolin Temple boxing). *Kung fu* has become the generic name to describe martial arts inherent to China, including Chuan fa.

There is evidence that martial arts existed in China long before the arrival of Bodhidharma. Fighting techniques may have been developed as early as 500 B. C. Cave drawings and temple statues created centuries before his arrival show subjects in martial arts like stances. Monks residing in the temples were continually plagued by bandits plundering anything they could. It was necessary to practice self defense.

China was comprised of many small countries, many of them in feudal conflict with each other, prior to 500 B. C. Caravans conducting lucrative trade between these countries, constantly threatened by bandits, required trained body guards for protection. Guards trained in martial combat also guarded temple gates and local warlords. It is logical that extensive interchange about defensive techniques went on between the fighting men of this profession, spreading martial arts knowledge throughout China.

Some believe the Chinese health exercises and fighting forms were developed by observing animals. At that time the general health of the Chinese people was poor. Scholars believed diseases were caused by inactivity. They observed that animals were very fit and began watching their living habits. This method of observing animals was also used by ancient civilizations to distinguish edible wild vegetation from poisonous plants.

Regimens of stretching exercises and deep breathing called *Doin* and *Tonoho* (called *Kikoho* in Chinese) were developed based on animal behavior, particularly the tortoise. This system greatly increased the health and lengthened the life span of the Chinese people.

Evidence of *Doinjutsu* was discovered in the 2000 year old silk painting *Hague*, found in the Royal Tomb *AB Tai*. The painting is divided into three parts. The first describes various diseases and ailments. The second part shows drawings of animals such as birds with wings spread wide. The third is a series of exercises, among them a man bending in different directions with a long stick in his hand. Only twenty-eight of the positions are legible. They closely resemble modern physical and neuro-therapeutic exercises.

The people of China have always sought everlasting youth and long life. They believe their close association with nature is the key to that health and longevity. This belief developed *Shinsenjutsu* (or *Senjutsu*), the practice to be god-like in the way one lives. *Shinsenjutsu* later combined with the philosophies of *Lao Tse* and became *Dokyo*, or *Taoism.*

This theology believes all things in the universe, nature and man, were created and are sustained by *chi* (*ki* in Japanese). Chi is a sort of electrical energy. Without chi all things would die.

Chi can be charged up and stored in the body by the practice of *Doin* or *Tonoho.* Better health, more strength and long life result from increased chi flow. When applied to the martial arts, this translates to increased power in techniques, stamina and an understanding and calmness in oneself.

The next step in this comparative development was to determine how animals fought against one another and who most often survived. Fighting moves emulating jungle animals such as the tiger, snake, monkey, dragon and birds native to China is one source of origin attributed to their fighting systems. The ferocity and deadly seriousness in the way animals fought one another was a missing factor in human combat. Emulating the fire in the eyes of animals as they fought for their lives became a factor in martial arts training.

Written evidence supports the existence of martial arts systems in China in 92 A. D. In 1727, martial arts practice and demonstrations were abolished by the Ch'ing dynasty. Sixteen hundred years of development and documentation were obliterated. Martial arts practice became clandestine and went underground.

Chuan fa and kung fu developed differently in Northern China than it did in the South. Northern China is rather flat and expansive so generations of people walked or rode horses as the primary means of transportation, developing strong legs. Southern China is broken up by many rivers and waterways. Communities developed along these waterways. Southern Chinese often rowed or poled boats for transportation which developed strong arms. It is surmised kicking techniques developed in the North while punching and striking techniques were emphasized in the South. Although simplified, this theory explains the difference in martial art systems in Northern and Southern China.

The evolution of Chinese boxing has resulted in five major styles: Choy, Hung, Lau, Li and Monk, each named after their founder.

Okinawa enjoyed 500 years of cultural education and trade with China. Emissaries and scholars resided in Okinawa and taught the ways of China while selected young men from Okinawa traveled to Peking for extensive education in culture, government and art.

In the seventeenth and eighteenth centuries young men from Okinawa traveled individually to Southern China, some for long periods, to study Chuan fa, the Chinese fighting systems. They did not enjoy the comforts of the scholars such as government sponsorship, or a place to live and food to eat.

The Southern Chinese province of Fukein lies directly West of Okinawa. It is geographically the closest province to Okinawa. Fuchow was the port of arrival in Fukein province (also called Bin province) for all Okinawans.

An Okinawan fellowship hall, *The Ryukyu Jueneki*, was established in 1439. The community that developed there and served as a temporary haven of familiarity before new arrivals embarked on lonely and unfamiliar travels into Southern China. Most notable among these adventurers are:

Kanga (Tode) Sakugawa (1733-1815)
Sokon (Bushi) Matsumura (1809-1901)
Kosanku Matsumora (1829-1898)
Kanro Higaonna (1853-1915)
Kanbun Uechi (1877-1948)

OKINAWA TE
沖縄手

These historic individuals are the forerunners of the modern karate styles found in Okinawa and around the world. Government sponsored research published by the Okinawa Prefecture Board of Education recognizes three organized systems of karate as the roots of all Okinawan styles of today. They are *Shuri te*, *Naha te* and *Uechi ryu*.

The oldest type is Shuri te (formerly pronounced *Sui dee*), today known as the various Shorin styles. Second is Naha te (formerly pronounced *Naha dee*) which developed into the Goju system. The third style, Uechi ryu (pronounced way chee ru), was known in China as Pangainoon ryu.

Shuri is an area of low hills and valleys overlooking Naha Port. Shuri was also the seat of Okinawan government and royalty for over 500 years. The style of karate that developed there focused on external strength and offensive techniques. The style was suitable for small or weak people. It emphasized evasive body moves and fast footwork.

The karate style that developed in Naha was considered more internal and defensive. It was popular among the larger, stronger men. This system held the belief that a person's body should be trained to absorb blows during combat rather than avoid them. Crushing power in punches and kicks was also emphasized.

Tomari is a small village near an inlet just north of the Port of Naha. Tomari te (formerly pronounced *Tomai dee*), a blend of Shuri and Naha te, influenced many instructors from both areas.

Uechi ryu, formerly Pangainoon ryu, emerged from China thirty eight years after Kingai, the style that would become Goju ryu. Uechi ryu was first taught in Japan and later in Okinawa.

The systems of Chinese Kempo taught in Okinawa became known as *tode* or *tote* which means "China hand". *To* represents the T'ang dynasty (618-906) and refers to all of China.

To can also be pronounced *kara*. Therefore the words tote and karate are interchangeable. The word karate replaced tote, written with the same kanji character, in about 1888. *Tode* refers to the open handed methods used in Chinese systems, as opposed to the fist methods of Okinawa te.

Kempo, the Okinawan translation for Chuan fa, is spelled *kenpo* in Japanese.

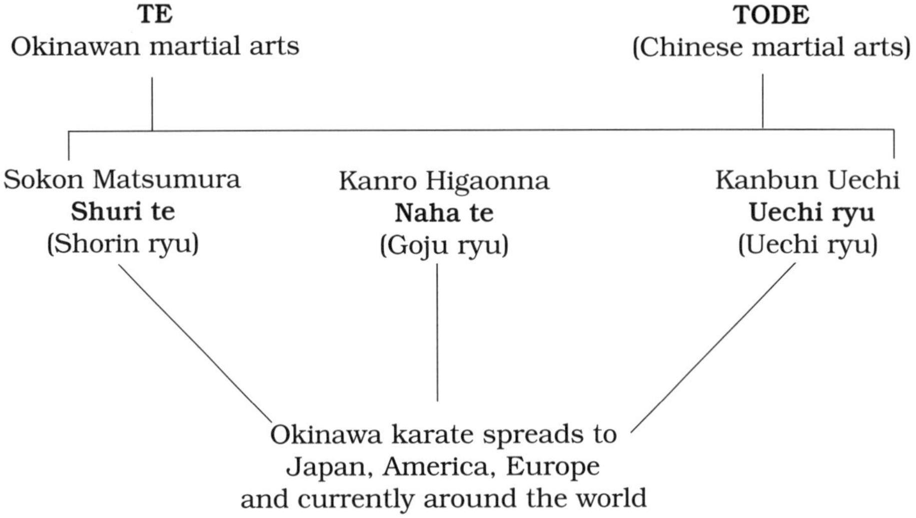

MASTERS OF OKINAWAN KARATE

One method of chronicling the development of Okinawan karate is from the scarce remaining documentation and extensive folklore that surround the lineage of the people who have perpetuated the individual systems of study. It is necessary to remain open minded about the history of karate. Dates, facts and stories differ from one source to another. Masters often disagree on past history and much conjecture has already been mixed with truth.

The spelling of names and places vary from source to source. Describing an ancient Okinawan art, with roots in China, in the Japanese language of today does create confusion. *Kanji* (the Asian method of writing using symbols rather than letters) characters can be read two or three different ways. For example the name Higaonna in the Okinawan *Hogen* dialect can be spelled Higashionna in Japanese. Mr. Shinjo in Okinawa becomes Mr. Arashiro in Japan. Forms, or formal exercise are called *kata* in Japan but were referred to as *te chikate mani* in Okinawa. *Kumite*, the word in Hogen for two man exercises became *bunkai* when karate spread to Japan, and so forth. The most commonly accepted terminology will be used throughout this book. All Japanese and Okinawan names will be written in the American family name system, first then last name. This is a departure from the Japanese system of placing the family name first and personal name second.

The lineage charts shown in this chapter were developed from information provided by the Okinawa Prefecture Board of Education.

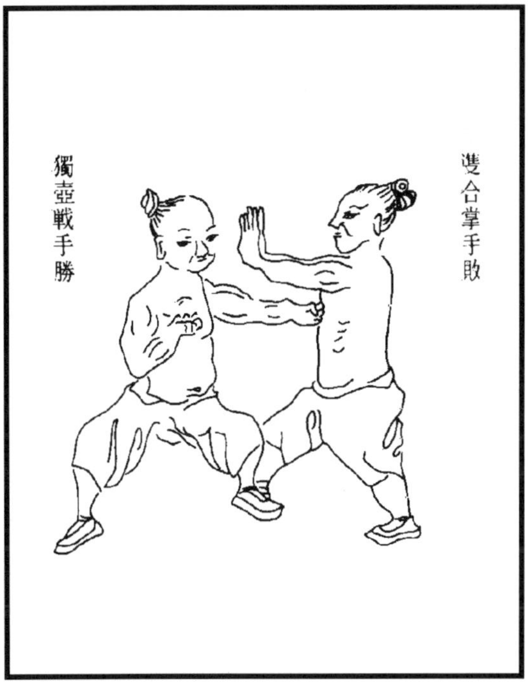
隻合掌手敗
獨壺戰手勝

後背伏宄手敗

存一朵手勝
獨角牛手敗

扠当胠手敗
捧後撞手勝

SHURI TE MASTERS LINEAGE

首里手

OKINAWA TE – CHINA (Kusanku)

Sokon *(Bushi)* Matsumura

- Anko Asato
- Anko Itosu
- Chostu Kuwae
- Sanda Chenin
- Chochu Itarashiku
- Penchin Kinyo
- Pechin Sakihara
- Chofu Kyan
- Chossho Chibana
- Pechin Kiyuna
- Ryosei Kuwae
- Nabe Tanme (Matsumura)

Anko Asato / Anko Itosu:

- Gichin Funakoshi (Shoto kan)
- Kentsu Yabu
- Chomo Hanashiro
- Kenyu Kudeken
- Chotoku Kyan (Shobayashi ryu)
- Choki Motobu
- Choren Yamakawa
- Moden Yabiku
- Chosin Chibana (Kobayashi ryu)
- Anbun Tokuda
- Choujyo Oshiro (Yamane ryu)
- Kenwa Mabuni (Shito ryu)
- Shinpan Shiroma

- Ankichi Arakaki
- Zenryo Shimabukuro
- Shoshin Nagamine (Matsubayashi ryu)
- Tatsuo Shimabukuro (Isshin ryu)
- Heltaro Shinjho
- Jyoen Nakazato

Chosin Chibana:

- Ankichi Arakaki
- Chouzou Nakama
- Yuchok Higa (Kyudo kan)
- Katsuya Miyahira
- Seitoku Ishikawa
- Katsuyki Shimabuku

Nabe Tanme (Matsumura) — Hohan Sokon (Matsumura Seito) — Seiki Arakaki

SHURI TE

Kanga "Tode" Sakugawa (1733 - 1815)

Kanga "Tode" Sakugawa (1733-1815)

The enthusiastic young student was given the nickname "tode" which refers to Chinese martial arts, by his teacher in Okinawa, Peichin Takahara. He also studied kempo in Okinawa and China, from a Chinese envoy named Kusanku, who reportedly spent time teaching in Okinawa.

Sakugawa, sometimes called the father of Okinawan karate, is considered by many to be Okinawa's first real karate teacher and the author of the first dojo codes called *kun*. He created the kata Sakugawa no Kun, a bo kata. Sakugawa's largest contribution was passing his vast knowledge to his star student, Sokon Matsumura, whom he nicknamed *Bushi* (warrior).

Sokon "Bushi" Matsumura (1809-1901)

Sokon Matsumura came to live with the aged Sakugawa as a child. He earnestly studied te until Sakugawa's death. He then traveled to China to further his studies. Matsumura was the first person to combine Okinawan te and Chinese Chuan fa into an organized system. He named this system Shuri te. All of the current Shorin styles originated with this man.

Matsumura served as a bodyguard to three successive Okinawan kings. He wrote the book "Matsumura Bucho Ikko", in which he stressed Chinese culture, education and martial arts.

He was reputedly involved in many fights but was never beaten. Matsumura was once attacked by a group of drunken sailors. He merely rolled up into a ball in the road and remained there unharmed until the attackers became wary and backed off. As he stood up and straightened his clothing the group realized they did not want to challenge this man and ran away.

Matsumura's wife was fond of martial arts and strength contests, which she often won. She was once seen lifting a bag of rice weighing over one hundred pounds with one hand while sweeping under it with the other.

Matsumura's most prominent student is another legend in the annals of Okinawan karate history, Yasutsune "Anko" Itosu. When Matsumura died he passed control of his system to his grandson Nabe.

Anko Itosu (1832-1916)

Yasutsune Itosu, a stout and very strong man became a phenomenal karate man. His nickname *Anko* means iron horse, and refers to the incredible strength of his stance. It was his desire to popularize karate, in spite of objections from other karate masters. The first public demonstration of karate in Okinawa was performed by Anko Itosu and Gichin Funakoshi. The demonstration, performed for Japanese dignitaries, created a lot of controversy with conservative karate masters who wanted to keep karate instruction secret, for selected students only.

Sokon "Bushi" Matsumura (1809-1901)

Monument to Anko Itosu, located in Shuri, Okinawa

The Japanese officials took note of the superb physical condition of the karate men. Itosu convinced them that karate training in the public schools was an excellent way to develop the health of Okinawa's youth. Japan saw this as a way to insure fit young men for service in Japan's military.

Itosu began teaching karate in elementary schools in 1901 and by 1905 he was teaching at the Okinawa Instructors College. The veil of private karate instruction had been lifted at the beginning of the Meiji era in 1868, however, karate did not gain popularity until its historic introduction into the school system.

Itosu emphasized kata practice in karate training. The advanced katas he had learned and developed were simplified to facilitate mass learning of karate techniques. Itosu created five beginners katas called *pinans* (*heian* in Japanese). He established the foundation for future instruction of Okinawan karate in all schools in Okinawa and mainland Japan.

Anko Itosu taught many students. The most prominent in the dissemination of Shuri te were Chosin Chibana, Chotoku Kyan, Gichin Funakoshi, Kenwa Mabuni and Chotoku Kyan. A world organization of Itosu kai Shito ryu is run from Santa Ana, California, by world renowned Fumio Demura.

Chosin Chibana (1885-1969)

Chosin Chibana, who also studied under Bushi Matsumura, continued the teachings of Anko Itosu but renamed the style Shorin ryu. The Chinese translation for *shorin* is "small wood". The Japanese translation for *shorin* means "Shaolin". The characters can also mean *kobayashi.* Kobayashi Shorin ryu became known as the style of Anko Itosu, distinctive from other Shorin and Shaolin styles that would develop.

Chibana was a strict traditionalist who believed karate was a martial art, not for sport or fitness. He was the first President of the All Okinawa Karate Federation, *Zen Okinawa Karate Renmei.*

Gichin Funakoshi (1868-1957)

Gichin Funakoshi studied under Anko Itosu and Anko Azato. He is called the father of Japanese karate because of his profound influence in introducing and propagating Okinawan karate in Japan. He became one of the first Okinawan masters to teach karate in Japan, along with Choki Motobu, Kanbun Uechi and Kenwa Mabuni.

Funakoshi was known for organizing and performing public karate demonstrations with other masters in different parts of Okinawa. In 1917, he performed the first demonstration of karate outside of Okinawa at the *Butokuden* (martial arts center) in Kyoto. In 1921, he demonstrated karate at Shuri castle for Crown Prince Hirahito. The Prince was so impressed he invited Funakoshi to Japan.

In 1922, Gichin Funakoshi performed demonstrations in Tokyo and soon began teaching karate in Japan for the first time in history. He taught at universities and police departments and in 1934, opened his own dojo, the second Okinawan karate dojo established in Japan. The first was by Kanbun Uechi who had been teaching Uechi ryu privately in Japan since 1925. Uechi opened a public dojo of Pangainoon in 1932, in Wakayama.

Funakoshi altered his system of karate and changed the names of the katas to gain acceptance by the Japanese and to accommodate mass learning. He emphasized low stances for beginners training while teaching advanced students more upright stances.

Gichin Funakoshi's style became known as *Shotokan. Shoto* was the pen name used by Funakoshi, who was a prolific writer. Kan means house. Shotokan has grown to become one of the most popular styles of karate practiced in the world.

The Japanese people applied their samurai approach to karate creating explosive and continuous direct-line attacks found in *kendo.* The four major karate styles of Japan are *Shotokan, Shito ryu, Goju ryu* and *Wado ryu.*

Kenwa Mabuni (1889-1953)

Kenwa Mabuni learned the Sanchin kata from Kanryo Higaonna, and studied briefly with Gokenki, a Chinese white crane expert residing in Okinawa. Mabuni then studied for many years under Chojun Miyagi. He was so devoted to Miyagi that it is said he stayed by Miyagi's grave, practicing kata, for one year after Miyagi's death.

Mabuni moved to Osaka and began teaching karate. He had a deep understanding of many katas from Okinawa te because of his extensive study. He studied at Kanbun Uechi's dojo in Wakayama, Japan, in 1925. After studying with Uechi, Mabuni created the kata *Shinpa.*

In 1937, he created the name *Shito ryu* by combining the Chinese characters for the first syllables of Itosu and Higaonna, to honor his two teachers. Mabuni's style of Shito ryu is carried on in Japan by Teruo Hiyashi (Hiyashi ha Shito ryu) of Osaka.

Chotoku Kyan (1870-1945)

Chotoku Kyan's life is explained in Chapter III, as a karate master from Kadena village.

Hohan Sokon (1889-1953)

Hohan Sokon, the only student of his uncle Nabe Matsumura, was a contemporary of Anko Itosu's students. He established Matsumura Seito (Orthodox) Shorin ryu. He also trained in unique group sessions with Gokenki, Kenwa Mabuni and others. Sokon was a staunch traditionalist. He was unhappy with the changes being made to Okinawan karate to accommodate its increasing popularity.

Choki Motobu (1871-1944)

Choki Motobu was an unorthodox street fighter who had been refused formal instruction by many Okinawan instructors. He was accepted as a student for a short while by Kosaku Motsumora of Tomari te and Anko Itosu from Shuri te. He was soon expelled because of constant street fights.

He also attempted to learn Motobu ryu, the family style, by spying on his brother during his practice. This private family style was taught only to the first born son. Sometimes called "Motobu the monkey" because of his massive body and arms, Motobu spent extensive time training on the makiwara and lifting large stones.

Motobu went to Japan in 1922, looking for employment. He gained a reputation there for the strength of his fighting. The style he taught was a combination of his techniques learned in many street fights. He never established a dojo but taught in Tokyo and Osaka until 1938, when he returned to Okinawa.

Choki Motobu (1871-1944)

Shinken Taira (1897-1970)

Shinken Taira's life is discussed in Chapter IV, Kobudo.

Shoshin Nagamine (1907-)

Shosin Nagamine studied under Chotoku Kyan, Arakaki Ankichi and Iha Kodatsu from Tomari te. Nagamine established the *Matsubayshi* (pine forest) system of Shorin ryu.

The list of ethics displayed in his Kodo Kan dojo stress courtesy, cleanliness and diligence. This is accomplished by purifying your mind and cultivating power, strength and perseverance through karate training. It states:

"The Dojo is the sacred place where guts are fostered and superior human natures are bred through the ecstasy of sweating in hard work. The Dojo is the sacred place where the human spirit is polished."

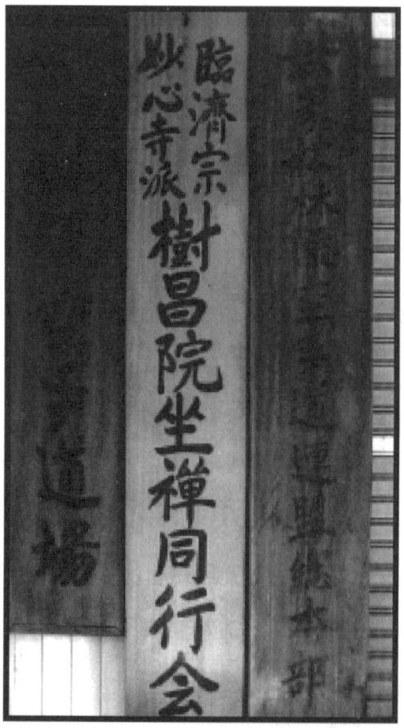

The sign in front of, and portrait from inside, Shoshin Nagamine's dojo.

Eizo Shimabuku (1925-)

Eizo Shimabuku, called Shimabukuro in Japanese, first studied under Chojun Miyagi then under Chotoku Kyan. He was named successor of *Shobayashi* (small forest) Shorin ryu when Kyan died. His dojo is near Camp Hansen Marine Base in Okinawa where he has taught many servicemen, most notably Former World Karate Champion Joe Lewis.

Tatsuo Shimabuku (1908-1975)

Tatsuo Shimabuku studied under the same two instructors as his brother Eizo. He also received extensive teachings in Motobu ryu. Tatsuo combined what he learned and created *Isshin ryu* in 1954. Like his brother, he also taught many U.S. Marines during his teaching career. Tatsuo

Shimabuku is known for changing the type of fist used in Okinawan karate by placing the thumb on the side of the hand. This was considered a weak technique and was very unpopular among other karate instructors.

Chinese military envoys to Okinawa who influenced some Shuri te instructors were Kusanku, Iwah, Ason and Waishinzan.

Each subsequent generation brings with it an ever growing number of individual karate styles and organizations. Detailed presentations of modern karate instructors are available in publications written specifically about Okinawan karate masters.

Alan Dollar in the Okinawa Kenritsu Budokan

NAHA TE MASTERS LINE

那覇手

Okinawa te - China *(Liu Liu Kung)*

Kanryo Higaonna

Juhatsu Kyoda
(Toon ryu)

Chojun Miyagi
(Goju ryu)
Koki Shiroma

Kenwa Mabuni
(Shito ryu)

Choko Iraha

Judo Kyoda

Jinan Shinzato

Seiko Higa
(Shodo kan)

Meitoku Yagi
(Meibu kan)
Jitsuei Yogi

Yukinori Uechara
(Saburo)
Kei Miyagi

Eichi Miyazato
(Jundo kan)
Koshin Iha

Seiko Fukuchi
(Senbu kan)
Masayoshi Toguchi

Yasuhide Tamaki

NAHA TE

Kanryo Higaonna (1853-1915)

Sometimes called *Toona*, Higaonna began training to avenge the death of his father who had been killed in a karate fight. He first studied karate on Okinawa from Arkakai, who had learned in China.

After several years of study, Higaonna, at about twenty-two years old, went to China to further his training. He stayed in China about thirteen years during which time he studied under Chinese master *Liu Liu Kung*, pronounced *Ryu Ryu Ko* in Japanese, who is believed by some to be the same *Ru Ru Ko* of Ryuei ryu karate.

Higaonna returned to Okinawa in 1881, but refrained from teaching karate for a while. As a result of karate training and maturity his quest for vengeance had been put aside.

As Japanese interest in karate grew, so did its popularity in Okinawa. Higaonna eventually began teaching publicly and his ability quickly became renowned. He was highly respected by other karate masters and was named instructor to the royal family. He also taught martial arts at the Naha Commercial High School. This milestone in karate history is one of the first examples of the acceptance of karate as a positive entity in the education of children.

Monument to Kanryo Higaonna and Chojun Miyagi

His style of karate became known as *Higaonna te*, and later was called Naha te emphasizing the difference from the system taught at Shuri or Tomari.

Kanryo Higaonna was a small man with lightening speed, agility and enormous power. He was known for the power of his legs, kicks and evasive ability. He emphasized the kata Sanchin and rigorously taught students this kata exclusively during the first years of training. He changed Sanchin kata from the open handed method practiced in Uechi ryu, to closed fist striking to match the emphasis placed on hard breathing. It is believed he also wanted to de-emphasize the killing power of fingertip strikes.

Higaonna demanded perfection from his students. The intensity of training and boredom from doing only Sanchin, weeded out all but the strongest few. Higaonna's most prominent students were Chogun Miyagi, Juhatsu Kyoda, Seiko Higa and Kenwa Mabuni.

CHOJUN MIYAGI (1888-1953)

Chojun Miyagi was one of the greatest karate masters of Okinawa. He first studied under Ryuko Aragaki, then under Kanryo Higaonna. He trained relentlessly to match the extraordinary ability of his teacher. Miyagi traveled to China to learn more of his teachers system. He was unable to find any remnants of the style or school. Everything had been disrupted and changed by the Boxer Rebellion. (Chapter I) He searched until he found a teacher in China who taught him a Chinese boxing style called *Kingai* (hard-soft).

Miyagi was legendary for his strength and stamina, *chikara*, prompting stories of him tearing bark from trees with his bare hands, or kicking holes in fuel cans with his toe. His popularity in Okinawa grew rapidly.

He was a martial arts scholar who regularly consulted the *Bubishi*, a text on Chinese boxing. He helped organize a study group of martial artists, the *Ryukyu Tode Kenkyukai* (Okinawa Karate Research Group). The focus of the group was to increase public understanding of karate, as well as their own.

Chojun Miyagi

Chojun Miyagi taught at the Prefectual Police Department and at the Okinawan Masters Training College. In 1905, he began teaching in the public school system. He developed an approach and techniques specifically for teaching children.

In 1928, he demonstrated karate in Japan. He wrote "An Outline of Karate *Do*".

and presented it to the governing body of martial arts in Japan, the *Dai Nippon Butoku Kai*, in 1933. Due to Miyagi's efforts and the help of his friend Kodukan Judo founder Jigiro Kano, Goju ryu became a martial art of Japan that same year. The Butokukai awarded the first title of Karate Do Master to Chojun Miyagi.

The tomb and headstone of Chojun Miyagi

Naha te became so popular in Okinawa during that time that Miyagi's best students began teaching Miyagi's style, known for a short time as *Kanko ryu*, half hard style. Miyagi changed the name to Goju ryu in the 1930's. The word *goju*, meaning hard-soft, came from the poem "Eight Philosophies of the Fist" found in the *Bubishi.*

Miyagi visited Hawaii briefly to teach his art. He traveled to China a seond time to increase his understanding of martial arts. Goju ryu is practiced around the world today as one of the strongest karate styles to come out of Okinawa.

JUHATSU KYODA (1887-1968)

Juhatsu Kyoda received training from Kanryo Higaonna. He started training one month prior to Chojun Miyagi and continued studying until Higaonna's death thirteen years later. He later trained in Chinese kempo in Okinawa.

Kyoda, a school teacher, started many karate clubs in the school system and became one of the few masters of the time to teach his style of karate, Toon ryu, in public school. He named the style after the first letter of kanji in Higaonna's name.

Juhatsu Kyoda became the chief instructor at the Okinawa branch of the Dai Nippon Butoku Kai in 1934.

SEIKO HIGA (1898-1966)

Seiko Higa studied under Kanryo Higaonna for four years. After Higaonna's death he learned from Chojun Miyagi until Miyagi's death. He was a school teacher, then a police officer teaching karate when he could arrange the time. After retiring from both professions, he dedicated all his time to teaching karate. Higa moved to Japan where he taught for many years before returning to Okinawa.

Upon his return to Okinawa, Higa opened the Shodokan dojo where he taught Goju ryu while Shimpo Matayoshi (Chapter IV) taught Kobudo.

KENWA MABUNI (1889-1952)

Kenwa Mabuni's life is described earlier in this chapter with his training in Shuri te under Anko Itosu.

Ichi Ka - Ichi Kai, one generation, one group
Calligraphy by Tetsuhiro Hokama

CHOJUN MIYAGI'S SENIOR STUDENTS

EIICHI MIYAZATO (1921-)

Eiichi Miyazato was constantly at Chojun Miyagi's side throughout his life. After Miyagi's death, he assumed responsibility for teaching classes. He later opened the Jundokan where he still teaches today. Miyazato, a former police officer, is also an accomplished judo master.

Miyazato's most notable student is Morio Higaonna, an exemplary instructor of Goju ryu karate. Higaonna first taught in Tokyo, Japan and now resides and teaches in America. Teruo Chinen, also a student of Miyazato, assisted in teaching at the Tokyo dojo. Chinen was the first Okinawan karate master to move to America and teach karate. Morio Higaonna runs a world organization of Goju ryu which he holds to a high standard, from his dojo in San Marcos, California.

JINAN SHINZATO (1901-1945)

Jinan Shinzato was a valued assistant to Miyagi. He also demonstrated Naha te in Japan. Shinzato was a civilian casualty of the Battle of Okinawa.

MEITOKU YAGI (1910-)

Meitoku Yagi was the recipient of Miyagi's gi and belt. He still teaches in Okinawa and runs an international organization.

Shinpo Matayoshi and Morio Higaonna

UECHI RYU MASTERS LINEAGE CHART

上地流

OKINAWA TE – CHINA *(Shushiwa)*

Kanbun Uechi

- Ryuyu Tomoyose — Numerous students in Japan
- Saburo Uehara — Takenobu Uehara
- Shuei Sakihama
- Kai Akamine
- Isamu Uehara
- Kanei Uechi
  - Takenobu Uehara
  - Yoshitoku Iraha
  - Soryu Furugen — Tokyo
  - Seiko Itokazu
  - Ryuko Tomoyose — George Mattson
  - Kosuke Yonamine
  - Seiki Itokazu
  - Ken Nakamatsu
  - Shigeru Takamiyagi
  - Kansei Uechi
  - Kanmei Uechi
  - James Thompson
  - Arbie Kinnifick
  - Mark Breslford
- Seiryo Shinjo
- Seiko Toyoma
- Seiyu Shinjo
  - Shinyu Gushi
  - Tsutomo Nakahodo
  - Seiki Ire
  - Minoru Miyagi
  - Kiyohide Shinjo
  - Narihiro Shinjo
  - Yoshisurne Senaga
  - Takayasu Takemi
  - Johnny Author
  - Peter Kellogg
  - Alan Dollar

UECHI RYU KARATE DO

Kanbun Uechi (1877-1948)

KANBUN UECHI (1877-1948)

Kanbun Uechi studied te and bo techniques in Motobu as a child. He lived in China, learning and teaching *Pangainoon chuan fa* from 1897 to 1910. Pangainoon means half hard, half soft. Unlike his predecessors he refused to teach karate, for personal reasons, after returning to Okinawa. Masters of Naha te and Shuri te knew his reputation and implored him to teach. He

Tomb and headstone of Kanbun and Kanei Uechi

was offered a position at the Okinawa Teachers College by Anko Itosu. Uechi declined and moved to Wakayama, Japan in 1924.

Kanbun Uechi was persuaded to teach in the Okinawan community in Wakayama. He taught selected members privately until 1932, when he opened a public dojo. The *Pangainoon Ryu Karate-jutsu Kenkyu-jo*, located in the Tebira section of Wakayama, was the first dojo in Japan run by an Okinawan teacher. Kanbun Uechi taught Pangainoon ryu at that location until he left Japan in 1946.

Kanbun Uechi's students, Kanei Uechi (Kanbun's son) Seiyu Shinjo and Seiko Toyama taught his system of karate on Okinawa. The name was changed to Uechi Ryu to honor Kanbun Uechi after his death in 1948.

This late comer to the island of karate has experienced phenomenal growth and organization in Okinawa. American names appear in the second generation of lineage after Kanbun Uechi, unlike the lineage of Shuri te or Naha te where they would appear in the third generation. This is due to Uechi ryu being established in Okinawa after World War II. Only those who spent extensive time on Okinawa and are still teaching karate today are listed.

The route taken by Pangainoon ryu between China and Okinawa was different from its predecessors. Uechi ryu is considered one of the three major roots of modern Okinawan karate. One purpose of this book is to present the history of Uechi ryu in context with the chronology of other Okinawan karate styles. This is the most complete presentation of this comparitive picture that has ever been presented. The history of Uechi ryu karate is covered in detail in Chapters II and III.

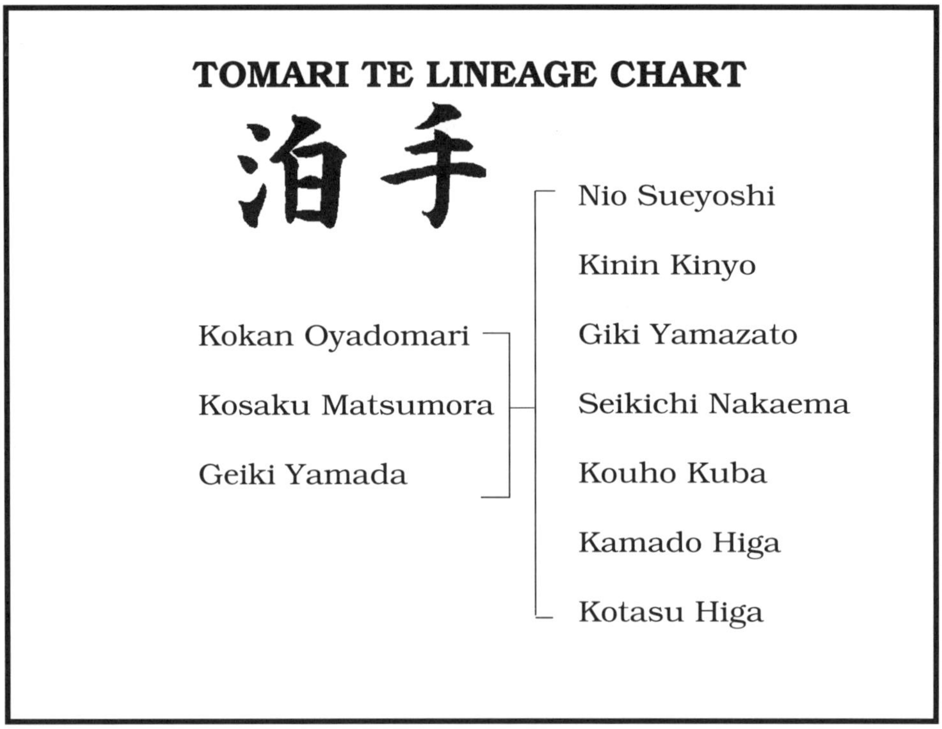

TOMARI TE

Another entity in the martial arts, *Tomari te*, emerged in the nineteenth century. Tomari is a small port village near Naha and Shuri. The type of karate developed there was a blend of both Naha te and Shuri te. Tomari te became assimilated primarily into Shuri te and both became the Shorin systems discussed earlier.

KOSAKU MATSUMORA (1829-1898)

Kosaku Matsumora, the primary exponent of Tomari te, reportedly learned from a Chinese man living in a cave in the hills around Tomari. Matsumora also studied under other Okinawan masters as did two other proponents of Tomari te, Kokan Oyadomari and Gikei Yamada.

Some Okinawan masters of Shuri te and Naha te such as Chotoku Kyan, Choki Motobu, Shoshin Nagamine and others, also studied Tomari te at some point in their lives. It was taught privately, even after most other styles opened to public teaching.

Kosaku Matsumora (1829-1898)

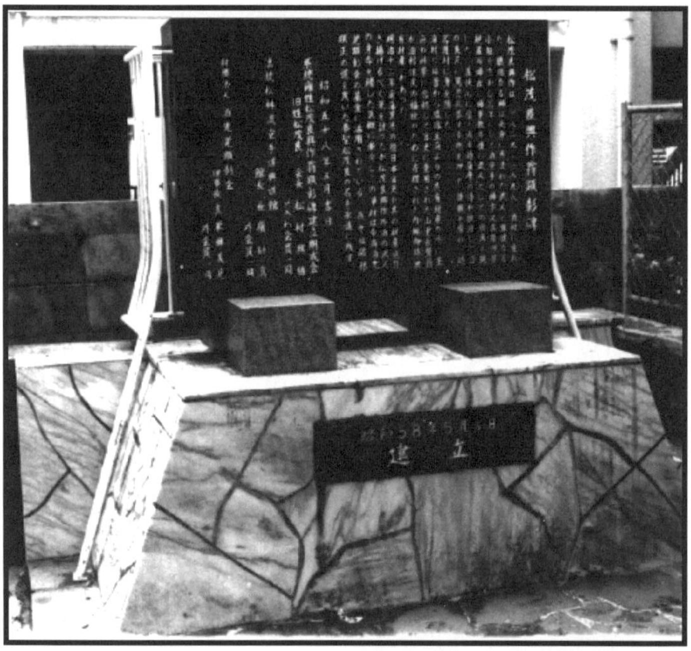

Monument to Kosaku Matsumora

RYUEI RYU KARATE

Ryuei ryu is one of the many smaller styles of Okinawa. The Nakaima family who perpetuated it, kept secret for many years. Ryuei ryu has its roots in Chinese Chuan fa, under Ru Ru Ko, and is a combination of many Okinawan systems. It utilizes the Sanchin kata used in Goju ryu and Uechi ryu, but emphasizes softness and pliability.

The best known proponent of Ryuei ryu is Tsuguo Sakumoto. Sakumoto teaches a brutal form of sport sparring. He is an avid fighter however he is best known for World Kata Champion titles. Tsuguo Sakumoto was the W.U.K.O. (World Union of Karate Organizations) World Kata Champion three times. He has also won the World Cup twice, the World Games twice and the All Asian Championship twice for an impressive record of nine world championship victories.

Mr. Sakumoto, formerly a high school physical education teacher, is now in charge of the karate division of the Okinawa Prefecture Board of Education.

TRADITIONAL OKINAWAN KARATE DO KATAS

Compiled by the Okinawa Prefecture Board of Education

SEISAN
SEIRYU
SEICHIN
SHISOCHIN
KURURUNFA
FUKYUGATA 1
NAIHANCHI
ROHAI
GOJUSHIHO
HOFA
SOCHIN
NUTUDE
ANAN
PAIHO
WUNU
SANSEIRYU
SANCHIN
GEKISAI
SEIPAI
SEIENCHIN
ANANKU
FUKYUGATA 2
WANSHU
CHINTO
CHINTI
NISESI
OHAN
BAIKU
SUNSU
KANCHIN
KANSHIWA
KANSHU
SAIFA
SANERU
SUPARINPE
PINAN
WANKAN
BASSAI
KUSANKU
JITTI
JICHIN
BACHU
HEIKYU
JION

型 形

The key principals who have developed and passed along Okinawan karate share certain commonalities. The famous karate masters all started training in their childhood or early teens and continued their karate involvement the rest of their lives. They traveled extensively and sought all the knowledge available at the time in order to improve their martial arts skill. They were often called upon to test their ability against challengers. Eventually all the icons of karate history were recognized by the Japanese Dai Nippon Butoku Kai as karate masters.

A common practice of the time was to require a potential student to perform months of menial chores for the instructor before being accepted into the dojo. This test of patience, humility and dedication weeded out the less serious students or those who did not yet possess the fortitude to undergo the rigorous, sometimes inhuman training in Okinawa te.

Martial arts have a long history however; *karate,* as the world knows it today, developed in rather recent history. It has spread world wide at a phenomenal rate and continues to enjoy growth and increasing interest.

The diminutive island of karate currently contains sixty-four different style names and three hundred dojos. The vast assortment of styles all share the same roots of three founding sources of organized karate recognized by the Okinawa Prefecture Board of Education. They are *Shuri te, Naha te* and *Uechi ryu.*

Many styles share the same katas but each one approaches the kata from a slightly different point of view. The same kata performed at two different dojos will differ depending on the priorities of the instructor. There are over seventy katas currently in Okinawan karate systems. The Board of Education research recognizes forty-four of them (previously listed) from the three original styles.

Karate on Okinawa in the past was a striking, joint locking and grappling art. Evasive body movements were prevalent among smaller karate teachers like Chotoku Kyan. Larger instructors, like Chojun Miyagi, believed a person should be able to withstand blows from an opponent and still be able to deliver powerful punches and kicks.

As ancient self defense movements became modernized, Chinese foundations and katas were altered and blended with *te.* Some changes were the natural result of the passage of time on an oral tradition. Others were to accommodate different types of teaching to different people, and lastly, to reflect particular specialties of the current instructor.

Protection to the Okinawans often meant defense against an attack with weapons. The unarmed Okinawan people faced armed authority throughout their history. A swift, one technique attack became the defense of these oppressed people. Penetrating seams and weak points in armor necessitated *makiwara* (Chapter VI) training to develop the crushing power in punches and kicks for which Okinawan karate is famous.

OKINAWAN KARATE IS INTRODUCED TO JAPAN

日本

When karate was introduced to Japan it became apparent that Japanese *jujutsu* was very similar to the grappling aspects of Okinawa te styles. It is surmised that rather than duplicate efforts, the Okinawans taught only the striking aspects of their art.

When Gichin Funakoshi introduced Okinawan karate in Japan he was very smart about the way he presented it. He taught karate "do" rather than karate "jutsu".

Jutsu means "technique" and refers to the method and purpose for studying karate, developing life saving techniques for self defence. *Do* (pronounced dough) means "way of life" in Japanese. Karate as a "way" implies a path toward personal and spiritual betterment. This concept brought karate practice into the realm of Buddhism as a means of attaining a greater level of personal awareness and compassion. Funakoshi taught karate as a method of health and fitness and for the development of one's character through training. Back in Okinawa the primary purpose remained self defense.

A common misconception is that karate is strongly tied to religion, as the martial arts of Japan are practiced in conjunction with Zen Buddhism. Okinawans traditionally practiced ancestor worship, however, Buddhism never became influential. The primary purpose of karate is self growth and moral and emotional development. This was approached from a personal and societal point of view, not a religious one.

The karate community shared mixed emotions about serializing and publicizing karate. The martial sport concept of karate that developed during karate's dissemination was offensive to some Okinawan masters. They felt it put their cultural art in second position behind the Japanese who were taking control over all martial arts.

Teaching karate to large numbers was very challenging. It was difficult for the highly proficient masters to balance group lessons with the combative specialties taught on a much smaller scale back home. Karate instruction in Japan became regimented and militaristic, unlike the small informal classes held in the courtyard of the Okinawan teacher's house.

The intricacies of *kata*, the forms that were the primary focus of karate training in Okinawa, were difficult to teach to large groups. A sparring system called *kumite* was developed which became a primary part of the new karate training.

The combative art of Okinawa gave way to the martial sport attitude of Japan. Free sparring had not been a part of karate practice in Okinawa because of the inherent danger. Japanese sport karate rules of sparring conduct changed karate techniques. Punching, striking and kicking techniques were allowed, while the more dangerous elbow strike, backfist and toe kick were prohibited.

Punches and kicks were now pulled short of contact for safety. This was in direct conflict with makiwara training and the mentality of defeating your opponent by any means. It did serve however to increase the popularity of karate practice.

Old katas were altered and new ones created with emphasis on looks and poise rather than combat. The new combative forms were viewed as karate dances by Okinawan masters.

In 1963, the first All Japan Karate Do Championship Tournament was held solidifying the direction toward sport karate and away from the defensive karate of Okinawa.

Okinawan karate miraculously became a tool in the shaping of young Japanese bodies and minds. This was an incredible accomplishment for Okinawa, Funakoshi and other masters who had helped accomplish the acceptance of Okinawan karate.

Acceptance included changing the perception of a Chinese martial art taught by Okinawan masters, to a Japanese martial art. A major step in the assimilation of karate in Japan was to eliminate the first kanji charac-

Elementary school boys and girls practice Karate in fornt of Shuri Castle— 1937

ter for "tode" meaning "China", and replacing it with the Japanese character meaning "empty".

The Dai Nippon Butoku Kai, whose mission was to identify and categorize Japan's martial arts, required the name change for styles to be accepted into their organization. In addition to "Nipponizing" karate, the change was aimed at removing Chinese culture from Japan. Japan and China went to war against each other in 1937.

The Chinese character used until that time can be pronounced *tode* or *karate*, as mentioned earlier. Changing the kanji did not change the pronunciation of karate but changed the concept from Chinese to Japanese martial arts.

Many karate instructors in Okinawa were furious. They considered the change insulting to their art and rejected it. Others, like Chomo Hamishiro had started using the ideogram for karate in the early 1900's.

In 1936, a conference sponsored by the Ryukyu Shimpo Press was held in Okinawa during which the power of Japan prevailed, and the name of the world recognized art from Okinawa officially became *KARATE.*

After World War II American occupation in both Japan and Okinawa became a new factor that would effect karate. American control first brought with it a ban on all martial arts practice, among other restrictions. When this was relaxed after a few years a new challenge was created.

"Karate Do" group formed in 1937

Seiyu Shinjo on Ie-jima Island wearing Chinese style gi.

American servicemen expressed increasing interest in learning the native fighting arts. The foreign presence and interest in karate was viewed differently in Japan and Okinawa, due to their different cultures and their vastly different roles in the war.

Karate had been in Japan a very short time before World War II, and was not practiced during the war. Many karate masters returned to Okinawa, while others became civilian casualties of the War. This left a vast shortage of qualified karate instructors. "Instant karate instructors" sprang up in Japan. Some of these pseudo teachers actually learned karate during the day from a reputable instructor and taught the same lessons at night pretending to be knowledgeable instructors. The shortage led to instruction that ventured further away from the art of Okinawa and more along the lines of Japanese martial sport.

KARATE BECOMES INTERNATIONAL

Military personnel stationed in Japan and Okinawa since the war were the primary source of karate's introduction and growth in America. Okinawa again became strategically important during the military operation of the Vietnam War. Military presence on the island increased, creating a new wave of interest in karate.

Okinawan teachers accepted the commitment of the Americans and realized that their art could be spread internationally. The dojos of Okinawa began changing. Some questionable instructors catering to Americans offered accelerated courses in which the training was not too difficult for the unknowing serviceman.

Other more reputable dojos began accepting Americans of good character into the same intense training that had always existed. Some instructors applied slightly different standards to the culturally inhibited Westerners, but still taught with much intensity. Staunch traditionalists refused to teach anyone other than Okinawan people.

During the mid-fifties the various karate styles adapted to wearing the white karate uniform, called a *gi*, that is familiar today. Prior to this, training was conducted in trousers normally worn during the day. The Chinese system of removing the trousers and tucking in the legs of the under shorts was used for more robust workouts.

The colored belt ranking system of white, green and brown was also created during that time. Advanced proficiency ratings were formalized into a black belt ranking system with multiple degrees.

A red belt was implemented to denote the master of each style. This system faced much abuse as styles diversified and was abandoned in during the 1960's. The red belt was replaced with gold stripes on the black belt. Currently there is no distinction on the black belt for ranks of first degree through fifth degree, *Shodan* through *Godan*. One gold stripe placed horizontally near each tip of the belt to indicate sixth degree *Renshi, Rokudan*. Two stripes denote both seventh and eighth degree *Kyoshi* and *Hanshi*. Three stripes denotes nineth degree, *Kyushi*. Tenth degree black belt is traditionally reserved for the *Grand Master* of the style.

The All Okinawa Karate Federation, *Zen Okinawa Karate Renmei*, was formed in 1956, as a governing body to aid in developing karate's rapid growth. It was made up of the four prominent styles of karate; Kobayashi Shorin ryu, Matsubayashi Shorin ryu, Goju ryu and Uechi ryu.

Okinawan karate history is viewed in five periods of development.

Cradle Period

This was the time before an official relationship was established in 1372 (Chapter V). Okinawa te and kobujutsu arts were being developed in various parts of Okinawa.

Assimilation and Harmonization Period

This period began when Okinawa became a sovereignty of China in 1372, and with the founding of *Kume Mura* Chinese settlement in Okinawa in 1392. It included karate development spanning a five hundred year relationship with China.

Modernization Period

This period covered the *Meiji Era* 1867-1910. The focus of the Meiji reign was the modernization of Japan which now included Okinawa. Karate styles were formalized and introduced into public schools

Popularization Period

This period, from 1910 to 1935, was one of growth in the awareness and popularity of karate in Okinawa. Karate was introduced to Japan.

Internationalization Period

This period began after World War II. It is during this latest period that the developed systems of karate are introduced first to America, then around the world.

Karate has been taught outside Okinawa and Japan for only forty-five years. Karate was introduced to Japan only twenty-eight years before that. It is necessary, to a certain degree, to change or update ancient martial arts in an ever changing world. The ways and methods of the past should not, however, be discarded because they are old. The defensive techniques of the past have been tried and proven true. With the exception of firearms, the manner in which unscrupulous people attack innocent people has changed very little.

Ineffective systems of self defense have died with their creators, while the strong, effective systems have survived. Their survival is credited to more than effective self defense. Karate has been a beacon of strength to an oppressed and deprived society. The historic national heroes of karate have inspired community strength and compassion in the face of oppression, aggression and holocaust.

Information about karate's mysterious past is just now coming to the forefront. This synopsis of Okinawan karate is only a sampling of the information available in print today.

The government of Okinawa has launched a campaign to consolidate and distribute the history of karate and kobudo styles of their country. A new martial arts training hall located in Naha, the *Kenritsu Butokukan*, was completed in 1994. The World Championship Pre-tournament was held in Okinawa in August of that year. It was attended by more than five hundred black belts from around the world. The World Tournament will be held there in August 1997.

A complete text, *The Karate and Kobudo Investigative Report* and a pictorial manual, *The Okinawa Karate and Kobudo Graph*, were published in 1995 by the Okinawa Prefecture Department of Education to aid in educating the world about the *ISLAND OF KARATE*.

The Okinawa Kenritsu Butokukan, Naha, Okinawa

UECHI FAMILY

上地流

KARATE HISTORY

Chou Tsu Ho — Shushiwa (1874-1926)

Kanbun Uechi (1877-1948)

Kanei Uechi (1910-1991)

In Wakayama, Japan during the summer of 1936 a young Okinawan named Owan decided to test Kanbun Uechi's martial arts ability. Owan lashed a cooking knife to the end of a two meter bamboo pole. He hid in the bushes along a path and waited for Kanbun who would be returning from the public bath. As Kanbun walked by, Owan thrust the homemade spear at the right side of Kanbun's body.

Kanbun, reacting with incredible speed, grabbed the spear and pulled it to him hand over hand as if climbing a rope. Before Owan knew what had happened, Kanbun had grabbed him by the throat and pinned him to the ground. Owan identified himself and cried out for mercy.

Kanbun spoke in a low, calm voice, and explained to Owan that he could have lost his life over such a foolish prank. He admonished Owan and warned him never to do such a stupid thing again.

Of the deadly techniques in Uechi ryu karate's arsenal, Kanbun used the one requiring the greatest karate development and ability: life-protecting defense combined with compassion. An impatient person might have hastily delivered a physical counter-attack. This incident demonstrates both the exceptional skills and gentle nature of Uechi ryu's founder.

Okinawa officially became a state, *prefecture*, of Japan at the beginning of the Meiji era in 1879. (Chapter V) The goal of Emperor Meiji's restoration was to modernize Japan and bring it into the twentieth century. This entailed, among other changes, the abolition of the samurai class in both Japan and Okinawa. Former Okinawan samurai were forced to move from Shuri, Naha and Tomari areas to become merchants, craftsmen, fishermen and farmers.

One of the disenfranchised samurai groups was the Uechi family who had served among others, Kings Shokei and Shoei from 1682 to 1728. The family moved north to Izumi, on the Motobu Peninsula and became farmers.

Conflicts often arose between the farmers of the common class and the former samurai who were now moving in to occupy lands. The Uechi family, despite their samurai background, were well liked by the villagers because of their tradition of hard work and family honor. The code of the Uechi family was one of immense pride and honor in their hearts, not to be shown outwardly.

The population of the Motobu peninsula in 1877, the year of Kanbun's birth, was about 11,500 people living in 2,300 houses or huts. The majority of the residences had relocated from the Tomari, Shuri and Naha areas.

Some believe Kanbun Uechi was born in Izumi, on the Motobu Peninsula, and moved to the tiny mountain village of *Takinto* at three or four years old. Evidence indicates that Kanbun's parents, *Kantoku and Tsuru Uechi*, had already moved to Takinto and it was in the mountain top village that Kanbun was born on May 5, 1877.

I have been fortunate to have had contact for over twenty years with several people who spent ten to twenty years with Kanbun Uechi, up to the time of his death. Seiryo Shinjo and his wife, Tsuru, became Kanbun's closest friends in Wakayama. Tsuru Shinjo, who still lives in Kadena, Okinawa, saw Kanbun almost daily for twenty years. Their son Seiyu, grew

Toguchi house and store near Izumi and Takinto

up around Kanbun and was his student for nine years. Seiyu's wife Yoshi, still lives in Kadena, Okinawa. Seiko Toyama, Kanbun's student for ten years, still teaches Uechi ryu in his dojo in Zakimi, Okinawa. These people provided details as to the location of Kanbun's birth.

Kiyohide Shinjo and I ventured into the mountains near Nago to find the founder's birthplace, formerly a farming village of eighteen to twenty houses. After an exhaustive search of every mountain road in a large area, we were unable to find the small lake and secluded farming area described to us. At dusk we found a small market at the base of a mountain. To our surprise and good fortune the store owner, *Taro Toguchi,* was a fourth degree black belt from the Nago Uechi ryu dojo, established by Kanei's younger brother, Kansei Uechi.

The farmland and overgrown lake of Takinto

Mr. Toguchi knew well the place we were seeking and offered to show us the way. His wife, riding a small motorbike preceded us into the mountains as night set in. We were taken directly to the place where the Uechi house had stood and where Kanbun was born.

It was a moment of intense pride to find this historic spot, so far above the rest of Okinawa. The lateness of the hour effected the view and the photos taken at that time. During a subsequent research expedition six months later I returned to Takinto.

In the daylight it was easy to see how the isolated spot had eluded us earlier. The tiny farming area is not easily seen from the road and the small lake is overgrown with vegetation. It is a tranquil and serene location with a breathtaking view of northern Okinawa.

Controversy may continue to surround Kanbun's birthplace, Izumi or Takinto. The exact location of the mountain top farming village of Takinto, where he grew up, has been established.

Kanbun Uechi grew up in this area, part of a proud, traditional Okinawan family of bushi (samurai or Shizoku) lineage. The Uechi family farmed daikon radishes and sold them in the village at the bottom of the mountain. Radishes are still grown there today.

Karate (te), kobudo and the samurai arts were a cultural part of rural life in Okinawa, especially on the Motobu peninsula. More organized martial arts were being taught in Naha, Shuri and Tomari. Those systems were greatly influenced by the martial arts of China (tote). Those areas, in the southern part of the islands, were an insurmountable distance for a farmer from Motobu to travel.

View of Ie-jima Island from Takinto

Kanbun learned *bojutsu* (staff arts) from exposure to Motobu experts such as Taru Kise and Kamato Toyozato, as well as his father, Kantoku. Kanbun often taught the younger people of his area and led bo demonstrations that accompanied holidays and festivals.

An aged martial arts master from Tobaru named Toyama instilled in Kanbun the desire to pursue martial arts training in China. Toyama had visited China many times to study the martial arts and bojutsu. He did not leave a historic mark on Okinawa, but influenced many young men in the Motobu peninsula, including Kanun Uechi.

The desire grew steadily by the day, despite objections from his parents. They explained the hardships a farmer from Northern Okinawa would face in the foreign land. Kanbun did not speak the language or understand the customs. Additionally, China was in an extreme state of social unrest.

Kanbun outwardly abandoned his idea to travel to China to become a martial arts expert but the desire continued to grow inside him. He listened and learned all he could to aid in fulfilling his dream and waited patiently for an opportunity.

By the time he reached young adulthood Kanbun had grown to about five feet five inches and possessed a strong, stout body from years of working the soil. He was considered a handsome young man, taking his facial features from his mother. Tsuru Uechi was a kind hearted, well-spoken woman. She was also tall, rather large and robust.

Kanbun's father on the other hand, was an average size man. He was a happy person with a perpetual smile who was well liked by the villagers. He enjoyed drinking, singing, dancing and sharing stories with his friends. Occasionally his wife, Tsuru, would arrive late in the evening to carry her husband home. The village saying was that Kanbun had inherited his strong body from his mother and his samurai spirit from his father.

There is a misconception that the former location of Takinto is on top of Mt. Yaedake that is now occupied by a Japanese military communication site. In reality, Takinto is located about four miles from that site.

The Universal Male Conscription Act, requiring military induction, came into effect in Japan in 1873, and in Okinawa in 1898. (Chapter V) The Okinawan people were against mandatory conscription, fearing it would invite the enemies of Japan to bring war against Okinawa. Their fears were proven correct during World War II and the Battle of Okinawa.

Kanbun and his family, like many in Okinawa, were strong antagonists of the Conscription Act. Kantoku Uechi, while descending from samurai roots, was a pacifist and objected to military ways. He had raised his son to shun war and to love peace.

Induction notices were unfairly issued. Those who worked in government offices, members of the medical profession and students studying abroad were exempt. Rural communities supplied most of the inductees resulting in a decrease in the farming labor force. Many young men of this time maimed themselves, feigned disabilities, or fled to China to avoid what they considered a socially unjust system.

Families of wealth could pay a fee of two hundred-seventy yen to exclude their son from induction. The cry in Okinawa was that the life of a young man was worth only two hundred-seventy yen! Conscription became an inflamed social issue in Okinawa. Seven hundred seventy-four Okinawans, a substantial number for that time, were convicted of attempted draft evasion during the enforcement of the Conscription Act. Conviction carried with it a one year prison term.

Kanbun's keen interest in karate and social objections to serving in the Japanese army provoked his decision to leave Okinawa. His parents abandoned their earlier objections against Kanbun traveling to China in the interest of their son's safety and life.

Kanbun and his family risked reprisal from the government with the decision for him to leave his homeland. At that time people were not allowed to live anywhere except the area where they were born and travel out of the country was illegal without permission.

Kanbun's father advised him of the many adversities he must overcome in the foreign land. He explained that the first step toward success would be to first overcome himself. He reminded Kanbun of an old book called *Hagakure*, written about *bushido* (the code of a samurai). The concept explained in the *Hagakure* is:

To win you must overcome your own side.
To overcome your own side you must overcome yourself.
To overcome yourself you must overcome body with spirit.

The Sino-Japanese war had just ended and relations between China and Japan were strained. The loyalties of Okinawan people were torn between the two countries. Foreign travel by common people was not allowed so Kanbun had to secretly make his way to China.

Kanbun Uechi left Okinawa not out of fear, but to solidify his conscious political objection to the Conscription Act. By the rules of the Japanese government, the young man had committed a treacherous act by leaving Okinawa to avoid military service. His decision would ultimately become a historic phenomenon, adding to the richness of the karate history of Okinawa.

ADVENTURES IN CHINA

In March 1897, Kanbun undertook the ten day excursion across the East China Sea to Fuchow City in Fukein Province. He was accompanied by *Tokusaburo Matsuda*, a friend from Motobu. The two young refugees, soon to be twenty years old, were uneducated and unfamiliar with the language and ways of China.

The pair stayed for a short time at the Okinawa Fellowship Hall, *Ryukyu Jueneki.* They experienced much difficulty and loneliness in the strange new land, a land embroiled in political upheaval.

The hills of Fukein Province in Southern China

During the collapse of the Ch'ing dynasty China was rife with revolution, civil wars and wars with Japan and Korea. This strife continued for ninety-nine years. In 1949, the People's Republic of China was founded by *Mao Tse-tung.*

Shortly after their arrival Kanbun and Tokusaburo began studying martial arts in the *Kugusku school,* located in the migrant Okinawan community. The school was run by an Okinawan named *Koho (Kogyo) Kojo,* who later founded *Kygyo ryu.* He is believed to be the first foreigner to open a martial arts dojo in China. His assistant was a man named Makabei Udon.

According to Seiko Toyama, Makabei took immediate notice of Kanbun's superior physique and muscular stomach and became jealous. He foresaw that Kanbun would become a great karate student. Kanbun's lack of formal education and the fact that he spoke with slight lisp, presented an appearance of being slow minded. Makabei ridiculed and criticized the quiet, gentle Uechi in an attempt to drive him out of the dojo. Kanbun soon defiantly quit, although his resolve to learn Chinese martial arts was stronger than ever.

It is unclear if Tokusaburo Matsuda stayed at the Kojo dojo or moved to another. He and Kanbun did learn similar chuan fa systems during their individual stays in China. *Chuan fa* (fist way), pronounced *kempo* in Japanese, is the predecessor of many Okinawan karate styles.

Chuan fa and *kung fu,* are two names used today to describe the martial arts of China. The Northern systems emphasize soft, flowing movements. The systems of Southern China that most Okinawans were exposed to, focused on strength and conditioning.

Formal association to a martial arts school was shrouded in secrecy. Admission was especially difficult for foreigners. Relations between China and Okinawa drastically deteriorated after Japan claimed Okinawa as their sovereign property.

Training was conducted in a clandestine manner during that time due to the political environment. The White Lotus Society, Shaolin Temple System and the Boxers, clandestine martial arts and political activists groups, were embroiled in campaigns against the oppressive *Ch'ing dynasty* (1644-1911).

In 1727, the Ch'ing dynasty had outlawed martial arts practice for private citizens in an attempt to squelch underground religious and political sects. Loyalties to the ways of the previous Ming dynasty remained strong.

The Ch'ing government twice set fire to the *Shusan Shaolin Temple,* considered to be the center of secret martial arts training. Eventually the Shaolin priests fled to other parts of China, particularly the South where oppression was not as severe. They established new Shaolin Temples, gathered comrades and again began conducting secret martial arts training.

The Boxer rebellion (*Hokushin Jihen*, 1898-1900) pitted the Manchurian run government against rebellious citizens and was centered on the martial arts factions. The eruption resulted in a fifty-five day occupation of Peking, by the United States Marine Corps. Kanbun experienced the rebellion after his arrival in China.

After the Boxer rebellion failed, the Ch'ing government increased enforcement of the restriction on martial arts practice and again burned Shaolin Temples. The expected results, the elimination of martial arts, did not happen. Instead, martial arts practitioners scattered themselves and continued teaching, secretly. For the first time in history chuan fa instruction was widespread and available to the peasant population of China.

During Kanbun's travels, selling medicine made from Chinese herbs, he searched for another school of chuan fa. He was familiar with many of the styles he viewed, having seen them practiced in Okinawa. Then he discovered a school run by a man named *Chou Tsu Ho* or *Chu Chi Wo* (depending on the translator). The Chinese characters for his name are pronounced *Shushiwa* in Japanese Ramanji. Kanbun called his sensei *Shuhabu*, perhaps due to his speech impediment.

Kanbun was impressed by the strength of the students there. He especially liked the body hitting and testing he witnessed during Sanchin kata so he requested admission to the school. He was denied entry, perhaps because he was not Chinese. It is also believed that Shushiwa's school was one of the headquarters for the underground Boxer rebellion. Kanbun requested entry several times and was repeatedly turned down.

Kanbun Uechi experienced extreme loneliness and dejection during that period. He reflected on his father's guidance in exercising inner strength and upholding ones honor. He applied patience and the determination he learned as a farmer and martial artist in Motobu to find the strength to continue.

Seiko Toyoma told this version of Kanbun's acceptance into Shushiwa's school. One day Shushiwa became ill with a massive headache. He did not look well so his alarmed students sought out Kanbun Uechi and insisted that he use his medicine to cure their teacher. Kanbun successfully healed Shushiwa with herbal mixtures. As a result Kanbun Uechi was finally accepted as an official disciple at the Fu Chuan Shin Temple in a secret ceremony called Pai Soo.

It has been surmised that Shushiwa was knowledgeable of herbal medicine and is believed to have taught them to Kanbun, however, this is conjecture and no other explanation of their meeting has ever been revealed.

Shushiwa, who was only three years older than Kanbun Uechi, had already developed an extraordinary martial arts reputation by the time they met.

Chou Tsu Ho - Shushiwa (1874-1926)

Chou Tsu Ho (or *Chu Chi Wo*) was born in 1874 in Nanko-chin Shibata village in the Zhitian area. Two different backgrounds have been established for *Shushiwa.* Both are explained here.

Among the priests who relocated after the burning of the Shusan Shaolin Temple was one named *Sosei Osho,* alias Shushiwa. He is believed to have founded the *Fukein Shoalin Temple* at Kurensan, in Fukein Province.

Sosei Osho changed his name to Chu Chi Wo to evade authorities when he relocated in Fukein Province. He was in charge of Shaolin Temple martial arts training under Shizan Osho.

The Fukein Shaolin Temple, and Southern China, hosted a growing number of anti Ch'ing revolutionaries training in the marital arts. The *Southern Shaolin Ken,* considered the strongest sect of Chinese kempo, consisted of hard body training and was offensive rather than defensive oriented. Emphasis was placed on fingertip, *nukite,* training. Practitioners were known for having fingers like iron.

Eishun Ken, another system developed in the South was a soft style known for its defensive skills. Shushiwa is believed to have combined the two styles to create a system that used hard techniques for offense and soft techniques for defense.

In the second version of his origins *Shushiwa* was known by several names such as, Yong Kuan (Eternal Vastness), Xunshan Doazhe (The Xun Mountain Taoist), Yeikan, and the samurai name of Azan-do-sha. He was born into a wealthy family and exposed to the best education possible, including martial arts, since he was a small child.

He learned Shu Haku in the Ei tai province and later learned Southern Shoalin Fist under Zhou Bei. He also studied Iron Fist under the tutelage of He Xi Di of Shandong Province and finally received instruction under a famous marital artist named Ko Sai Tei, from San To Province. He also became an accomplished painter and calligrapher.

Shushiwa, described as an intelligent and dedicated student, became proficient in several forms of boxing, particularly Tiger Fist, one of the Five Fists of Fujian. Legends attribute him with great strength. He could hold the weight of two people hanging from the fingertips of his outstretched arms.

Shushiwa contracted a severe illness and died in 1926, at the young age of fifty-two.

The first three years of Kanbun's training were devoted only to the kata Sanchin. Besides karate training he worked at farming on the temple grounds, pulling up daikon radish roots. The first two years focused on strengthening the student's body through hard work as well as martial arts practice.

Another chore he performed was the cleaning and husking of beans. The beans were placed in a large stone bowl and struck repeatedly with the fingertips until the husks could be blown away. With this type of work the fingertips were being trained for martial arts. In Okinawa and China building strength in daily work and karate training were closely related.

After three years practice Kanbun, who was lonely, visited the Kojo dojo to see the Okinawan people there. After Tokusaburo Matsuda returned to Okinawa he described the reunion.

Makabei insisted Kanbun demonstrate his karate. Kanbun performed Sanchin kata. Throughout the kata Makabei tested Kanbun's strength by pushing punching and kicking him. Kanbun performed his kata with smooth, flowing moves and lightning fast speed. Attempts to disrupt Kanbun's rock-solid stance were unsuccessful.

Makabei was impressed with Kanbun's incredible strength and piercing eyes, acquired in only three years. He humbly apologized for his previous rudeness and the two men became friends in the pursuit of pure martial arts.

In the spring of 1904, the same year that war began between Japan and Russia, Kanbun Uechi received the *Menkyo Kaiden* certificate naming him a master of Chinese Pangainoon (half hard-half soft style). It was a monumental event in his twenty-seven years of life. He had vowed to himself to become proficient in the martial arts of China, or never return to his homeland.

Kanbun felt he had accomplished his goals in China. He missed his homeland tremendously so he wrote to his father about his desire to return to Okinawa. The return letter from his father was emotionally devastating.

Kantoku Uechi felt it was unwise for his son to return then because of the continuing injustice of compulsory military service. In spite of a seven year absence, Kantoku's intense love for his son dictated that Kanbun remain in China.

Kanbun reluctantly followed his father's advice. He became an assistant to Shushiwa, continuing his martial arts training and lessons in Chinese literature and medicine, for three more years. Kanbun felt a strong obligation to perform and teach Pangainoon precisely as Shushiwa taught him. He was diligent about every aspect of his teaching.

Shushiwa taught that an opponent will attack when you are at an unguarded moment, when your mind and focus are not sharp. It is therefore important to maintain piercing eyes! Watch all four directions and listen to all eight directions, always. This will lessen the likelihood of an offensive attack. If it becomes necessary to move, move swiftly with hands and feet.

He scolded students for slackness and stressed swift moves when they detected the opportunity to attack their opponent. Kanbun's favorite words became "sharp eyes — quick hands!"

The following precept was taught by Shushiwa.

> *If you know yourself and know your enemy, you will win one hundred battles.*
>
> *If you know yourself but not your enemy, you may win fifty battles.*
>
> *If you know neither yourself nor your enemy, you can not win.*
>
> *To fight one hundred battles and win one hundred times is not virtuous. To achieve victory without a fight is true virtue.*

Kanbun had learned a great deal about the language and herbal medicine by that time. The speech impediment that affected Kanbun's Okinawan language was no hindrance to his Chinese speech. He became very fluent, specifically in colloquial Chinese.

Flower from Uechi gusuri on display in Tetsuhiro Hokama's Karate and Kobudo Museum.

The knowledge of growing, preparing and administering herbal medicine went hand in hand with martial arts teaching. A teacher was expected to heal his students when they were injured during training.

Chinese herbal remedies, when used as a drug, are called *Kanpo Yaku*. Since they are all herbal they are often called *Kigusuri* which means raw drug. *Kanpo Yaku* was the system of medicine used in Japan until the Meiji Restoration. After that time western medicine prevailed.

Kanbun's experience as a farmer was an asset in learning to grow medicinal herbs. He brought one form of herb with him when he later returned to Okinawa. The mixture made from this herb is known as *Uechi gusuri* (drug) and is effective in curing sickness, healing internal organs and the stopping of internal bleeding and bruising.

He passed the secret knowledge of this herb to only three of his students, Ryuyu Tomoyose, Kanei Uechi and Seiyu Shinjo. Seiyu Shinjo taught the process to his son Kiyohide Shinjo.

The process involves fermenting the dried roots of the plant in *awamori* (Okinawan sake). I have seen trays full of small pieces of the root drying in Master Shinjo's house.

I had the opportunity to experience the effects of Uechi gusuri in 1975. Master Shinjo became alarmed at the extreme bruising on my body, the result of another beating from his son Kiyohide. I was given about six ounces of noxious liquid to drink. Within two days all the bruising, and the accompanying pain, were completely gone.

Kanbun began selling medicine on the street as a means of income. In doing so he exposed himself to the challenges of martial artists who felt they had more skill than Kanbun Uechi.

His reputation as a remarkable martial artist became widespread. A warrior named Matsu Kinjo returned to his home in Itoman in 1909, after spending eighteen years in China. He told stories praising the magnificent ability and gracefulness of an Okinawan he met there named Kanbun Uechi.

During that time Shushiwa encouraged Kanbun to open his own school, but Kanbun had no desire to do so. Shushiwa's persistence prevailed and Kanbun finally agreed.

Kanbun, age thirty, opened his own dojo, the *Pangainoon Kempo Sho* (Martial Arts Institute) early in 1907. He chose a town he liked called *Nansei no cho (Nansoe)*, approximately 250 miles southwest of Fuchow.

During the time Kanbun Uechi was establishing his martial arts school in China a small pox epidemic, famine and a series of typhoons swept across Okinawa. On the other side of the world Albert Einstein was publishing his theory of relativity.

Kanbun Uechi was a warm hearted, affectionate man who was well liked by his students. His fierce martial arts ability was secondary to his easy, likable demeanor. Kanbun continued his instruction by making semi-annual visits to Shushiwa to continue his own dedicated training.

While in China Kanbun became good friends with a native of Fuchow named *Gokenki* (1886-1940) who practiced White Crane Boxing. Gokenki is the Japanese pronunciation of his Chinese name, which is *Wu Hsien Kuei.* Gokenki regularly visited Kanbun at Shushiwa's school and at Kanbun's school in Nansoe. The young man challenged Kanbun's enthusiasm and rousing exchanges of chuan fa took place when they came together.

White Crane Boxing expert Gokenki (1886-1940)

Ryuko Tomoyose once told a story about Kanbun Uechi that occurred about that time in China. Kanbun and three or four of his students visited a pub in a nearby village to drink and talk. At midnight Kanbun decided to leave while everyone else wanted to remain.

The dark path that Kanbun took was well known as a dangerous place, full of bandits. Before long a massive figure appeared in front of Kanbun on the path. The figure stretched out his long arms, blocking Kanbun's way, and demanded his money. Kanbun stated that he had spent all his money at the pub and had none left. The man angrily demanded that Kanbun take off his clothes and hand them over. Kanbun refused and anticipated the forceful punch launched at his face.

Kanbun blocked the strong man's punch and delivered a fingertip strike, *nukite*, to the man's chest. As the bandit lay motionless his companions scurried away in the bushes.

Fingertip strikes (*nukite, koken* and *kakushiken*) were Kanbun's favorite techniques. He reportedly became known in China by the saying; "One strike means certain death."

For three years Kanbun conducted classes at his school and sold medicine. His compassion, strength and martial arts ability became renown in his new area. At the age of thirty Kanbun Uechi was one of very few foreigners ever to teach chuan fa in China. Then a tragic event occurred that would cause Kanbun to leave China and refrain from teaching for fourteen years.

The established story is that during a period of extreme drought Kanbun's most promising student was involved in an argument over irrigation of parched rice fields. In the ensuing fight the student struck a fatal blow, killing the other man.

Villagers blamed Kanbun Uechi for his student's actions and their feeling about his school changed. The villagers turned against him, calling him a teacher of murderers. He took responsibility for his students' actions as if they were his own. He closed his school and left China forever.

More recent research indicates the possibility that Kanbun himself was involved in the dispute and delivered the fatal blow. Seiko Toyama, a devoted student of Kanbun Uechi for ten years, spent every opportunity listening to his Sensei and Ryuyu Tomoyose (Kanbun's first student, later in Japan) talk about karate. He heard Kanbun tell Ryuyu that he had once used a technique that he now disguised as the crane and had killed a man. He said he had to leave as a result.

In the conversation Kanbun revealed that he had accidentally killed someone in China using the cobra technique he had been taught in Pangainoon. The vertical downward strike resembled the striking method of the cobra. It was considered as dangerous as the snake's bite. Kanbun explained the fingertip strike, delivered the way he had been taught, would certainly result in death.

After the incident he vowed never to teach the technique the way he had learned it from Shushiwa. He explained that he used the crane to hide the cobra and placed less emphasis on the new version of the technique. The knowledge of the subtle differences of the two techniques died with Kanbun Uechi.

This point of view may be unpopular but when put into context, it would not be the first time karate men died in altercations with each other. No disrespect to the memory of Kanbun Uechi is intended.

This is a classic example of the dilemma of the martial arts. In the quest for self defense ability, the body is trained to the point of being a deadly weapon. That weapon of defense can become a weapon of destruction in the span of a heartbeat.

The development of self control and the building of character is more essential in the martial arts than learning techniques. An instructor's influence concerning this responsibility will always be limited due to the emotional and irrational side of human beings.

More than one master who returned to Okinawa after training in China refused to pass their art along to anyone. They cited the fear of a breach of self control resulting in the destructive use of their art.

Kanbun Uechi, despite requests from his students and Shushiwa to remain, closed his dojo in 1910 and left China forever. During his thirteen years in China Kanbun learned three katas. They were *Sanchin, Seisan* and *Sanseiryu*, along with body conditioning. Kanbun called the third kata *Sandairyu*.

The kata names represent Chinese numbers. Sanchin is three, seisan means thirteen and Sanseiryu, thirty-six. Kanbun did not stay in China long enough to learn the kata *Suparimpe* that was part of Shushiwa's system.

KANBUN UECHI RETURNS TO OKINAWA

A few Okinawans who had returned previously, including Kanbun's friend Tokusaburo Matsuda in 1901, had been arrested and imprisoned for one year for evading service in the Japanese army. Kanbun, whose Chinese name was *Shusaya*, anticipated this problem and took precautions. When he arrived in Naha in February 1910, Kanbun Uechi's appearance, dress, demeanor and language were Chinese. He avoided arrest upon re-entry to his homeland.

Kanbun had fulfilled his dream of becoming a martial arts expert. He should have arrived to a glorious and dignified homecoming. Instead the depressed, haggard Kanbun Uechi quietly arrived in Okinawa.

Kanbun was thirty-three years old and unmarried. He was formally introduced to Gozei Toyama, fourteen years his junior. They married in May, 1910, and began a life of farming in Izumi. Their first son, Kanei, was born June 26, 1911. His birth was followed by that of two daughters, Kame and Tsuru. Tsuru died as a child and a third daughter was named after her. Their second son Kansei, was born July 23, 1922.

Kanbun continued his quiet life at Izumi and *Ie-jima Island* (off the coast of Motobu) for fourteen years. He taught staff techniques to villagers as he had in younger days on Okinawa. He faced continuing pressure to teach the Pangainoon system. He always refused, claiming he had been mistaken for someone else. Kanbun, a very reverent, humble and serious individual, still felt the disgrace he had experienced in China. He also continued to be apprehensive about reprisals from the Okinawan government for service evasion.

Despite his quiet lifestyle Kanbun's reputation as an incredible martial artist grew, fueled particularly in the Naha area by his old Chinese friend. *Gokenki* had married and settled in Naha. He changed his name from Gokenki to *Yoshikawa* and established the Eiko Sagyo Tea Store in 1912.

Gokenki was involved in a fight with a Naha karate teacher and defeated him. Others challenged Gokenki, but no one could defeat him. He became popular, with many requests for instruction. He would speak of a great chuan fa expert in the northern part of Okinawa, who had been his friend and teacher in China.

Gokenki demonstrates White Crane chuan fa as Kenwa Mabuni looks on.

Although no one had ever seen him perform, the number of young men who approached Kanbun for instruction, with letters of introduction from Gokenki, increased annually. Kanbun learned of Gokenki's location from these men, allowing him to rekindle their old friendship.

Gokenki become very well known in Okinawa and became good friends with *Chojun Miyagi*. His Fukein White Crane system influenced the development of both Shuri te and Naha te.

Confronted with Gokenki's confirmation, Kanbun could no longer deny his martial arts expertise. Government officials traveled to Izumi to implore Kanbun to teach his martial arts in the public school system. He continued his refusal to teach, or even demonstrate a kata. He quietly worked his farm as if he had forgotten all about China and his ability.

There is a story that says the karate masters of the time were aware of Kanbun Uechi's reputation and were eager for him to prove his abilities. The opportunity presented itself one year at the annual Motobu Police Department Celebration at which local karate schools performed demonstrations. During the celebration the mayor asked him to demonstrate his style. Kanbun refused but was coaxed onto the stage. He demonstrated the kata Seisan with such speed, strength and ferocity that everyone in attendance was spellbound.

Seiko Toyama doubts the validity of this story, stating that Kanbun constantly refused to perform his art because he had seriously injured someone with his karate.

Kanbun's reputation was, however, very well known and *Anko Itosu*, founder of Shorin ryu, asked Kanbun to accept a position at the Prefectural Teachers College in Okinawa where Itosu was a karate professor. The Prefectural Governor, during a tour of northern Okinawa, also asked him to teach at the College. Kanbun respectfully declined both offers.

The constant pressure to teach karate made life difficult for Kanbun Uechi, who sought only seclusion. Combined with the economic strife of Okinawa, Kanbun again left his homeland. He followed the lead of many Okinawan people seeking employment during this time and at forty-seven years old decided to travel to the industrialized area of *Kansai* (Osaka and Kobe), *Japan*.

THE WAKAYAMA PERIOD

After the new year in 1924, Kanbun left his family in Okinawa and traveled to mainland Japan, stopping first in Osaka. Okinawan people living in Wakayama read about Kanbun's presence in Osaka and of his karate ability. Many people traveled to Osaka, asking Kanbun to teach them. He always refused.

Unable to find suitable employment Kanbun eventually traveled to Wakayama and secured employment in a textile mill, the *Hinomaru Sangyo Kabushki Kaisha.* The large mill, made of red tile, *akarenga,* produced boseki fabric used in Japanese clothing. The factory operated twenty-four hours a day.

Boseki is a fabric produced on a spinning machine as opposed to *bengata* that is hand made. Today, a large department store stands on the former site of the Hinomaru Sangyo Kabushki Kaisha.

It was the first time Kanbun and the other migrant Okinawans were employed by someone else. They lived in tenement housing and faced hardships and social discrimination at the hands of the Japanese locals.

Along with isolation from Okinawa and daily poverty, they were victimized by local hoodlums who had formed a criminal society called *Wabodan,* headed by an Okinawan named Kinjo, from Kakinohana Oroku. While most of the people pulled together to help one another in the new land the dark side of human nature caused some to take advantage of their own countrymen.

The Okinawan people were very small and quiet by nature, making them easy targets. These helpless people were regularly bullied, beaten, robbed and raped. The migrant community, deciding they had been victimized enough, formed the Okinawa *Kenjinkai* (Okinawa Citizens Association) in an attempt to strengthen their position against these hoodlums.

The Izumiya department store now occupies the site of the former boseki factory and Shataku Dojo

In 1925 a senior of the Kenjinkai, Bungoro Nakamura, approached Kanbun Uechi, Chosige Motobu (another known martial arts master) and a young man known for his sense of justice, *Ryuyu Tomoyose*, for help with the situation. Chosige Motobu is a nephew of Choki Motobu, of Motobu ryu karate.

Ryuyu Tomoyose, then in his twenties, constantly sought revenge on the hoodlums. Whenever the Japanese or Korean criminals would victimize a fellow Okinawan, Tomoyose would determine who the culprit was, hunt for him, and attempt to beat him up. His oldest son Ryusen, described his father as a "scrapper" who would sometimes challenge ten men. He did not always win.

Two other men living in Wakayama, Kai Akamine (an Okinawan sumo wrestler), and Susumu Tamaura had studied karate for two years from Kai's father, Kaho Akamine. These two men also fought back against the Wabodan during this time. Kai Akamine, then eighteen years old, was attacked by six Wabodan members, who he soundly beat one after the other.

These five men successfully defeated the Wabodan and ended the violence against their migrant community, gaining them tremendous prestige and respect.

left to right: Ryuyu Tomoyose (forty years old), Kanbun Uechi (sixty years old), Mr. Ganeko. Kai Akamine (twenty-nine years old) is standing in back.

Ryuyu Tomoyose was born on Ie-jima Island, near Kanbun's home on the Motobu Peninsula. He traveled to Wakayama in 1923, and knew of Kanbun's reputation from Okinawa and Ie-jima. The two men would become life long friends.

Tomoyose found entertainment fighting with the local Japanese. The exuberant young man lived in the apartment next to Kanbun and would frequently visit in the evenings, relating stories of his altercations. One evening Kanbun became excited while listening to one of the stories and explained the stance and techniques Ryuyu should have used in the fight. The young man persistently pleaded with Kanbun to teach him. Kanbun refused at first but little by little, began to teach only Tomoyose in his living quarters.

Ryuyu Tomoyose, Bungoro Nakamura and other Okinawans from the work community approached Kanbun formally, requesting that he teach his chuan fa system lest it be lost forever. Under continued pressure to teach, Kanbun explained what happened in China and his reason for not teaching. The delegation explained that they felt that fifteen years of repenting and remorse were enough to turn a bad situation of the past into a good one in the present.

They appealed to Kanbun's community spirit and social responsibility explaining that the great ability he had acquired through his hard work in China should not be lost in one generation. They believed his skill should be passed on to the Okinawan community for its protection and self growth. Considering the current problem with the Wabodan, he began to realize that the gentlemen were right. Kanbun changed his mind and agreed to teach for the first time outside China.

In April, 1925, Kanbun ended his fifteen year ban on teaching martial arts and opened his first school in Japan. It was at this point that Uechi ryu, taught as Pangainoon, was born. Kanbun used the living quarters (taku) in the company (kai-sha) compound for this purpose, naming it the *Shataku* (company quarters) *dojo*. Dojo is the name for a karate school. The words literally translate to "way place" and represents the place where the way of karate is taught.

Kanbun and his new students maintained regular patrols to keep the Wabodan in check, reducing violence against the Okinawans to a minimum. Kanbun and his senior students were given the name *gijin* or guardian angel.

Ryuyu Tomoyose was the first person to cross the threshold of the new dojo becoming Kanbun Uechi's first, student. Tomoyose was followed, in order of seniority, by:

Genmei Uezato (Kume-jima, Okinawa)
Saburo Uehara (father of Takenobu Uehara, Oroku)
Isamu Uehara (Ushigome Shubukan in Tokyo)
Kata Yamashiro (Ie-jima, Okinawa)
Yoshitada Matyayoshi (Urasoe)
Kanei Uechi (Motobu)
Shuei Sakihama (Ie-jima)
Bunkichi Tamaki (Motobu)
Kai Akamine (Itoman)
Susumu Tamamura (Naha)
Seizen (Seiryo) Shinjo (Ie-jima)

Kanbun taught the three classical katas he learned from Shushiwa: Sanchin, Seisan and Sanseiryu. Kanbun never taught or demonstrated a kata in its entirety. He taught a method he called *Ikyoryo*, meaning one move at a time with explosive power. He never performed an entire kata in front of his students during his years of teaching in Japan.

Along with kata Kanbun taught kote kitae (arm conditioning) and jiyu kumite (free sparring). Free style sparring was not part of karate practice in Okinawa. Sport karate sparring was being developed at this time in Japan. Kanbun explained that in China karate men would often seek out a school and challenge the instructor and students to fight. Kanbun wanted his students to be prepared in this event. He taught sparring moves from kata, unlike the sport type of point sparring prevalent today.

Kanbun intentionally limited the number of students he taught. New students had to be recommended by one of the original members. That member guaranteed the moral character and behavior of the candidate they recommended. All prospective students were carefully screened and scrutinized by Kanbun. All students were forbidden to display their martial arts outside the dojo. All training was conducted secretly behind closed doors and shutters.

Seiryo Shinjo spoke about how the young men of the area would peek through the cracks in the wall observing with enthusiasm the training going on inside. On the occasions when a visitor knocked on the door all activity inside stopped. The visitor was greeted by fully clothed men sitting on the floor engaged in social conversation. In spite of this secrecy Kanbun's reputation grew.

Kanei Uechi at thirteen years old

Kanei Uechi at twenty years old

It was during this time that Gichin Funakoshi began teaching Okinawan karate at colleges in Japan. As karate grew in popularity among the Japanese, Kanbun continued teaching secretly, to local Okinawans only.

Kanbun Uechi was historically the only Okinawan in Japan during this time to teach a Chinese-Okinawan martial art in a dojo environment. For six years the secret training continued at the Shataku dojo, while the carefully selected students became proficient in Pangainoon.

Kanbun Uechi's oldest son Kanei, lived in Okinawa with his mother until he was thirteen, then with his grandmother for three years. He was unhealthy as a child, often experiencing stomach difficulties. Kanei is a name in modern language. As a child Kanei was called *Sandee* (pronounced Sanday), from the older Hogen dialect.

In 1927, at sixteen years old Kanei traveled to Wakayama and joined his father. He found employment at the Hinomaru Industry Joint Stock Company. Kanei joined the Shataku dojo and began chuan fa training under his father.

Kanei soon realized he would be the successor of the martial arts legacy left by his father. He took this responsibility seriously and trained daily with great enthusiasm to become proficient in Pangainoon.

Tebira Dojo, Showa Dori - Wakayama, Japan

Some of Kanun Uechi's students in front of the Pangainoon-ryu Karate-jutsu Kenkyu-jo (Tebira dojo), 1936. back row left to right: Mr. Kishimoto, Mr. Ochima, Mr. Matayoshi, Mr. Gibo, Mr. Yabeku. front row: Mr. Oshiro, Ryuyu Tomoyose, Kanbun Uechi, Kanei Uechi, Ryukichi Tomoyose.

PANGAINOON GOES PUBLIC

In March 1932, Kanbun Uechi, at fifty-four years of age, changed the location of his dojo. He opened the *Pangainoon-ryu Karate-jutsu Kenkyu-jo,* in the Tebira section of Wakayama. The new dojo, located at Showa Dori (street), less than two miles from the former Shataku dojo, was dedicated to formalized training and personal development.

Gichin Funnakoshi who is generally credited with being the first Okinawan to open a dojo in Japan opened his *Meisei Juku dojo* in Koishigawa, Tokyo two years later in 1934. (Chapter I)

It is noteworthy that Kanbun used the word *karate* on the sign in front of his new dojo. This was four years before the reading of the kanji for "China hand," *tode*, was changed to "empty hand," *karate*, in Japan and Okinawa. (Chapter I) Kanbun's students referred to their art as karate from that time on.

The structure that served as Kanbun Uechi's house and dojo was very small, only about eight tatami mats (a tatami mat measures approximately three by six feet, totaling about 145 square feet). Only a few students at a time could train inside. Most of the training was conducted outside in the packed dirt practice area, hidden from view behind the dojo. The space measured about 20 tatami mats (360 square feet). When it rained, no one showed up. When it was cold the students, dressed only in shorts, moved around constantly to stay warm.

The clandestine atmosphere of the Shataku dojo was left behind and the new dojo was open to the public. Kanbun continued to screen potential students. Only persons of an unbalanced or deceitful nature were excluded. The student enrollment grew and Kanbun soon quit his job at the boseki factory.

Many of the factories and other industries in the area operated twenty-four hours a day. To accommodate work schedules, Kanbun taught three times a day, 365 days a year.

The morning session went from 10:00 A.M. and lasted three hours. The three hour afternoon session started at 2:00 P.M. The night session, beginning at 6:00 P.M. lasted several hours. About thirty to forty students attended each session. Besides the fixed class schedule, students would come in and out at all times.

The intense nature of Kanbun's teaching eliminated students who were of weak mind. Survival of the fittest was the universal rule applied to all practicing students. Many school children sought instruction during this time but there were many drop outs due to the rough training.

Showa Dori (street). Kanbun Uechi's dojo stood where cars are now parked.

View from the backyard training area. The building across the street remains from that time.

New students were charged with cleaning the dojo before daily practice. One of the duties of the *kohai* (junior students) was rinsing and wringing out the towels their *sempei* (senior students) used to wipe the sweat from their bodies. If the towel was not rolled to the satisfaction of the sempei, the kohai would be pummeled over the head with the towel.

Students who trained in the Tebira dojo described the respect and the fear they had for their sempei, who were very hard on the kohai. The use of full force kicks to the legs and body during sparring practice as well as brutal intensity used during body conditioning were common practice.

Seiko Toyama, spoke of being constantly slammed across the dojo. He recalled he was once hit with a shoken (one knuckle punch) in the middle of the forehead, which knocked him unconscious. He said today, over fifty years later, he can still feel that shoken punch.

Mr. Toyama said Kanbun used herbal mixtures to treat the bruising that often occurred during training but he never taught this aspect to his students. He remembers one concoction that also contained human urine. The combination of herbs and uric acid proved effective on the injuries.

The Pangainoon karate dojo became well known and very well respected by other martial artists in the area, including judo and kendo schools. They showed a keen interest in the unique style Kanbun taught. Many Okinawan people flocked to his dojo as well as the Japanese residents of Wakayama.

Okinawan karate master Kenwa Mabuni traveled to Wakayama in 1925 and studied for a while with Kanbun Uechi. After his exposure to Kanbun, Mabuni designed the kata *Shinpa*.

The dojo grew to between one hundred-fifty to three hundred students. Many became proficient enough to teach Pangainoon.

The most senior students of the Shataku dojo named earlier are followed by those of the Tebira dojo.

From Okinawa:

Seiyu Shinjo
Chigen Bise
Kazuo Kishimoto
Koshin Matayoshi
Shuka Izu
Seitoku Toyama
Natukichi Shimabukuro
Seiko Toyama
Sensuki Yabiku
Yamata Chinen
Seitoku Teruya
Choei Nakazato
Kotoku Takamine
Hachizo Oshiro
Takeo Gibo
Noboru Uchima
Eika Hirayama
Ryukichi Tomoyose
Hansei Yamashiro

From Wakayama:

Misao Kitamura
Tadamitsu Kamei
Kosei Nerai
Tsunejiro Akai
Kenichi Demizu
Seiichi Hosokawa
Takehsi Yamazaki
Seiji Kimoto
Ken Akunuma
Shunsho Yabuta
Chuichi Kameyama
Seiro Enomoto
Karikei Minemoto
Ryuzo Nishitani

The most conspicuous students of the Wakayama period of Pangainoon, and those credited with contributing to the founding of Uechi ryu karate are:

Ryuyu Tomoyose, Genmei Uezato, Saburo Uehara, Kata Yamashiro, Yoshitada Matayoshi, Seizen Shinjo, Kanei Uechi, Shuei Sakihama, Bunkichi Tamamura, Hachizo Oshiro, Takeo Gibo, Kazuo Kishimoto, Kaei Akamine, Susumu Tamamura, Noboru Uchima, Eika Hirayama, Ryukichi Tomoyose, Natsukichi Shimabukuro, Kotoku Takamine, Seiko Toyama, and Seiyu Shinjo.

THE TEBIRA DOJO BECOMES A FORMAL ORGANIZATION

As the student structure grew, the need for a formal organization became apparent and in November 1933, the Shubukai (Organization of Martial Arts Training) was formed. The Shubukai created a governing constitution containing six articles and five items. The constitution consisted of *Chuko no hongi*, a pledge of loyalty and filial piety, and *Chino no kenma*, the development of intelligence. The Shubukai felt that *Shubu no seishin*, the spirit of mastering the martial arts, was common sense and did not include it in their constitution. Among the governing rules were the following principles:

Third annual Shubukai organizational meeting, January 1, 1936
Notice the western attire worn by Kanei Uechi, front row - right

This damaged photo shows Kanbun Uechi with Ryuyu Tomoyose and two of his children in 1935. The boy, Ryuwa, took over the teaching responsibilities of the Wakayama Uechi ryu dojo until his death in 1994.

We will embody the principles of filial piety and make efforts to be upright citizens.

We will deepen our understanding of everyday life and pursue a hardworking, humble and frugal lifestyle.

We emphasize physical exercise and bodily health.

We will cultivate moral behavior and increase our appreciation of others.

We will promote social spirit and contribute to public well being.

PANGAINOON SPREADS TO OSAKA AND OKINAWA

After ten years of rigorous study Kanei Uechi received a Certificate of Instruction and Full Proficiency from his father in 1937. At age 26, he opened a branch dojo of his own on Tsurumibashi Dori, Nishi-Nariku, Osaka. Two years after opening the *Osaka dojo* he married Shige Nakahara from Izumi, Okinawa.

In 1940, Kanei Uechi moved again and opened a dojo in his home at Hyogo-ken, Amagasaki-shi, Osaka. In 1941, he was promoted by his father to Master level. In May of the same year Kanei's first son, *Kanmei*, was born.

Kanei Uechi, thirty years old, and student of his Osaka dojo.

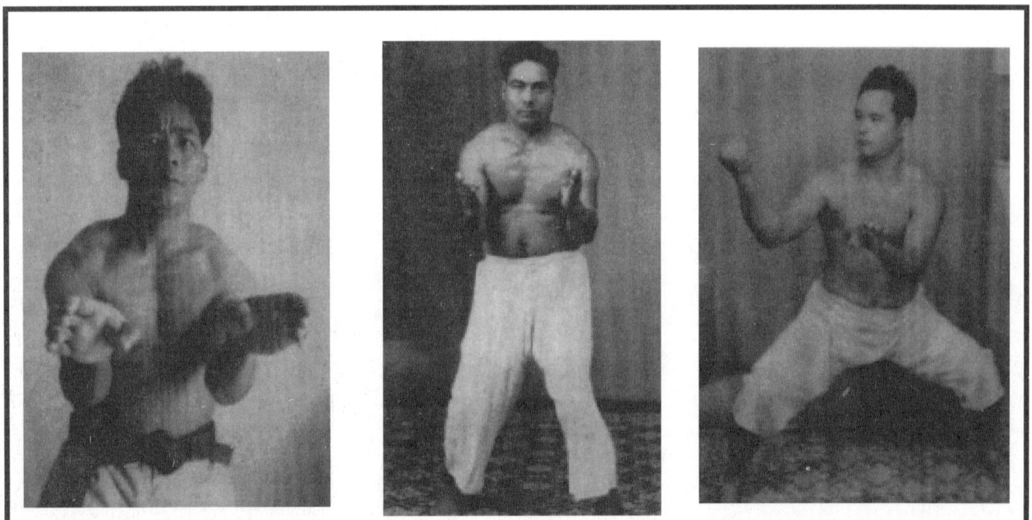

Kanei left the Hyogo dojo in the care of senior students Soryu Furugen, Kotoku Iraha and Seiki Itokazu.

The Osaka dojo is now run by Mr. Fukushimia, a student of Soryu Furugen. One of the signs reads Uechi ryu karate while the other says Pangainoon jutsu.

The start of World War II saw most of Kanei's students called into the war effort. In 1942, Kanei, with his wife and family, returned to his mother's new home in the village of Miyazato, near Nago, Okinawa.

Kanei Uechi began teaching his brother Kansei, twenty-five years old, and other young men from the village in the yard of his home. This was the first time Pangainoon (Uechi ryu) was taught in Okinawa. Kanei closed his dojo after only two years. He and his students responded to the government call into the war effort to defend Okinawa.

Kanei, thirty-three years old, was assigned to the Ie-jima garrison commanded by Major Tadashi Igawa. He was then transferred to the Kungami ground support unit where he remained until the end of the War in 1945.

Osaka Castle

Shubukai members anniversary photo taken August 16, 1945. It was the last photo taken before Kanbun Uechi and others left Wakayama to return to Okinawa. Third from the left is Seiko Toyama, third from the right is Seiyu Shinjo.

Pen and ink etching of Osaka Castle by Alan Dollar, 1992

Kanei Uechi in front of the Tebira dojo, 1936

Seiyu Shinjo at 16 years old in Wakayama, 1945

The Tomoyose Wakayama Uechi Ryu Dojo

Alan Dollar, Ryusen Tomoyose (Kiyohide's uncle), Kiyohide Shinjo

KANBUN UECHI LEAVES JAPAN

Due to post war strife in Japan, Kanbun decided to return to Okinawa. In October, 1946, Kanbun Uechi, accompanied by students Seiryo, Tsuru and Seiyu Shinjo, Seiko Toyama and a few others, returned to Okinawa together. Several others later returned separately and settled in the northern portion of Okinawa. Kanbun left the Tebira dojo in the care of Ryuyu Tomoyose.

The post war occupation by American forces brought with it a ban on martial arts practice as well as restrictions on other group gatherings. Ryuyu taught only family members and close friends until the occupying forces relaxed the prohibition in 1948.

In 1957, he moved the dojo to a location nearby on *Kokutae Dori*, where it remains today. He continued to teach Uechi ryu karate until his death in 1971. The dojo was taken over by his son Takayoshi (also known as Ryuwa) until he died in 1994. The Wakayama dojo is now run by another of Ryuyu's sons, Takahiro Tomoyose.

Ryusen Tomoyose, the oldest son of Ryuyu, was born in Okinawa in 1924. He joined his father in Wakayama when he was sixteen years old. He did not study karate from his father, but describes himself as a "scrapper", as his father was. He married *Sayako Shinjo*, the daughter of Seiryo and sister of Seiyu Shinjo. They are both kind and generous people with a strong family tradition. They still live in Wakayama.

Ryusen and Sayako Tomoyose, Wakayama, Japan

CONDITIONS ON OKINAWA AFTER THE WAR

Kanbun's second son, *Kansei* had been captured in Manchuria by Russian forces near the end of the war. He spent two years in a Siberian prisoner of war camp. He was released and returned to Okinawa in 1947. He established a dojo in Nago.

Upon returning to Okinawa, Kanbun Uechi, the Shinjo family and Seiko Toyama were interned in a prisoner of war camp on the Motobu peninsula. Kanbun and the Shinjos shared the same tent as their living quarters for six months. Morale was very low in the camp so to lift spirits Kanbun began demonstrating his karate.

Wakayama Castle first built in 1585. It was destroyed in 1945, while Kanbun Uechi lived in Wakayama.

Ie-Jima Island near Motobu, Okinawa.

Kanbun Uechi died on this farm on Ie-jima Island.

This garage occupies the site of the small house where Kanbun Uechi died.

While in Japan, as described earlier, Kanbun taught by showing individual moves from kata rather than the whole kata. Kanbun's morale boosting performances in the prisoner of war camp were the only times senior students Seiryo and Seiyu Shinjo and Seiko Toyama had seen their Sensei perform all the kata in their entirety.

The entire group relocated to Ie-jima Island after being released from the prisoner of war camp.

Conditions in Okinawa after the war were deplorable (Chapter V). Famine and disease were rampant. There was no oil in which to boil tempura, a mainstay of the Okinawan diet. In desperation, motor oil that had been drained from American military vehicles was used for cooking. Survivors of the Battle of Okinawa have described to me the foul taste and devastating effect on the body of what they call, "Mobil tempura".In January, 1948, Kanbun Uechi became ill with nephritis that he fought for eleven months. Kanbun, 71 years old, died on Ie-jema Island on November 25, 1948. The Shinjo family were the only ones present when Kanbun died.

THE CREST OF THE UECHI RYU KARATE-DO ASSOCIATION

The *Octagon* represents the eight katas of Uechi ryu.

The *Circularity* denotes the eternal circularity, with no beginning or end, of self completion, of heaven and earth, justice and peace, harmony and fairness.

The *Chrysanthemum petals* stand for prosperity and long life.

Hidari gomon is the Japanese translations for the three commas in a circle spiraling to the left.

The symbol was developed in opposition to the Satsuma invasion of Okinawa in 1609. In the Hogen dialect it is pronounced hijai gumun. This symbol is often confused with *mitsu domae* that is a similar Japanese symbol that swirls to the right.

Ue represents the first character of Uechi ryu karate. Ue means upper level or top.

Seiyu Shinjo once described Kanbun's agonizingly painful death. Sieyu's pregnant wife, Yoshi, was asked to leave the dying man's room because of the belief the experience might damage her unborn baby. Later that night their first child, a daughter named *Toshiko*, was born.

The next day Seiryo Shinjo contacted Kanei Uechi with the news of his father's death. Kanei, Seiryo and Seiyu Shinjo took Kanbun's body, in a small sabani boat, back to Okinawa.

Kanbun Uechi has been described by many people who knew him as a kind, gentle, quiet man in day to day life but a fierce, intense and strict instructor of Pangainoon ryu. His life was as unique and eventful as other forefathers of karate, as was his influence.

Ryuko Tomoyose, twenty years old, learned from his father, Ryuyu, that Kanei was back in Okinawa. In April, 1949, he helped Kanei Uechi establish the *Uechi ryu Karate jutsu Kenkyu-jo* in Ginowan-son, Aza Nodake, known as the *Nodake dojo*. The style name was then changed from Pangainoon karate jutsu to Uechi ryu karate jutsu in honor of Kanbun Uechi.

Previous publications have stated that the name change occurred in 1940 while Kanbun was still in Wakayama. Seiko Toyama and Seiyu Shinjo clarify the style was still called Pangainoon when they returned to Okinawa with Kanbun and that the name was changed after his death.

The Nodake dojo was a small, thatched roofed building. A little later the *Oroku dojo* was opened by Saburo Uehara and the *Kanzatobaru* (Naha) *dojo* was established by Seiki Itokazu.

Photo taken in a field behind the Nodake dojo in 1950. At the front right are Ryuko Tomoyose and Seiyu Shinjo

Kanzatobaru dojo established by Seiki Itokazu.

Annual meeting of the Uechi ryu Shubukai, 1952

The Shubukai started in Wakayama, was updated in 1953 with a new constitution, the *Chino no kenma.* In the same year Kanei Uechi and Seiyu Shinjo started a new job as night security guards for the Japan railroad in Okinawa, the *Nihon Tetsudo Koyogyo.* The employment would last three years.

In 1955, Seiyu Shinjo, twenty-six years old, established the *Asato Uechi ryu dojo* in Naha. Also in 1955, Kanei moved his dojo from Nodake to Futenma.

In 1957, Kanei combined the Futenma dojo and the Kanzatobaru dojo and relocated a short distance to a new site. Uechi ryu karate and the *Futenma dojo* were open to the public, including American servicemen in 1958. The first American student, and black belt, of Uechi ryu was George Mattson.

Kanei Uechi was very ambitious about organizing and teaching his father's system. He recognized the difficulty in teaching newer generations in the rough manner of the past. His desire was to make Uechi ryu karate available to the public at a level at which they could participate, without compromising the integrity and authenticity of Pangainoon.

Asato (Naha) dojo of Seiyu Shinjo, 1955

Photo taken after a karate demonstration for the Yaeyama Island Police Department in 1955. Kanei Uechi, Seiko Toyama, Seiyu Shinjo and Ryuko Tomoyose, among others are seen here.

Photo taken after training at the Futenma dojo in 1956. Listed by last names only, back row left to right: Shirada, Yonaha, Komesu, Kinjo. Front row: Kinjo, Toyama, Sakihara

Sparring practice on Ie-jima Island between Seiyu Shinjo and Mr. Yohena as Kanei Uechi looks on, 1951

Toward this end Kanei created four new katas, between 1954 and 1958, to be used as stepping stones between the three brought from China. Kanei Uechi, with assistance from other seniors, created katas *Kanshabu, Daini Seisan, Seirui* and *Kanchin.* Kanshabu kata was named after Shushabu and Kanbun. The name was later changed to *Kanshiwa* when the pronunciation of Shushabu's name was changed to Shushiwa. Daini seisan, or second seisan, was changed to *Kanshu,* also named after Kanbun and Shushiwa. Seirui is the number sixteen and Kanchin means the tactics (chin) of Kanbun.

In June, 1958, Kanei Uechi held the first dan test and awarded the first belt ranks in Uechi ryu karate. Students of Kanbun Uechi such as Seiko Toyama and Seiyu Shinjo were promoted to Godan (fifth degree), while others received first through fourth degree promotions depending on their seniority and ability.

In July 1959 Kanei Uechi was awarded the Master Instructor Certificate by Ryuyu Tomoyose.

The short, Chinese style *gi* (karate uniform) had been traded in for heavy gi used in judo in 1954. The new belt ranks brought with them the wearing of the first karate gi, similar to those worn today. Sport sparring karate was gaining popularity and was being added to traditional training during that time.

Second Futenma dojo, 1957

Shubukai group in front of the Futenma dojo, 1957

Kanei Uechi in front of his Futenma dojo.

Construction of a dojo and house began in December 1963, at the site in Futenma. The new Uechi ryu dojo was named *Soke Shubukan*, style headquarters. The same year a new kata created by Saburo Uehara, *Seichin*, (ten conflicts) was added to the style.

Kanei Uechi, Ryuko Tomoyose and others visited Taiwan in 1966 to discuss with Chinese kempo experts the origins of Uechi ryu.

There was an occasion during this time when the *All Japan Karate Team* visited Okinawa to spar with various dojos. The first few dojos contacted declined to become involved. The delegation eventually called Kanei Uechi at the Futenma dojo. He politely and enthusiastically encouraged them to visit his dojo that evening. Kanei then called around to the Uechi ryu dojos to recruit a team for that evening.

The young Okinawans, anxiously awaiting the arrival of the prestigious team, were startled by loud clacking sounds outside. Peering out the window they saw the All Japan Karate Team, in formation, marching up the hill toward the dojo carrying flags and banners. The traditional geta (wooden sandals) were making the loud noise. The Okinawans were excited and intimidated by such a formal display.

Yaeyama Island Police Department demonstration, 1958. Front row left to right by last name: Inada, Itokazu (Seiko), Toyama, Miyagi,(Seiki Itokazu's son), Yohena. Back row in gi: Takara, Shirado, Yonaha, Kinjo, Uehara, Shinjo. All the men in dark clothing are Yaeyama police officers except Seiki Itokazu, middle right and Kanei Uechi in the middle.

Following introductions Kanei suggested they demonstrate kata for each other. The response was that the team from Japan did not practice kata, only sparring. Kanei then directed them to sit and watch as Uechi ryu kata was demonstrated. The strength displayed during kata and the body testing during Sanchin in particular, instilled anxiety in the visitors.

Kanei arranged the young men in a line with *Toshiyuki Itokazu* to fight first and the younger Kiyohide Shinjo second. "Tosh" beat his opponent soundly and quickly. The second visiting fighter lined up expecting a new opponent, but Itokazu remained. He pummeled the second opponent worst than the first, kicking him with such force that he flew across the dojo. Permission had been given by Kanei Uechi to use shoken (one knuckle punch) and sokusen (big toe kick) techniques that evening. These techniques are compared to the tiger's teeth (Chapter X).

The visiting team bowed out after the second fight. They left more quietly than they had arrivcd. Kanci Ucchi respectfully bowed to them as they left and invited them to return any time.

In February, 1967, Kanei, at age fifty-six, was promoted to Hanshi Judan (tenth degree) by the Japanese Karate-do Federation, *Zen Nihon Karate-do Renmei.* In August of the same year Kanei, accompanied by Ryuko Tomoyose, visited America for the first time. The visit was sponsored by George Mattson and other instructors in Boston, Massachusetts.

More dojos opened and the number of people practicing Uechi ryu in Okinawa and America grew. In January, 1971, the Shubukai was renamed the *Uechi Ryu Karate-do Kiyokai*, Uechi Karate-way Association.

The structure of the new Association and the methods of teaching were refined to preserve traditional budo from the past and combine it with the increasingly popular competitive karate.

An annual tournament of all Uechi ryu black belt competitors had begun in 1968. The first year both the kata and kumite divisions were won by *Kosuke Yonamine* of the *Koza dojo*. He won the kumite championship the second year while *Ken Nakamatsu* placed first in kata. The third year Kiyohide Shinjo, son of Seiyu Shinjo won the kata and kumite titles and began a nine year reign as the Uechi ryu Champion of Okinawa. (Chapter III)

In May, 1975, Kanei, sixty-four years old, was elected President of the All Okinawa Karate-do Federation, *Zen Okinawa Karate Renmei*, which had been founded in May, 1956. In April, 1977, Kanei was promoted to Hanshi Judan by that association, ten years after his promotion from Japan.

Kadena dojo black belts depart for the Futenma dojo to compete in the 1975 Uechi ryu tournament.

The strength and harmony of the organization in the 1970's and early 1980's were impressive. The semi-annual dan tests held in Futenma, brought with it an inspiring unity and brotherhood shown by the various dojos. The magnitude in the training and testing was sometimes frightening. The intensity established by Kanbun Uechiís methods was still the standard in the dojo.

Kanei Uechi always sat quietly observing the activities before him. Seiyu Shinjo barked orders and darted around at moments of disorganization. The senseis, black belts and students always conducted themselves with the utmost dignity and respect for one another and their karate style, and they were tough. This is a great tribute to the teaching of both Kanbun and Kanei Uechi.

The Uechi ryu Association gained momentum in the international dissemination of Uechi ryu karate. There were many American servicemen training at the various dojos and an increasing number of visitors came from the states. In 1979, the Association began sponsoring the *Zen Okinawa Karate Championships*. The tournament champion the first year was Kiyohide Shinjo. Competitors of all Okinawan styles from around the world continue to compete in the annual event.

Seiko Itokazu split from the Uechi ryu Association in 1980, and started the *Pangainoon Ryu Kiyokai.* Takenobu Uehara established the Uechi Ryu Oroku Shinkokai in 1983.

The Soke Shubukan (Futenma dojo) in the early 1970's

Alan Dollar and Kanei Uechi

Kiyohide Shinjo and Alan Dollar— Futenma Dojo

The following is a listing of Uechi ryu dojos and head instructors listed in *Uechi Ryu Karate Do*, the master text for this style, published by the Uechi ryu Karate Association in 1975. Over five hundred pages of that manual were translated during research for this book.

SHUBUKAN (Dojo)	***KANCHO (Head Instructor)***
OKINAWA AREA	
Soke	Kanei Uechi
Nago	Kansei Uechi
Kadena	Seiyu Shinjo
Koza	Kosuke Yonamine
Tobaru	Seisho Yonaha
Noborimata	Seisho Komesu
Ohira	Seiko Kinjo
Nakanishi	Seishin Shirado
Urasoe	Nobuhide Asato
Aja	Sheshu Maeshiro
Wasaka	Seiko Itokazu
Nah	Tsutomu Nakahodo
Matsugawa	Katashiro Kasawa
Sakashita	Kiyoushi Komesu
Hantagawa	Takashi Kinjo
Oroku	Takenobu Uehara
Haebaru	Seiki Irei
Kyan	Shinsei Omine
Yaeyama Island	Masaharu Shinzaki
KAGOSHIMA AREA	
Amani	Katsuhiko Kasawa
TOKYO KANTO AREA	
Shinjuku	Isamu Uehara
Hachioji	Yasuo Shimoji
OSAKA and KANSAI AREA	
Kansai	Mr. Arakaki
Toyonaka	Koichi Mori
Tsukaguchi	Mr. Fukushima
Ikeda	Miki Kohigashi
Wakayama	Ryukichi Tomoyose
Hanshin	Omasu Takenaka
Kishiwada	Hiroshi Sugihara

Additional to this list in Okinawa are:

Seiko Toyama, Yomitan	Shinyu Gushi, Oroku
Ken Nakamatsu, Kitanaka	Yotsune Senaga, Nakagusuku
Minoru Miyagi, Yomitan	Tigeru Tkamiyagi, Chatan
Masakazu Kinjo, Kubagawa	Kazunori Maemaya
	Takahiro Gaja

Robert Trias visits the Futenma Dojo

THE STRONG FIST GROUP OF SEIYU SHINJO

KEN - FIST 拳
YU - SEIYU 優
KAI - GROUP 会

In 1981, Kiyohide Shinjo started the *Kenyukai* fraternity, within the Uechi Ryu Association, in honor of his father who died that year.The new emblem was worn on the left sleeve of the gi by all black belts from the Kadena dojo. This innovation soon caught on in the Association and various dojo names began appearing on Uechi ryu gis.

In April, 1984, Kanei and Kansei Uechi, Ryuko Tomoyose, George Mattson, John Mills and Marty Dow underwent an expedition to Fuchow City, China. They attempted to retrace Kanbun's life there and search for the origins of Pangainoon. Most of what is known about Shushiwa was obtained on this expedition. All information about Pangainoon or Kanbun Uechi had passed from existence.

Kansei Uechi, Hachi dan (eighth degree) died in November, 1987, during one of my visits to Okinawa. Classes at the Nago dojo are now taught by three of his sons.

Kanei Uechi was hospitalized during that time with a severe stomach ailment. During a visit with him it was apparent he was gravely ill. I lingered by his bed side for some time when I realized this would be my last opportunity to see him alive.

Kanei Uechi was not receiving visitors during my return in 1990. He remained in that frail condition until his death on February 21, 1991. He was eighty years old.

Kanei was a kind, gentle person like his father. His soft spoken manner was in direct conflict with the expressiveness of his karate. He dedicated his life to his father's style of karate and directed his efforts to its propagation. Kanei Uechi's vision and years of tenacious work have created a karate system that is practiced in many countries throughout the world.

The Nago Uechi ryu dojo

In the relatively short time Uechi ryu has been on Okinawa it has risen to the forefront of karate history. It has been named by the Prefectural Board of Education as one of three original styles of Okinawan karate.

Kanei's passing caused the inevitable; the splitting of the Uechi ryu Association. It became increasingly difficult for all the egos to co-exist and most of the Association members left the Soke dojo in 1988.

They formed the Okinawan Karate Do Kiyokai, *Okikukai.* The first President was Ryuko Tomoyose. He retired in 1993 and the position was filled by Tsutomu Nakahodo. Since the original separation in 1988, several dojos have severed affiliation with any Association and operate individually.

In 1995 the Okikukai organization changed the name of the style they practice from Uechi ryu to *Shohei ryu.*

Kansei Uechi's class

Three generations of family ties and loyalties to the Uechi family left Kiyohide Shinjo with no choice but to remain with the Soke dojo. He upheld the honor of the Shinjo family by remaining loyal, in the face of adversity, to the Soke and the Uechi family until Kanei's death. In 1992, he too left the Soke dojo and formalized the *Uechi Ryu Karate Kenyukai Association.*

Explaining the political infighting that accompanies the downfall of an organization of such great stature serves no purpose here. Fragmentation of karate's lineage and roots, of many styles, plagues Okinawa, Japan, and America.

There are many outstanding instructors and students of Uechi ryu throughout the world. The traditional style of Uechi ryu karate, fortunately, continues to grow in numbers and strength, despite personal and political fragmentation. It is a unique style of karate!

Futnema Uechi ryu dojo in the early 1990's

Shintoku Takara (R) 1965

Shintoku Takara 1995

Shintoku Takara and Seiko Toyama

Ryuko Tomoyose

Ken Nakamatsu and his Kitanakagusuku dojo

Kanei Uechi presents Nidan promotion certificate to Alan Dollar, May 1977.

SHINJO FAMILY

新城

KARATE HISTORY

Seiryo Shinjo (1908 - 1976)

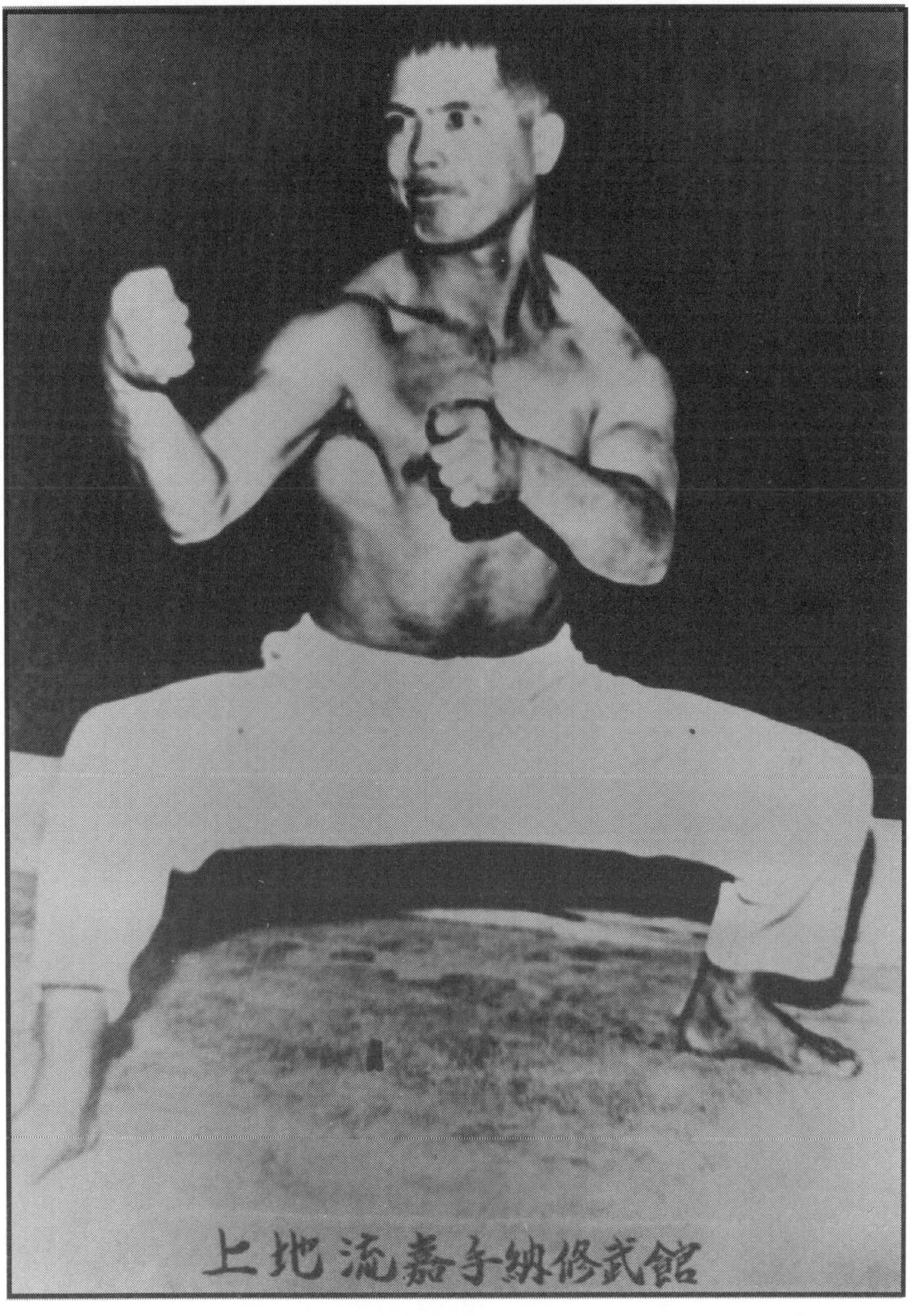

Seiyu Shinjo (1929- 1981)

Kiyohide Shinjo (1951 -)

At the karate demonstration commemorating the third anniversary of the death of Seiyu Shinjo, Grand Master Kanei Uechi spoke these words of praise:

> *"It already has been three years since the great loss to our Association. Unfortunately, once Seiyu Shinjo became seriously ill, modern medicine could not help him.*
> *He worked actively as a teacher and as a board member of the Uechi Ryu Karate Do Association. Karate was not recognized by society during the 1940's to 1970's. Mr. Shinjo made great efforts to popularize, develop, and organize karate.*
> *Moreover, I could say that he was one of the persons who made the greatest strides toward karate becoming internationally known as a cultural inheritance of Okinawa. He was instrumental in making the Uechi Ryu Karate Do Association, one with an international stature.*
> *There are many of Mr. Shinjo's students actively teaching Uechi ryu karate all over the world. I can rely on Mr. Kiyohide Shinjo, son of Seiyu Shinjo, to carry on his father's will."*

The Shinjo family is one of the most dynamic and renowned names of traditional Okinawan karate. Three generations of Shinjo men have helped mold the history of this unique karate style. The history of this karate family parallels the growth of Pangainoon and Uechi ryu karate from the time Kanbun Uechi first taught martial arts outside China.

With the exception of Kanei Uechi, no one has had more influence on the development of Uechi ryu karate and the Uechi Ryu Association than Seiryo, Seiyu and Kiyohide Shinjo. In the Japanese dialect their names can be pronounced Kiyoshi, Kiyoyu and Kiyohide, respectively. The last name, Shinjo, can also be Arashiro.

The information presented here, combined with that of Chapter II, Uechi Family Karate History, will provide a complete picture of the development of Uechi ryu karate in Okinawa.

WAKAYAMA PERIOD

Seiryo Shinjo (formerly called Seizan Shinjo) was born on Ie-jima Island, June 10, 1908. His father, Seisan Shinjo was a well-known bo expert on Ie-jima. Seiryo traveled to Wakayama seeking employment in 1923, one year before Kanbun Uechi. Seiryo found a job with the same company that Kanbun later would, the *Himomaru Sangyo Kabushki Kaisha*, a boseki factory. He worked at a different location but eventually heard stories of Kanbun and that he was now teaching. He introduced himself to Kanbun, and requested permission to become his student. Kanbun checked on Seiryo's background and observed his character before accepting him as a student.

Seiryo Shinjo entered the *Shataku dojo* early in 1927. He and his wife Tsuru, whom he had met in Wakayama, were married later the same year. Tsuru is the daughter of Seisho Toyama, a famous karate expert of the time, from Motobu, Okinawa.

Seiryo Shinjo was a small, agile man who became known for his incredibly fast kicks. *Hisaguwa Seizen* (fast kicker Seizen) was the nickname given to him by his peers.

Kiyohide Shinjo and Alan Dollar stand on the site of the former Shinjo home, Wakayama, Japan.

Ryusen and Sayako Tomoyose

Yoshi and Tsuru Shinjo

Tsuru Shinjo describes her current home as being very similar in size and appearance as Kanbun Uechi's Wakayama house and dojo.

Seiryo was a quiet, gentle man who would not quarrel with anyone. Kanbun grew to like him very much and they became the best of friends. Kanbun felt comfortable with Seiryo and Tsuru. Their house was the only place he could relax and express himself. It became a gathering place for Seiryo's friends including Kanbun, who was present for the birth of their daughter, Sayako. Sayako Shinjo later married Ryusen Tomoyose, the oldest son of Ryuyu. (Chapter II)

Tsuru Shinjo, now eighty-seven years old, lives in Kadena, Okinawa. She speaks with vigor and humor about her life around the karate men. She said the men would gather at her house and talk well into the night about karate and women.

Wakayama Kogyo (Technical High School)

One evening Seiryo and Kanbun talked so late into the night that Kanbun went to sleep there. Kanei Uechi (called Sandee at that time) became alarmed the next morning when he found his father gone. He feared Kanbun had been in a fight with rival karate men and lay beaten or dead somewhere.

He searched the many rivers and waterways that surround Wakayama, to no avail. As evening approached, he pondered where his father might be and went to Seiryo's house. He found Kanbun and Seiryo seated around a small table, still deeply engaged in conversation.

Tsuru Shinjo, who was very frugal, occasionally managed to obtain beef, which she would salt and store under the house. Meat was scarce in Wakayama. There was a law in Japan that prevented the killing of cattle because of their importance in farming.

Kanbun did not eat meat, but liked the tendons and cartilage. He believed eating them made his tendons strong. Tsuru often gave Kanbun the sinew from the meat she stored.

Their first son Seiyu, born July 10, 1929, was named after Ryuyu Tomoyose. Seiyu was born premature, at seven months, and was so small his mother compared his head to the size of a teacup. He caught diphtheria when he was three years old and beat death by only ten minutes, according to doctors at the hospital. Seiyu was never sick, even with a cold, after that.

Kanbun became fond of the exuberant young Seiyu, who pleaded for years with his father to let him study karate. Seiyu became a student at Kanbun Uechi's Tebira dojo in 1939. He was ten years old.

Seiyu, and other new students performed cleanup and other duties around the dojo. The first three months of training consisted of doing Sanchin steps across the dojo. Holding his arms in the proper position was added to the stepping, the following three months.

The rambunctious young man complained daily to his father that they had done the same thing in class again. Seiyu remained determined to learn karate. Eventually Seiryo began teaching his son at home, in addition to Kanbuns teachings. Seiyu Shinjo was exposed to an unprecedented learning opportunity for nine years.

Classes at the elementary and high schools were taught in shifts, so children could work. Seiyu went to the *Miyamae Shogoko* elementary school, only a few hundred yards from the Tebira dojo. He later attended *Wakayama Kogyo* (Technical High School) at night. He trained in the morning sessions at the Tebira dojo and worked at a job making pots and pans during the day. The high school is still in operation today. Wakayama was relatively undamaged during the war and many buildings of that era remain.

Seiyu Shinjo at sixteen years old in the Tebira dojo, Wakayama, Japan

Uechi Ryu Shubukai anniversary photo August 16, 1945. This is the last photo taken before many of the students returned to Okinawa. Shown left to right are Misters: Koyena, Seiko Toyama, unknown, Ueda, unknown, Tomoyose, Nakazima, Seitoku Toyama, unknown, Seiyu Shinjo, Miyagi, unknown.

Seiyu Shinjo was drafted into the war effort by the Japanese military. He attended pilot school, including *kamikaze* (divine wind) pilot training. Fortunately the war ended shortly after his military training began and Seiyu was released from duty.

Seiryo became ill with a respiratory problem toward the end of their stay in Wakayama. He had to quit his karate training.

The harsh conditions in Japan after the war facilitated the decision to return to Okinawa. The Shinjo family traveled with Seiko Toyama and Kanbun Uechi. Seiyu was leaving the only home he had known.

RETURN TO OKINAWA AND IE-JIMA ISLAND

The group was interred in a prisoner of war camp for six months, when they returned to Okinawa. They lived in tents and fought starvation and depression.

To lift moral in the camp, Kanbun demonstrated karate. It was the only time his students saw him perform all the katas in their entirety. In Japan he always taught explosive individual moves from a kata, *ikyoryo*, but never demonstrated the entire kata.

After release from the camp, Seiko Toyama moved to Naha. The Shinjo family and Kanbun Uechi relocated on Ie-jima Island.

Seiyu Shinjo met and married Yoshi Kohama there in 1947. They built a house on the property of the Shinjo family, a few hundred yards from the home of his parents. Hokonoto, a monument to the people who died on Ie-jima Island during World War II, now occupies the site. Members of the Shinjo family still live on Ie-jima Island, which has a current population of 5,500 people.

Kanbun lived less than a mile away, where he died on November 25, 1948. The Shinjos were the only ones present. They contacted Kanei the next day and using a small sabani boat, assisted him in returning his father's body to Okinawa. (Chapter II) On November 3, 1951, three years after the passing of the great karate master, Ie-jima Island produced a modern day karate legend named Kiyohide Shinjo.

The Shinjo family moved to Naha in 1953. Seiyu Shinjo continued his karate training under Kanei Uechi. The two men, who had grown up as brothers, worked for three years as security guards for the Okinawan railroad (Nihon Tetsudo Koyogo). They worked the night shift preventing theft from the train yard. Okinawa was impoverished after the war, and American relief was slow in coming. Some people took what they could to survive.

Hokonoto, a monument to those who died on Ie-jima Island during the war.

Kiyohide Shinjo, born on Ie-jima Island

Seiryo and Tsuru Shinjo soon moved to Kadena, a small village at a focal point in the road between Naha and Nago to work in the laundry shop owned by Seiryo's parents. The laundry business was booming because of the occupying American forces.

Seiyu Shinjo stayed in Naha and at twenty-six years old, opened the *Asato Uechi ryu dojo* in 1955. It was the fourth Uechi ryu dojo established in Okinawa. Three years later the first black belt promotions in the Uechi ryu system were awarded. Seiyu Shinjo was promoted to Godan (fifth degree).

Asato (Naha) Uechi ryu dojo established in 1955. Shinyu Gushi is sitting to the right of Sensei Seiyu Shinjo.

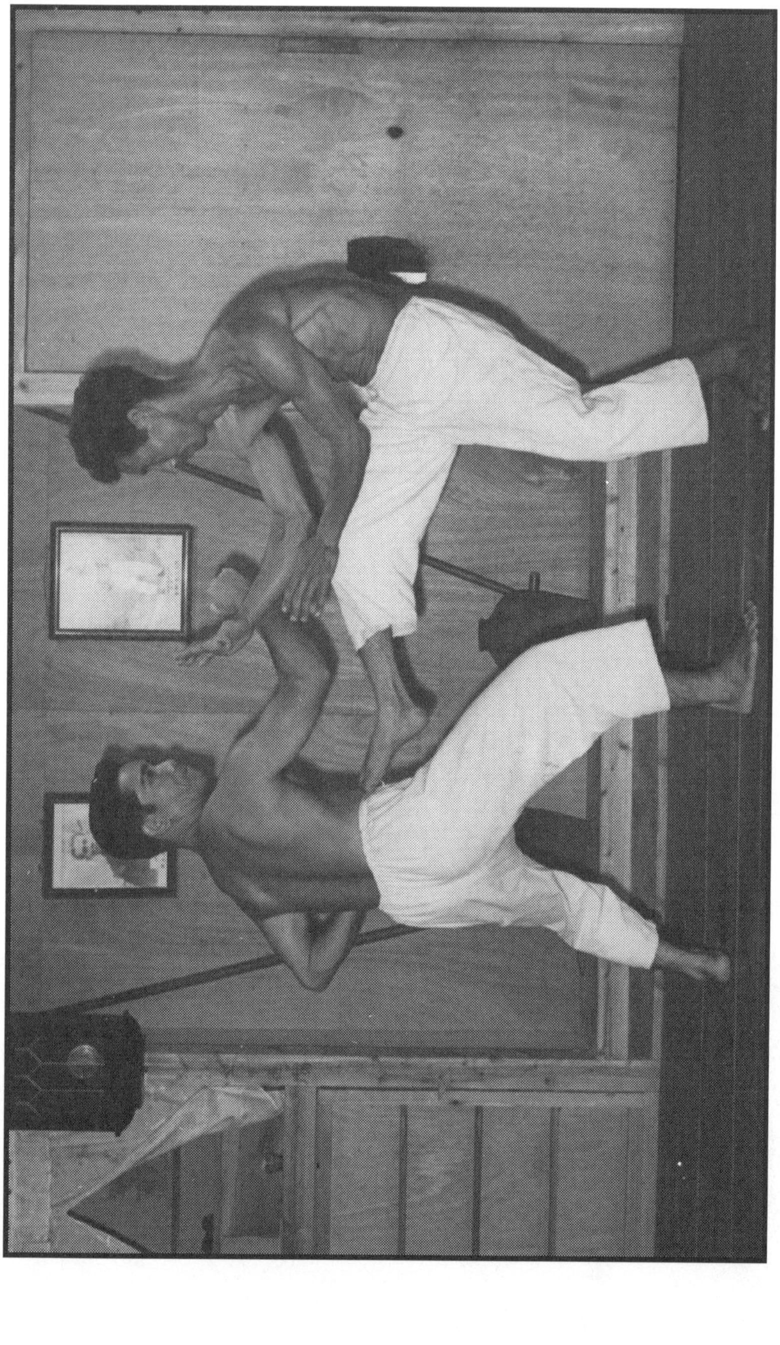

Omine Yoshiro and Kameijiro Uechara in the Kadena dojo.

Tsutomu Nakahodo and Seiki Irei receive Nidan promotion, 1964

THE KADENA ERA OF UECHI RYU KARATE

The land on which the Asato dojo stood was appropriated by the government for a new thoroughfare (Highway 58) connecting the southern and central parts of the island. In 1960, Sieyu Shinjo and his family moved to Kadena, and opened the Kadena Uechi ryu dojo. His second son, Narahiro, was born the same year. The Shinjo dojo has operated at the same location for thirty-five years as of this writing. The Kadena Shubukan is the only one in which three generations, grandfather, father and grandchild have learned karate in the same dojo.

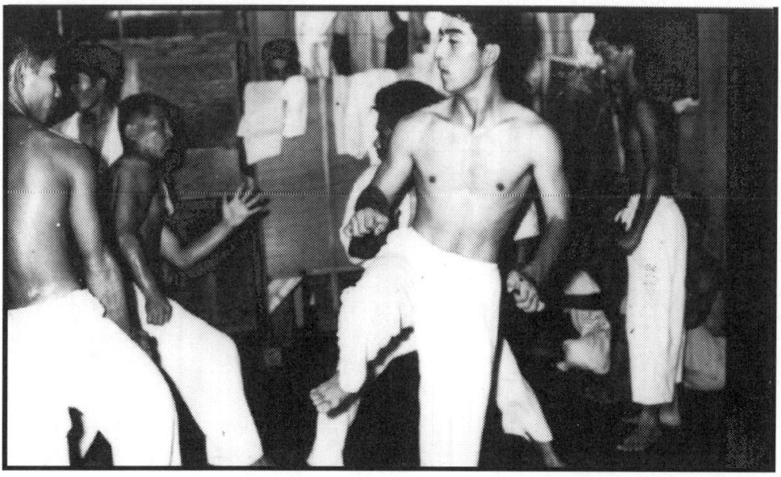

Minoru Miyagi, Seiyu Shinjo and Fumio Higa practice sparring.

Kiyohide Shinjo at twelve years old, with his father.

Kiyohide Shinjo began karate training, not by his own choice, when he was ten years old. Kiyohide did not like karate practice for several years, and probably for good reasons. Six o'clock in the evening was the starting time for karate class and Kiyohide's favorite television variety show, Golden Hour. His father would grab him by the ear and forcibly lead him into the dojo.

Seiyu was a hard man concerning karate. He also maintained the uncompromising, and sometimes inhuman, standard of training established by Kanbun Uechi. As the young man became accustomed to the training regime he was given the added responsibility of cleaning the dojo for thirty minutes before class began. On one occasion, when Kiyohide was fourteen years old, he and some friends went to the river after school. They cut bamboo swords and played at being samurai warriors. Kiyohide kept a keen eye on the setting sun, as a reminder to return to the dojo on time. He misjudged the time and arrived home after class had already begun.

He put on his gi (uniform), slipped into the dojo, and joined the group exercise. He was not called on all night to perform individual kata, as the other students were. He knew his tardiness had been noticed. After all the students left, Seiyu Shinjo went into a rage over his son's lack of responsibility. Mr. Shinjo took a large knife and cut the gi top down the back and ripped it from his son's body. He did the same to the belt and pants, telling his son that since he did not take his karate training seriously, he no longer had to practice. The incident passed and Kiyohide was allowed to resume his training.

Intoxicated servicemen often found their way into the dojo, challenging the Okinawans to fight, in those days. Seiyu Shinjo often ordered his son to fight the belligerent Americans. For many years the skinny young Okinawan was beaten by the challengers. As Kiyohide's size, strength, and karate ability increased, so did his dislike for American servicemen. In time Kiyohide won every fight, with great pleasure.

Kiyohide was promoted to Shodan (black belt) in 1968, eight years after he began training under his father. He established karate clubs in high school and college. He was promoted to Nidan (second degree) in 1970 and Sandan (third degree) in 1973. He also studied kendo for seven years during that time, earning the rank of Nidan.

Nobomasu Tomoyose

Kiyoshi Shinjo

Kiyoshi Shinjo (born in 1932) once opened a laundry shop with Ryuko and Nobomasu Tomoyose. They also trained under Kanei Uechi.

By 1969, the Shinjo family was complete with three daughters: Etsuko (1954), Kazumi (1956), Kiromi (1964), and four sons: Kiyohide (1951), Narahiro (1960), Hidonori (1968), and Masaru (1969).

The Shinjo's oldest child, Toshiko, born the night of Kanbun Uechi's death, died as a young child. Five of Seiyu's children are black belts in Uechi ryu karate, as are his brothers Seiho and Kiyoshi.

TOURNAMENT HISTORY

In 1968, The Uechi Ryu Karate Shubukai held the first annual Uechi ryu tournament. It included kata and kumite competition for black belts. Seiyu Shinjo was the organizer and tournament director. His son Kiyohide, placed third in kata in the inaugural tournament. (Chapter II)

At the third annual tournament in 1970, Kiyohide Shinjo won the championship in both kata (forms) and kumite (sparring). He continued to do so for a record nine years. He became a legend in Okinawa in the process and is often called "Okinawa's Superman".

The annual Uechi ryu tournament was held in two parts. Kata competition was held in the Futenma dojo under the watchful eyes of Kanei Uechi and all the senseis and seniors of the style. Sparring competition was conducted the following week.

In 1978, the eighth year of his championship reign, the first All Okinawa Championship Tournament was held. The champion of this historic sparring event, open to black belts of all karate styles, was Kiyohide Shinjo. He retired from competition after the 1980, Uechi ryu tournament, due to the ill health of his father.

By 1970, the Kadena dojo of Seiyu Shinjo contained the most students and had become the most popular dojo of Uechi ryu karate in Okinawa.

Senshu Sensei Opening Ceremony

Narahiro Shinjo placed first in kata in five of the eight Uechi ryu tournaments following his brother's retirement.

The Uechi ryu tournament ran uninterrupted for twenty years until the break up of the Uechi Ryu Association in 1988. The Kadena dojo won the championship in fifteen of the twenty tournaments.

On May 15, 1972, the United States gave up control of the island and Okinawa reverted to Japan. The All Japan Sports Festival, *Kokutae*, was held at the Naha Stadium, (near the site of the new Okinawan Martial Arts Kenritsu Budokan) as part of the Reversion celebrations. Massive demonstrations of Okinawan karate and dance (odori and eisa) were performed. The Japanese government gave every karate practitioner a new karate gi. The patch on the gi was patterned after the Olympic torch.

Kokutae, All Japan Sports Festival, in celebration of Okinawa's Reversion to Japan, April 1972.

Trophies and awards of nine time Okinawan Champion Kiyohide Shinjo

Kadena dojo tournament competitors

Kadena tournament winners in front of Futenma dojo

Seiyu Shinjo directs the annual Uechi ryu karate tournament

Kadena Dojo Victory Party, 1974

Kadena Dojo Tournament Winners, 1975

Kiyohide Shinjo— a decade of Tournament Victories

Kadena dojo victorious on the twentieth anniversary of the Uechi ryu tournament, 1987

Seiyu Shinjo was adamant about increasing public awareness of Uechi ryu karate and expanding its practice in America. To this end, he was one of the first sensei to open his dojo to American servicemen. He performed many demonstrations, for Okinawans and Americans, to propagate Uechi ryu karate.

Minoru Miyagi breaks boards for the Army Special Forces, 1964

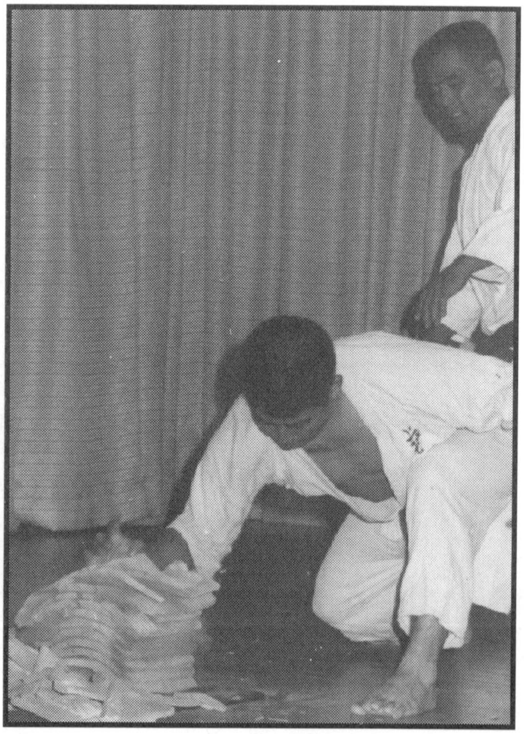

The rank structure had been developed and refined by the Association since the first promotions in 1958. In 1972, Seiyu Shinjo was awarded the title of Shihan, Master Instructor (certificate number six). Seiyu and his father Seiryo Shinjo were promoted to Hachi dan (eighth degree), May 16, 1974. Seiryo received the first Hachi dan certificate ever issued by the Uechi Ryu Karate Association.

Tsutomu Nakahodo breaks a 2x2 pole over the arm of Seiho Shinjo. Seiki Irei then does the same to Mr. Nakahodo

Seiyu Shinjo breaks a 2x2 pole on the arm of green belt Alan Dollar

Yako Shinjo toe kicks three boards held by Seiyu Shinjo, Minoru Miyagi and Tsutomu Nakahodo

Kiyohide was promoted to Yondan (fourth degree) in 1974, as a result of his continuous tournament victories. He also received Shihan certificate number thirty-one the same year. He was promoted to Godan (fifth degree) in 1977. Kiyohide Shinjo, although younger than his contemporaries, tested for Rokudan (sixth degree) and Nanadan (seventh degree) with Masters Nakamatsu, Takamiyagi, Gushi and Senaga.

Seiryo Shinjo, the founder of the Shinjo karate dynasty, died March 5, 1976, from a lung disease he contracted in Wakayama. He was sixty-eight years old.

The dojo-house structure in Kadena was very small. There was a small living room and kitchen adjacent to the dojo. The dojo area itself served as the sleeping quarters for the entire family. The small house and dojo were torn down and replaced in 1976. The new house was built on top of the new dojo, dramatically increasing the training and living area.

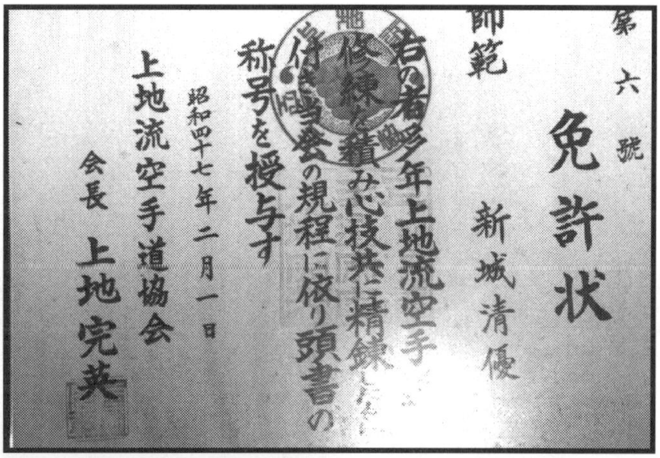

第六號
免許状
新城清優
師範
右の者多年上地流空手修練を積み心技共に精錬したるに付き当会の規程に依り頭書の称号を授与す
昭和四十七年二月一日
上地流空手道協会
会長 上地完英

Shihan (Master Instructor) certificate (#6) issued to Seiyu Shinjo

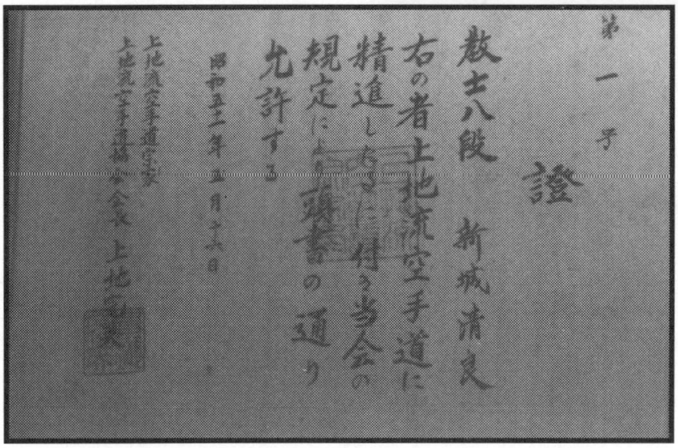

第一号
證
教士八段 新城清良
右の者上地流空手道に精進したるに付き当会の規定に依り頭書の通り允許する
昭和五十二年五月二十八日
上地流空手道協会会長 上地完英

The first eighth degree black belt certificate (#1) ever issued by the Uechi Ryu Karate Association. Presented to Seiryo Shinjo.

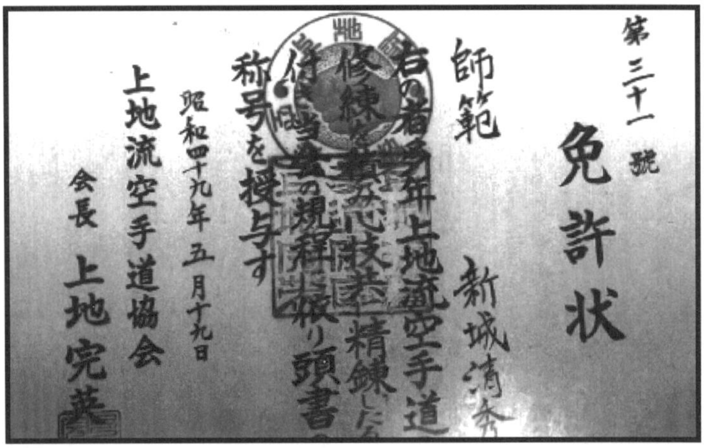
第三十一號
免許状
師範　新城清秀
右の者多年上地流空手道
修練を重ね心技共に精錬したる
に付き当会の規程に依り頭書の
称号を授与す
昭和四十九年五月十九日
上地流空手道協会
会長　上地完英

Shihan Certificate of Kiyohide Shinjo

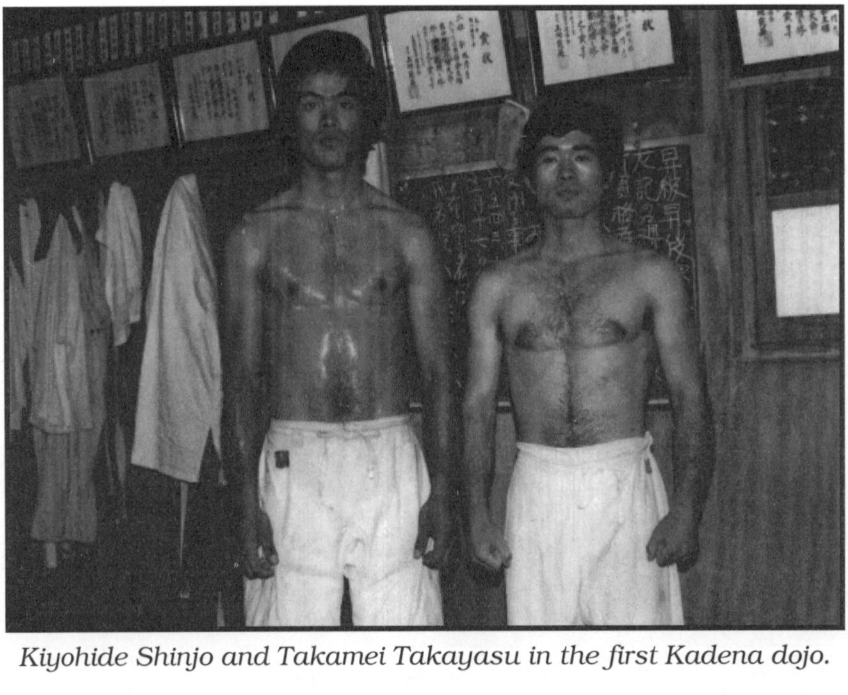

Kiyohide Shinjo and Takamei Takayasu in the first Kadena dojo.

上地流空手道

The first Kadena Dojo, established in 1955

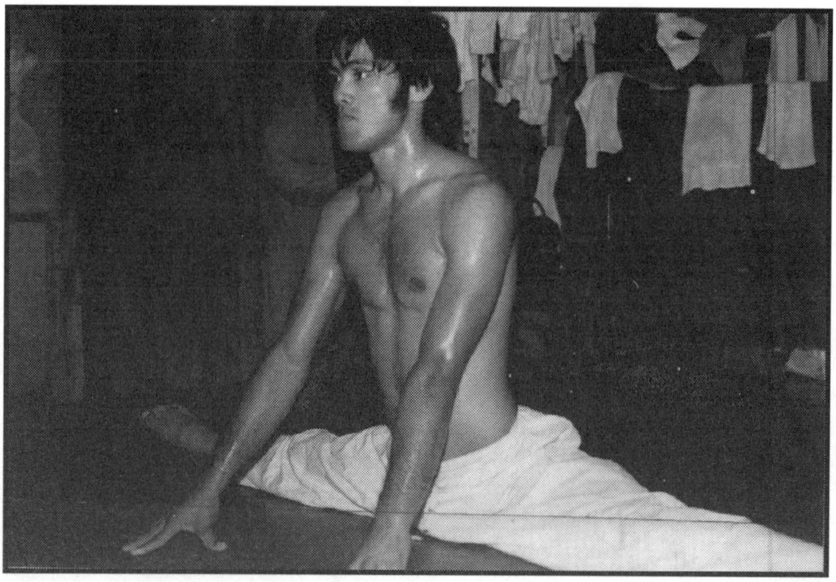

Sieyu Shinjo in front of, and inside, the second Kadena dojo, 1977.

上地流空手道

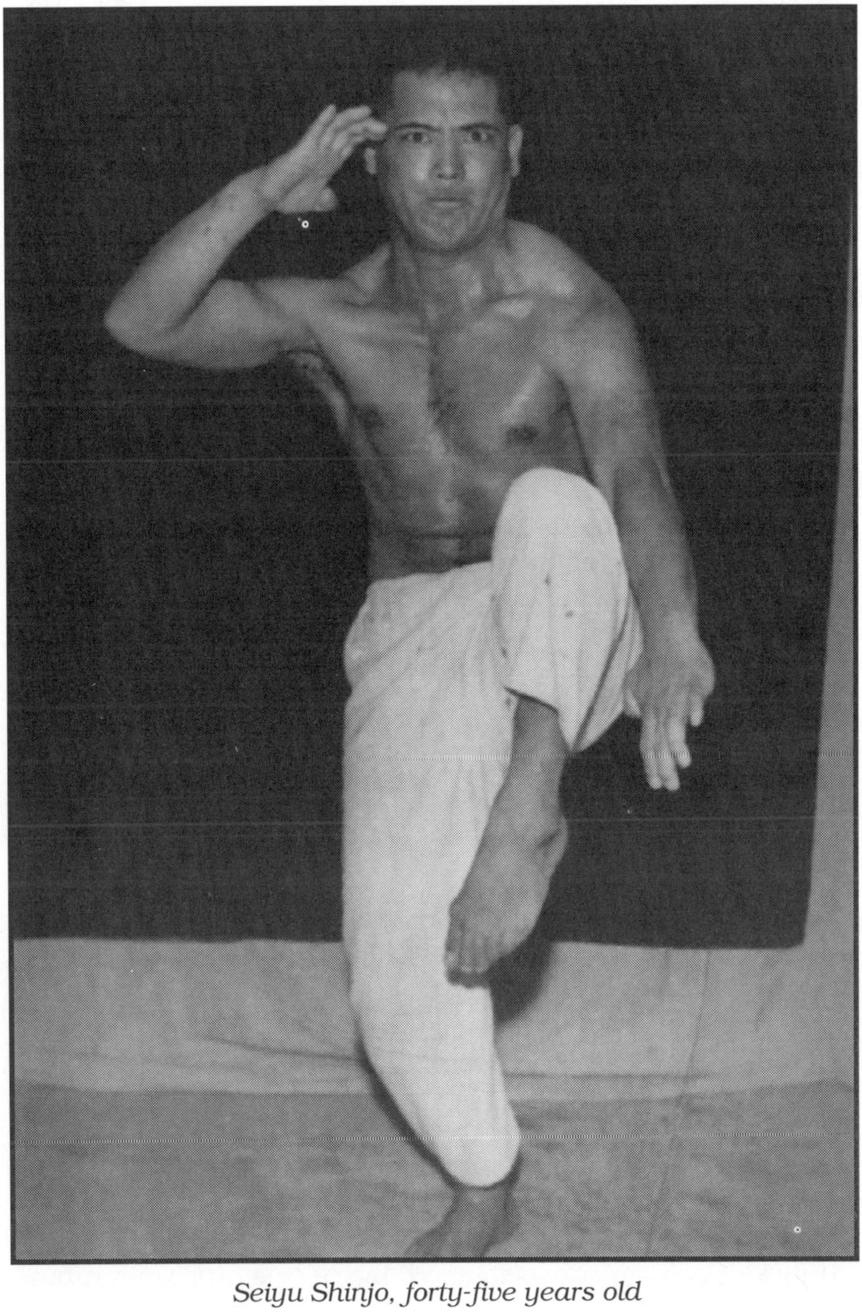

Seiyu Shinjo, forty-five years old

Seiyu developed diabetes in his late forties and his health deteriorated rapidly. He underwent two operations and died during the second operation on October 23, 1981. He was only fifty-two years old. Seiyu Shinjo was posthumously awarded the rank Kiyoshi (ninth degree black belt) by the Uechi Ryu Karate Association and the All Okinawa Karate Federation on November 26, 1981.

The premature death of Master Shinjo brought with it a dark cloud over the world of Uechi ryu karate. His strength of presence and organizational expertise may well have prevented the breaking up of the Uechi Ryu Karate Association in the years to follow.

After his death, the following speech was delivered by Mr. Nakazato, then President of the All Okinawa Karate Federation;

> "Mr. Seiyu Shinjo had the good fortune to be a disciple under both Kanbun Uechi, the founder of Uechi ryu karate, and his son Kanei Uechi. He became *Tatsujin* (Master of the highest skill of karate). Sensei Shinjo was an intelligent, gentle, respectful and open-minded person, who always tried to understand karate do, both philosophically and technically.
>
> After he opened the Uechi Ryu Karate Do Kadena Shubukan, he taught not only karate to his students, but also the philosophy of human life. He helped the development of children's physical and mental health in his neighborhood. He was like a second father to both youth and adult karate students.
>
> Besides teaching his own students at his dojo, he spent his time helping to develop the Uechi Ryu Karate Do Association and the All Okinawa Karate Federation, where he served on the Board of Directors.
>
> I sincerely show him my respect for his great achievements toward the prosperity of Okinawan karate.
>
> Unfortunately in the world there is no perfect thing or person, and even a strong person like Mr. Shinjo could not defeat his death. However, his philosophy and knowledge of karate have been inherited by his oldest son, Mr. Kiyohide Shinjo, and other students. I hope Mr. Seiyu Shinjo is watching his son's and student's development of karate ability, from heaven."

The Shinjo karate legacy was fostered by the teachings of Kanbun Uechi. Four generations of Shinjo karate men have dedicated themselves to the physical and spiritual teachings of Kanbun and Kanei Uechi.

上地流
沖縄

Kiyohide Shinjo is a graduate of Okinawa Kokusai University, majoring in law. He married Michio Nakamura in 1977. Their first son, Shuichi, was born in 1978, followed by Kiyohito in 1979.

After his father's death, Kiyohide Shinjo reluctantly assumed the teaching responsibilities at the Kadena dojo. At the time he expressed the opinion that he needed ten more years training under his father to properly prepare him to be a karate teacher. He also worked at two jobs to meet the family's financial responsibilities.

Late one night while working as a taxi dispatcher, he received a call for help from one of the drivers. When Kiyohide arrived he saw the driver arguing with three Americans. When he approached them, the men challenged him. He defeated all three men in short order.

He founded a fraternity within the Uechi Ryu Association to honor his father and called the group *Kenyukai*. Ken means fist, yu is part of the name Seiyu and kai means group. Kenyukai stands for "Seiyu Shinjo's Strong Fist Group".

拳
優
会

Kiyohide Shinjo has served on the Board of Directors of the All Okinawa Karate Federation since 1980. He was voted Chairman of the Board from 1991 to 1994, and is the youngest person in the history of the Federation to hold that position.

He has pursued the growth of Uechi ryu karate as fervently as his father did. He has traveled to Spain, twice to France, three times to Brazil and Canada, four times to Argentina, and to America ten times in his efforts to present the Kanbun Uechi-Seiyu Shinjo combined methods of teaching Okinawan Uechi ryu karate. Kiyohide's compassion toward foreign practitioners has increased with each exposure. He admires the long-term devotion and ever increasing ability he has witnessed outside Okinawa.

Seiyu's second son, Narahiro Shinjo, is often lost in the shadow of his famous brother. Narahiro also inherited his father's vigor and relentless approach to karate and is every bit as accomplished as his older brother. He has also traveled internationally teaching and demonstrating Uechi ryu karate.

Narahiro sparring in Futenma dojo, 1975.

In August 1995, Narahiro Shinjo placed fourth in kata in the All Okinawa World pre-tournament, an event of over five hundred black belts from around the world.

The Shinjo family is one of vigorous strength who live by the code of *Gosatu Bokuto* (live life easy and peacefully, but when it is time to fight become ferocious).

Kadena Uechi Ryu Karate Kenyukai dojo, 1995

SHINYU GUSHI

Shinyu Gushi, born May 25, 1939, first began karate training in the Oroku dojo under Saburo Uehara. Mr. Gushi, as a high school student, wanted to start a karate club at his school. Sensei Uehara was against the idea, wishing to keep his instruction more secret.

Mr. Gushi discussed the situation with the more progressive thinking Seiyu Shinjo, who supported the idea of a high school karate club.

Impressed by Mr. Shinjo's students and his goals of Uechi ryu development, Mr. Gushi joined the Asato dojo in 1956. After Seiyu Shinjo moved to Kadena, Mr. Gushi trained in Wakasa under Seiko Itokazu. For ten years he taught class and performed demonstrations at the Naha ginza dojo. He opened his own dojo in Oroku in 1985.

Shinyu Gushi and his family moved to California in 1988. He is currently the only Okinawan master of Uechi ryu living in the United States. He is currently eighth degree black belt in Uechi ryu karate and seventh degree in Okinawan kobudo. (Chapter IV)

TSUTOMU NAKAHODO

Tsutomu Nakahodo spars with his Sensei, Seiyu Shinjo, 1964.

One of the most senior black belts of Seiyu Shinjo is Tsutomu Nakahodo, born November 25, 1933. He first started karate training under Seiko Toyama in 1955, and became a student of the Kadena dojo in 1960.

Mr. Nakahodo is referred to as "Popeye," because of his massive forearms and brute strength.

Tsutomu Nakahodo in the Kadena dojo

Mr. Nakahodo at sixty years old

Mr. Nakahodo at the first Antioch, California Uechi ryu Dojo

He started the *Onason Sonogari dojo* in 1970, then moved to the Naha ginza dojo in 1974.

Mr. Nakahodo opened the *Migushiku dojo*, in a Naha taxi garage, after the closing of the seven story ginza in 1986.

He is currently a ninth degree black belt and President of the Okikukai, one of the current Uechi ryu organizations in Okinawa. Now in his mid sixties, he still smashes through 2x2 inch poles during nightly dinner demonstrations next to his dojo.

Tsutomu Nakahodo and Seiyu Shinjo were like brothers. Mr. Nakahodo recalls with enthusiasm the body conditioning and sparring he used to do with his teacher.

Mr. Nakahodo delivered this speech commemorating the death of Seiyu Shinjo:

> "I was one of Mr. Seiyu Shinjo's first students when he opened the Kadena Shubukan and was under the respectful but strict care of him. I am very much obliged to Sensei Shinjo for his hard but helpful karate lessons. He emphasized *kote kitae* (arm conditioning), *tai gitae* (body toughening), coupled with speed and power in training. That helped a small person like me to develop karate ability.
>
> The daily practice, under his keen insight, was incredibly hard, but rich in content. As a karate teacher he was as scary as a Buddhist evil-looking god.
>
> He never compromised his teaching methods and technique. However in his personal life he was a gentle, helpful, respectful and open minded person. Without his help and two different approaches (one was tough and strict as a teacher, the other was kind and open minded as a friend), I do not think I could have kept my karate discipline. Moreover, I could not have deeply understood the meaning of karate do.
>
> It is too sad that I can no longer see the active and energetic Mr. Shinjo. I respectfully and sincerely thank Mr. Shinjo, who spent his life teaching and developing Okinawan Karate."

The *Naha dojo* was located on the third floor of a seven story shopping mall, *ginza*. Bus loads of Japanese tourists were shuttled through, several times a day, to watch demonstrations of Uechi ryu karate. Day and evening classes were also taught there.

The daily demonstrations were performed by Tsutomu Nakahodo, Yoshitsune Senaga, Minoru Miyagi, Kiyohide Shinjo and Shinyu Gushi, all black belts of Seiyu Shinjo. Other American and Okinawan practitioners were invited to join the demonstrations when they visited the dojo. For ten years the katas and body conditioning methods of Uechi ryu karate were performed for thousands of Japanese tourists.

The Migushiku Dojo of Master Nakahodo

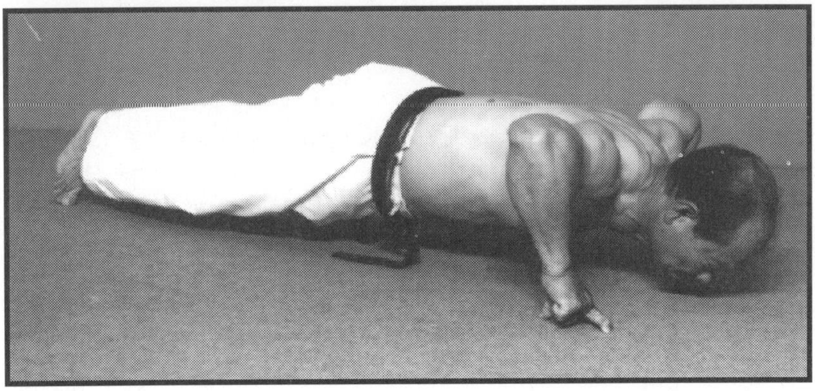

Mr. Nakahodo performing finger tip pushups at sixty three years old.

SEIKI IREI

Another senior black belt from the beginning of the Kadena dojo is Seiki Irei. It was Mr. Irei who persuaded Seiyu Shinjo to quit his regular employment in construction and only teach karate. This decision sealed Seiyu's fate to a life of poverty (as was historically common with karate masters), but allowed him the time and energy to create his karate legacy.

Seiki Irei began training under Seiyu Shinjo in 1960. He established his own dojo, *Irekan*, in Chatan, in 1980.

Seiyu Shinjo vigorously told a story about Seiki Irei one evening. The following version of that story is an excerpt from an article about Uechi ryu karate that appeared in the May, 1989, issue of *Black Belt Magazine*.

> When the large American entered the Kadena dojo of Seiyu Shinjo, he said he wanted to learn Uechi ryu karate. What the U. S. Marine Boxing Champion of Okinawa really wanted to do was show the so-called martial artist at the school what a real fighter was like. It wasn't long before he got a chance to spar.
>
> He was pitted against a much smaller Okinawan named Seiki Irei. It was obvious from the start that the marine wasn't interested in light sparring practice. He was launching full-force blows which Seiki initially tried to parry without reaching into his store of disabling methods. Finally Seiki felt he had put up with enough from the disrespectful American.
>
> He knew he would have to put some devastating moves on the larger man to stop him. He approached his Sensei and asked for permission to use such tactics. Permission was granted. (Seiyu Shinjo's English words when telling the story were, "Hospital is O.K.")
>
> The next time the marine came in to attack, the Okinawan delivered a front kick, toes first, to his thigh. The kick ripped through muscle tissues, and the big man left in an ambulance.
>
> Several months later, the same man, thigh now healed, returned to the dojo. He had begun practicing kicking techniques and insisted on a fight with Irei, who he felt had only landed a lucky shot in their first match. (Challenges such as this by servicemen were not uncommon)
>
> The rematch was almost an instant replay of the first bout, except that Irei used a different technique. As the American kicked at him, Irei planted a shoken (one knuckle) punch on top of the boxer's foot. Again the man went to the hospital.

To the boxer's credit, he returned once more, this time on crutches, to apologize for his behavior and acknowledge the Okinawans as fighters of the first rank. He continued karate training and became a black belt in the Kadena dojo.

Seiki Irei and Seiyu Shinjo spar in 1961.

Irekan dojo, Chatan

Young black belts of the Kadena Dojo
from left— Tsutomu Nakahodo, Seiki Irei; from right— Minoru Miyagi, Seiho Shinjo

MINORU MIYAGI

Minoru Miyagi began studying under Seiyu Shinjo in 1960. He opened the Yomitan Uechi ryu dojo in 1976, and still teaches there today.

YOSHITSUNE SENAGA

#Yoshitsune Senaga, born October 1, 1937, began training in the Oroku dojo. While in high school, in 1958, he saw Shinyu Gushi, a Kadena black belt, break fifteen roof tiles in a demonstration. He was so impressed he began training under Seiyu Shinjo. More information about Mr. Senaga can be found in Chapter IV, Kobudo.

Dojo and Makiwara training of Yoshitsune Senaga

STRUCTURE OF THE UECHI RYU KENYUKAI ASSOCIATION SEIYU SHINJO (1929-1981)

Black Belts of the Uechi Ryu Asato Kenkyusho (Research Institute) Naha Dojo 1955-1960

Shinyu Gushi
Keisho Tamaki
Seisho Arakawa

Black Belts of the Uechi Ryu Kadena Shubukan 1960-1981

Kiyohide Shinjo
Minoru Miyagi
Takayasu Takemei
Isamu Wakugawa
Keiko Tomori
Yoshio Ohmine
Kenjiro Miyagi
Tadamatsu Teruya
Keishin Shimoji
Kiyomitsu Shinjo
Seiichi Matsuda
Kenei Nakama
Ken Yamanoha
Jitsumori Tsuha
Masakazu Izena
Yasunobu Teruya
Masayoshi Irei
Choki Hamamoto
Seiki Irei
Narahiro Shinjo
Fumio Higa
Shinzen Irei
Seiki Gisushi
Risho Shiohira
Norikazu Kishimoto
Seishi Henna
Kenko Chibana
Kenei Gushi
Yoshiharu Kamiya
Takeshi Yamashiro
Chosin Kyuna
Masahiko Izena
Toshio Okuma
Seisho Aguni
Akira Tsukayama
Monoru Nakamura
Tsutomu Nakahodo
Genki Matsuda
Yoshimitsu Matsuzaki
Chyoshin Kyuna
Hideo Taira
Seisho Nakaza
MasamitsuYamauchi
Kensei Chibana
Minoru Kamiya
Genkichi Matsuda
Nobumasa Takara
Kenji Ura
Yukihiro Kamiya
Masahide Izena
Tshio Irei
Hirokazu Koja
ChyokoMakabe
Genwa Higa.

NON OKINAWANS

Johny Author
Henry Hooper
Alan Dollar
Mike Knebel
Mark Sullivan
Frederick Norris
James Daily
John Ray
Marty Dow
Julious Scott
Peter Kellogg
James Foley
Charles Shultz

These black belts have produced many black belts of their own, insuring that the teachings of Kanbun Uechi, Kanei Uechi and Seiyu Shinjo will be perpetuated around the world.

Mr.Takayasu, second from left, consistent winner in the Uechi ryu tournament series

TAKEMEI TAKAYASU

Takemei Takayasu is a black belt of the Kadena dojo who has gained prominence in France. Mr. Takemei finished second, behind Kiyohide Shinjo in the annual Uechi ryu tournament year after year. He moved to France in 1985 to pursue his education in art. He is currently a well-known artist and karate instructor in France, with branch dojos in Italy.

1995

1975

Seiko Toyama at sixty-eight years old

SEIKO TOYAMA

Seiko Toyama was born in 1928. By the time he was five years old his family had moved to Wakayama, Japan. He learned Shorin kai for five years from his father, who had studied on Okinawa for several years. He was a very small child and was constantly picked on at school. The harassment was so bad that he quit school at an early age. His father watched a training session at Kanbun's dojo and was so impressed with the strength and hardness of Uechi ryu that he put his son's karate training in Kanbun's hands. Toyama and Seiyu Shinjo, who started training under Kanbun one year later, became friends for life. They both listened intently for years as Kanbun and Ryuyu Tomoyose talked. He is a wellspring of information about the history of Uechi ryu karate and a robust story teller.

Seiko Toyama trained under Kanbun Uechi for eight years in Wakayama. He accompanied his Sensei and the Shinjo family from Wakayama to Okinawa. They were all interned in a prisoner of war camp in Nago for six months upon their return.

He then moved to Naha and in 1960 opened a dojo in Urasoe. In 1975, he moved to Zakimi, a remote part of Yomitan, and began farming.

The industrious Mr. Toyama built his own house and the *Zakimi dojo.* He teaches a handful of selected students and continues to work on his farm as he approaches seventy. Part of that work includes catching habu (a deadly nocturnal snake indigenous to Okinawa) with his bare hands.

Poisonous Habu Snake

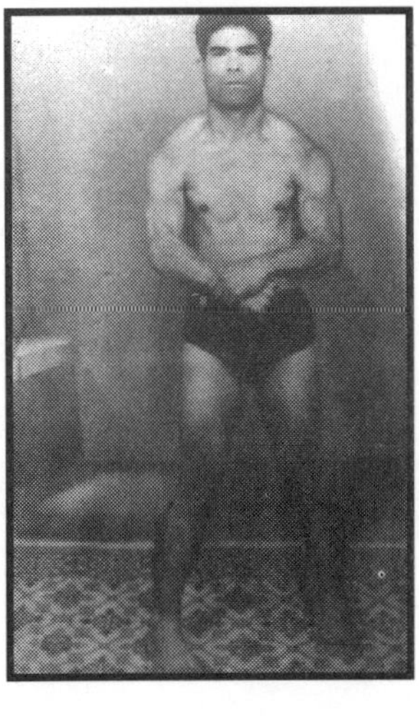

Seiko Toyama at forty years old

In June 1995, Mr. Toyama visited America for the first and only time in his life, as the guest of honor at the Twelfth Annual International Uechi Ryu Karate Black Belt Championship Tournament, in Antioch, California. More information about Seiko Toyama can be found in Chapter II.

Seiko Toyama, sixty eight years old

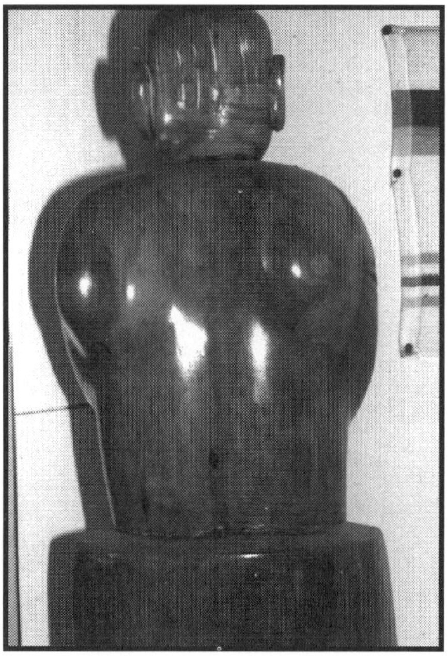

Wooden sculpture by Mr. Toyama emphasizing the importance of the back muscles in Sanchin kata.

I would like to extend my special thanks to Yoshi and Tsuru Shinjo and Mrs. Toyama the backstage women of Uechi ryu karate, for their invaluable information and insight about the dynamic men who make up the history of Uechi ryu karate.

Seiko Toyama built his Uechi ryu dojo in Zakimi.

Sieko Toyama and Alan Dollar in the Antioch Kenyukai Shubukan, 1995

The author with Mr. Tomoyose and Mr. Nakahodo at the opening of the new headquarters of the Okinawa Karate Do Association, December, 1995.

CHOTOKU KYAN
A KADENA VILLAGE KARATE MASTER

Okinawan karate bujin are like brilliant sparkling stars. One of those stars is Chotoku Kyan. Even though he was a small man (4' 10," 110 lbs.), his name shines in Okinawan Karate History.

Chotoku Kyan was born in 1867, in Gibo village in Shuri. His father, Chyofu Kyan, was a martial arts expert (Bugei), and a valued body guard to King Sotai. Chyofu Kyan guarded the King during his frequent diplomatic excursions to Edo (Tokyo) during the installation of the new Meiji government (Chapter V).

Chotoku began studying karate under his father when he was three or four years old. He eventually accompanied his father on the frequent trips to Edo, where he broadened his knowledge and education, while assisting with the protection of King Sotai.

The *Big Tsunami* as the Meiji restoration was called, swept through Japan and Okinawa, ending the Ryukyu Kingdom. Most of the government officials were dismissed from their duties. The newly unemployed royalty and dignitaries moved from Shuri into the countryside in an act called Inaka Ori.

An edict called Niyu Shoku, granted permission to clear forests and begin farming. Chotoku Kyan relocated to Makihara Yomitan village. The area had been used as grazing land and stables for the horses of the Kingdom. Chotoku secured a job as a caretaker for horses.

He became friends with young men from neighboring Yaro village. Problems often arose between the existing village farmers and the new Inaka Ori people. Association between the two groups was difficult. Chotoku Kyan successfully bridged this gap with his karate knowledge, his education and his genuine heart. It wasn't long before he was teaching karate to his new found friends.

He once gathered five or six students at the Hija Bridge, in Kadena, and ordered them to try to push him off the bridge with a bo (six foot staff). The students reluctantly picked up the bo and pushed against their teacher. They stared at each other in amazement as the small man did not move. All the men then pushed with all their strength, to no avail. He remained as a statue on the bridge, immovable.

When faced with difficulty he would always remember the time he spent with his father at Edo. They had practiced karate in the Snow Fall Garden and he never forgot his father's teachings. Chyofu had told his son, "Your

Hija River in Kadena

body is physically small but you have guts. With training you can polish your technique with a kata that best suits you."

While searching for his technique, he sought those he admired. He received training undcr Sokon Matsumura and Anko Itosu from Shuri, and Koukan Oyadomari from Tomari. He fought many challengers but never lost. Chotoku Kyan became well known in Shuri and Naha, and later Kadena, where he was known as Chyan mi-guwa.

Chotoku married the daughter of the Rindo family from Naramura village. They built a house near the Hija Bridge in Kadena. He quit his job at the stables.

Hijagawa was a major port. Horses, cattle and lumber from Yamabaru and brown sugar grown in the central part of the island were shipped daily from Hijagawa to Naha. Mr. Kyan secured a job as a buggy driver, hauling these goods for shipment.

The *bashamuchya*, as they were called, resembled the early American teamsters. They were rough, burly men, who struck fear in the local villagers. They fought for the right-of-way on the narrow roads and for first position to unload their brown sugar at the warehouse.

One day Chotoku Kyan was waiting in line to unload the large bags of sugar from his buggy. Behind him were five or six known bullies, who were feared by everyone. They did not want to wait in line and began to pick on the people in front of them. As they worked their way to the front of the line, the leader yelled "Move over old man!". In a very calm manner Chotoku replied "Even though you told me to move, I will not because it is my turn." This calm reply angered the man further, and he attempted to start a fist fight, not knowing who the small man was.

The group shouted, "It is not worth it to fight a runt like you," and suggested a bet. "Let's see who can move a bag of brown sugar the fastest." The heavy bags usually required two men to carry them. "What are you going to do?" one man shouted. The group knew the man was too small to carry the heavy bag and expected him to give up his place in line.

Chotoku said in a confident manner, "If you lose what are you going to give me?" The men felt confident they were going to win and replied "If we lose we will carry all your bags into the warehouse for you, old man!" Chotoku stared deep into their eyes and agreed to the bet. "Are you ready?" shouted the crowd. "Yo-shi!" they shouted and the race began.

Two big men picked up a bag and started carrying it into the warehouse. Chotoku grabbed his bo (six foot staff) from the buggy. He lifted the heavy bag with the bo and threw it through the air. It landed inside the warehouse, in front of the two men. The men stopped abruptly, frozen in disbelief of what they had just seen.

Chotoku threw his bo on the ground and yelled at the crowd, who was trying to sneak away. "Hey young men, are you trying to sneak out on your promise?" Then he added softly, "Keeping a promise is the perfection of a human being." Still stunned by what they had just seen, the group began unloading Chotoku's bags of sugar.

Later that day they found out who the small man was. They realized how foolish they had been when they learned he was a karate expert. They were impressed, not by the strength of his fist, but with his technique. After the incident, the men caused less trouble and started working harder.

On February 28, 1922, the Kadena railroad opened, taking many jobs away from the buggy drivers. Chotoku Kyan, again unemployed, decided to continue teaching karate.

At first he taught only the village youth. As his popularity increased, so did the number of people wanting to learn karate. Eventually his teaching became part of the curriculum for school and was taught at the Kadena police station.

Chotoku Kyan died on September 20, 1945, while interned at the Ishikawa concentration camp. He was seventy-six years old.

Headstone of the Shinjo family tomb located in Yomitan

Nintai—
Patience-perseverence

Black belt training in the Naha ginza Dojo, 1977

Seiyu Shinjo's black belts in the Futenma Dojo

上地流

KOBUDO

古武道

OKINAWAN WEAPONS

Since the first human used a weapon to protect himself against attack, weapons systems, both primitive and sophisticated, have been developed by many countries around the world. Differences are determined by the size and strength of the people and the topography in which they live.

When a weapon is developed, an adequate defense against it soon follows. This facilitates a more sophisticated or powerful weapon, then a stronger defense. This developmental see-saw has taken mankind from crude stone age clubs to the massive overkill ability of today's nuclear weapons.

Most of the weapons currently popular in martial arts training originated in Okinawa. Awareness of these weapons comes mostly from martial arts movies and karate tournaments. The public knows little of the origin, history, or cultural importance of these crude, yet magnificent innovations.

Kobudo history, like karate's history, has been shrouded in secrecy from oppressive rulers. What little is known, or can be traced, is embroiled in controversy. The history of a particular weapon or kobudo system will vary from one master to another, depending on his instructor's history or lineage. There is agreement as to the history or method of handling some of the weapons discussed, while others have more than one theory about their source of origin or proper application.

Controversy surrounds the origins of the weapons discussed here. It is generally accepted that ancient people of Okinawa used long tree branches as weapons of defense against wild animals. Some masters explain that in later times the weapons developed from farming tools in order for citizens to defend themselves against animals and human attackers. While other countries have developed different weapons such as the spear, knife, sword or guns, the weapons of Okinawa differ in that they can be used against an opponent without causing death or serious injury.

King Sho Shin ordered weapons confiscation at the beginning of his reign in 1477. (Chapter V) The Satsuma invasion of 1609, brought with it a re-enforcement of this edict. Additionally, they deprived the Okinawan people of any metal for fear they would fashion weapons. The industrious Okinawan people soon found ways for their daily tools to double as effective defensive weapons.

The Okinawans were already known for their empty handed defense systems, called te. This advanced martial arts ability was vital in the effective use of such crude weapons against the armed and well-trained samurai oppressors. Formidable fighting methods using weapons, called *Kobu-jutsu* or *Ryukyukobu-justsu*, were born when karate was suppressed and went underground.

Some historians explain the migration of young men to Southern China in the 1800's, is the source of Okinawa's weapons systems. These young men (which included Kanbun Uechi) studied chuan fa, weapons systems and medicine, some for more than ten years. Historically, kobu-jutsu techniques have long been displayed in village dances in Okinawa. They were refined into fighting applications and systematized when the Okinawans returned from China with their advanced weapons ability. Kanbun Uechi was well known on the Motobu peninsula for his performance with the bo at village festivals and holidays, before his training in China. (Chapter II)

There is no question that China influenced the culture, government and education of Okinawa for hundreds of years. It is a safe assumption that martial arts and weapons exchange also occurred during this time. (Chapter IV)

A few weapons katas are hundreds of years old. The formalizing of kata and kobudo organizations, however, has occurred mostly in the twentieth century. As weapons practice became as organized and systematized as karate, it was rare to find an individual who practiced both. It was not until after World War II that the lines were crossed and karate practitioners actively pursued kobudo and vice versa. The pioneers discussed at the end of this chapter worked diligently at perfecting both arts.

Weapons indigenous to the Ryukyu Islands explained in this chapter are the bo, sai, nunte, nunchaku, tonfa, eku, tekko, kama, suruchin and tinbe. Many other implements of daily life have been converted to use as a weapon by the Okinawan people.

These weapons are no longer carried for protection or used for work. Their continued use and practice have become art forms, of great importance to the culture and history of the Ryukyu Islands. Many excellent texts have been written about Okinawan kobudo. Presented here is an overview.

ROKUSHAKUBO

棒(棍)

コン

Roku means six in Japanese, shaku is a measurement of about one foot in length and bo translates to mean a staff. Therefore rokushakubo means six foot staff. The length of the staff in Okinawa was originally determined by the height of the ceiling in the small thatched roof houses. The bo was placed standing straight up in a corner of the house for quick access if needed.

This weapon, more commonly called a bo, is the most frequently used weapon in the Okinawan kobudo systems. It is primarily a long range weapon used in open spaces. It is effective in blocking the full length of the body, while providing a hard striking surface. It greatly increases the reach of attack and allows effective striking to 360 degrees. It can be used to defend a large area with a wide swinging motion.

The first staff was probably a long tree branch used as a walking stick and to protect oneself against wild animals. As civilization developed Okinawan fisherman used long poles called kushakubo, or ocean bo, to navigate their boats around the roots of mangroves where oars proved ineffective. Stories are told of the bo being used to scale castle walls. The bo was inserted between the stones and used as a step.

Farmers placed a staff (tenbin), measuring from five to nine feet, across the shoulders to carry their loads. Baskets hung from each end of the staff for carrying everything from fish and farming harvest, to human waste. When faced with an altercation the staff could be disengaged from the load and used as a defensive weapon. To carry the heavy loads of the Okinawan peasants, the staffs of ancient times were thicker and more stout than today.

TENBIN

The thickness of the modern bo is about 1 1/4 inches at the center tapering to approximately 3/4 of an inch at the ends. It is made of hardwood, generally oak. The tapered construction maintains the fulcrum of the bo at the center, keeping the bo balanced and easier to handle. The tapering of the bo gives it more tensile strength, making it more flexible and less prone to breakage. The taper also facilitates powerful whipping of the bo during striking and block.

The Chinese staff, *kun*, has been combined with the character of the Okinawan people since the beginning of the eighteenth century. The Chinese staff is not tapered, but maintains the same diameter from end to end. Balance at the center is not essential as the Chinese systems involve handling the kun more from one end or the other. Kun can also measure eight or nine feet in length

Early practitioners of bo-jutsu used a variety of bo shapes such as square, *marubo*, hexagonal, *rokkakubo*, or octagonal, *hakkakubo.* When fighting the multiple edges proved effective in breaking the opponent's weapon and delivering a deadlier blow. The hard bamboo of Okinawa was often used and called *takebo.* Many cultures throughout history have employed the staff, in some form, as a tool and weapon. None have achieved the refinement of effectiveness, power and art, as have the Okinawan people.

SAI

釵(サイ)

The sai was brought to Okinawa from Indonesia over three hundred years ago. The sai exists as a weapon in many countries throughout Asia. It was probably introduced to Okinawa through trade with one of these countries. The sai did not become popular in Japan. It developed primarily in the kobudo styles of Okinawa. The sai was used by the police, *Chichi saji* of the Ryukyu Kingdom.

The Chinese character for sai means hair pick, creating conjecture that the sai was either designed after a hair pick or named after one because of its similar appearance. Other theories of origin are that it was fashioned after a pitchfork, after the shape of the human body, or after a religious symbol.

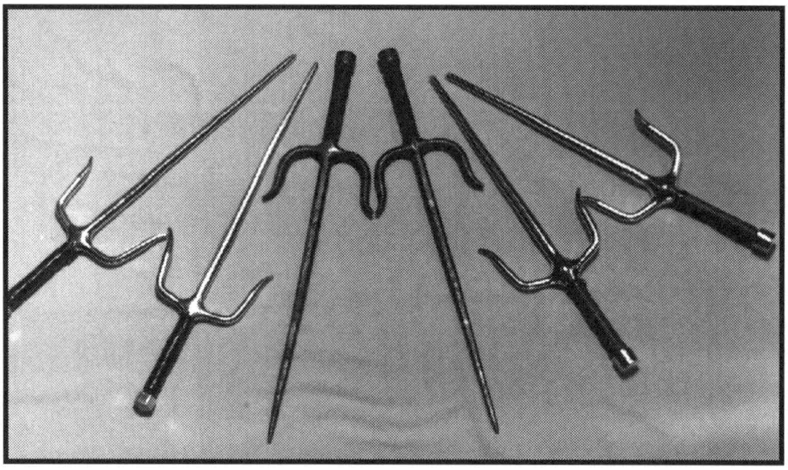

The sai is a pronged truncheon weapon whose purpose is primarily defensive. It can be used to block, trap, jab, strike and punch. It is useful against strikes and thrusts from a staff or spear, and against cuts from a sword and other bladed weapons. The sai, usually made of iron, weighs two to three pounds. The length of the sai varies between 15 to 20 inches. When held in the natural position, it should be long enough to extend to the elbow to protect the entire forearm, with the index finger extended to the pommel.

The sai is held in two primary positions (shown above). Flipping the sai from the reverse grip to the natural grip is a method of blocking the opponent's weapon and a method of striking.

The sai can also be held by the shaft, using the forks to hook the vital areas of an opponent's body.

Three sai were often used in combat. One in each hand and a spare kept in the belt to be used as a projectile. Ancient weapons masters could impale an opponent or pin his foot to the ground, by throwing the sai. The tip of the shaft and forks of ancient sai were sharpened. The sai used in kobudo arts of today are more blunt.

Use of the sai develops strong wrists and forearms, as sai techniques closely resemble the techniques of karate. The sai is the second most popular Okinawan weapon after the bo.

責任

The natural grip, honte mochi, is used to jab, strike, flail and parry.

The reverse grip, gyakute mochi, is used to punch, poke and to protect the arm when blocking.

The forks can also be used to trap the opponent's weapon.

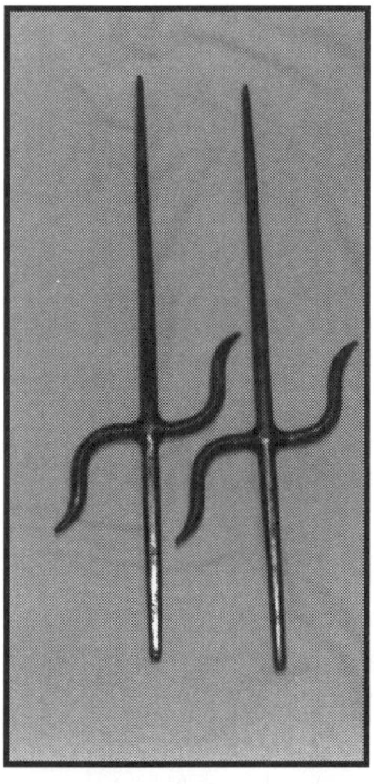

A variation of the sai is the manji sai, or nunte. Nunte sai were used primarily as a throwing weapon. One of the forks is reversed to facilitate sticking no matter which end hits the opponent.

The manji sai, when lashed to a bo, creates a different weapon called a nunte bo. The range of the weapon changes when lashed to a bo. Although bo techniques are used, the method of handling the nunte bo is different, relying less on power and more on finesse with the sai portion of the weapon. It is used to hook and stab the opponent or his clothing.

While some believe the nunte bo was used as a fisherman's gaff, Shinpo Matayoshi believes in a different origin. Nunte means "horse's hand". Sensei Matayoshi teaches that the nunte bo was a weapon of the mounted police of Okinawa. It was effective from horseback or from the ground.

The highly trained horses used by the police in older times reportedly assisted the rider when he dismounted to fight multiple attackers. As the police officer dispatched assailants approaching from the front or side with a nunte bo, the horse would place his head near the man's shoulder and protect his back by kicking at assailants from that direction with its rear legs.

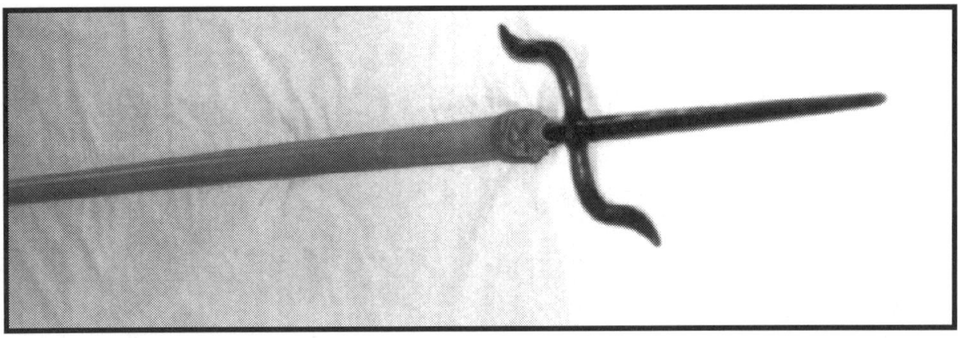

Nunte bo

NUNCHAKU

ヌンチャク(双節棍)

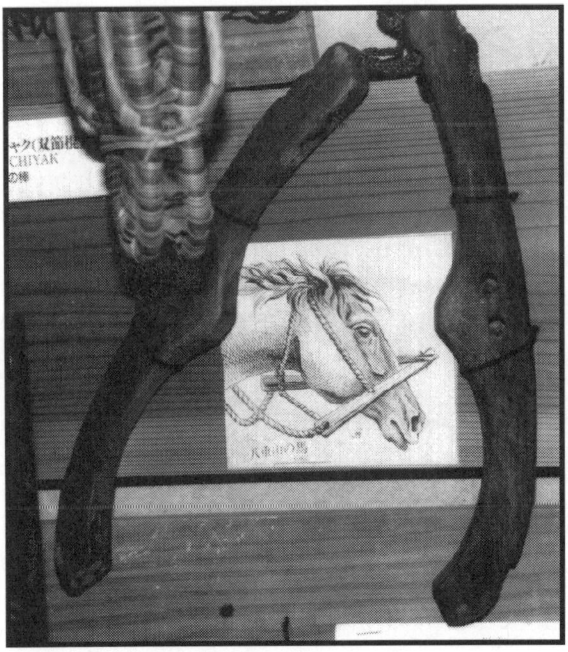

There are several theories about the development of the nunchaku, *nunchiyaku*, from tool to weapon. The most credible version attributes its origin to a traditional Okinawan harness, or horse bridle, made of wood and rope. In the Okinawan language nunchiyaku means horse bridle.

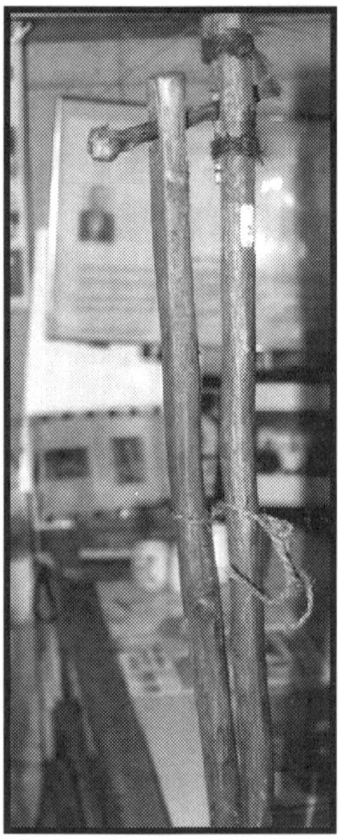

Another source of origin of the nunchaku is a tool called *utsu*. Utsu means to thrash, pound, or flail. It was formerly an agricultural flail used to pound harvested rice, separating the grain from the husk or straw. It was also used to take bark off trees Women performed the majority of this type of work, bringing forth the theory that the utsu was first used as a weapon by Okinawan women.

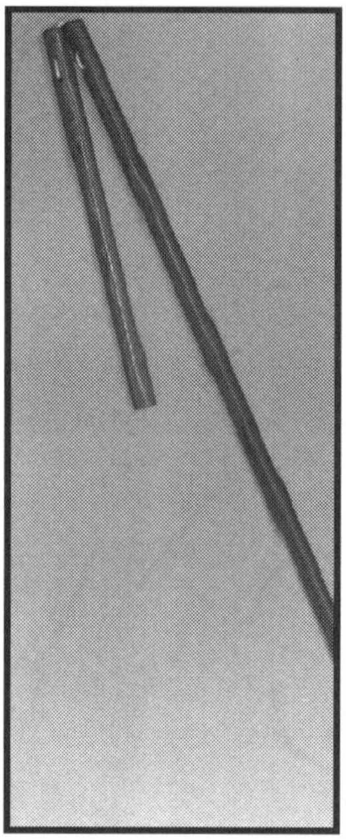

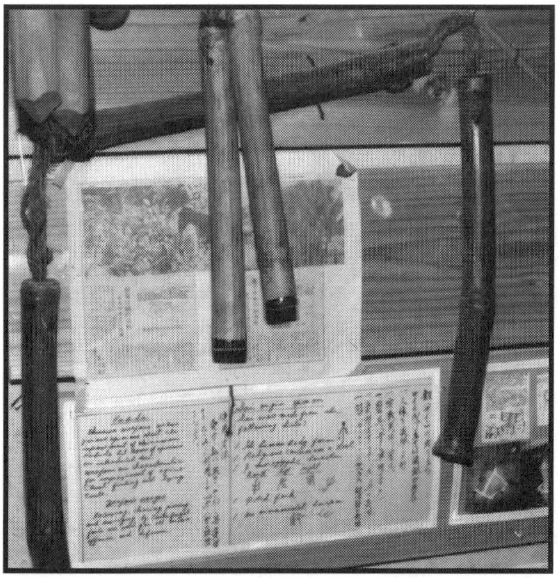

The three section staff, *sansetsukun*, made popular in Chinese marital arts movies, is an Okinawan weapon derived from the removable rails of a farmers cart. The three section implement prevented the large stacks of sugar cane from slipping off the cart. When needed for self defense the rails were quickly removed to become a formidable weapon of protection. These implements made an easy transition from working tools to defensive weapons in the hands of the tenacious Okinawan people.

Modern nunchaku are constructed of two pieces of wood of equal length. "Nun" also means identical or twin, "chaku" means section. They may be round, square, hexagonal or octagonal and measure between 12 and 15 inches in length. Some taper, others maintain the same diameter from end to end. The method of connecting the two pieces of wood at the end is a work of art in itself. The method of attachment is designed so each piece of wood swivels from one central point.

Early nunchaku were connected by silk, rope, women's hair, horse hair or vine. Modern versions use nylon rope or chain. There are no ancient katas for nunchaku, although a few have been created by kobudo masters of the last few decades.

Popularized by Bruce Lee in his movies, the nunchaku is the most well known karate weapon in the world. The weapon is not manipulated in the flamboyant manner of martial arts movies, but with a more practical approach. Handling the nunchaku is difficult and requires a high degree of karate skill.

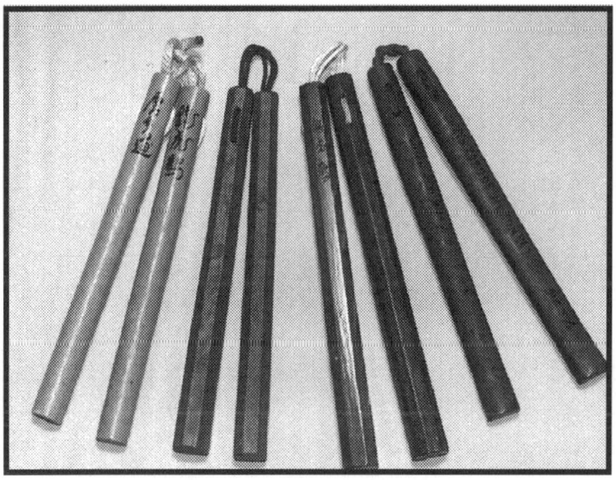

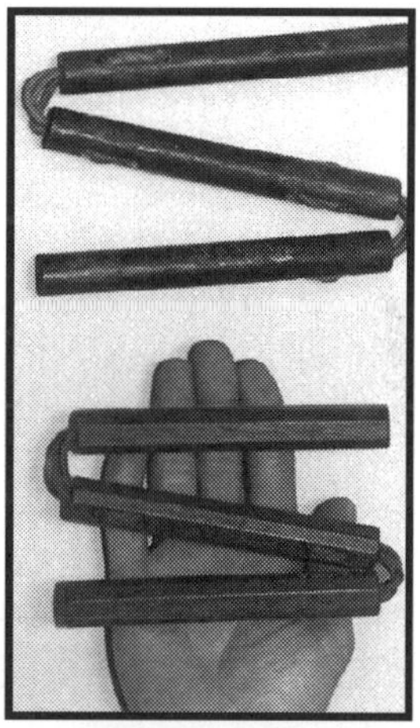

Pocket nunchaku made by Masakazu Kinjo.

The nunchaku is swung in large vertical or horizontal circles, or in a figure pattern in front of the body to attack opponents, or keep them at bay. An cnormous amount of force develops because of the swivel action of the free-swinging piece of wood. The force developed and speed of delivery making this a very deadly weapon.

Upward and downward diagonal slashes are stopped against the user's body and trapped with the hand. Because of this range ability the nunchaku is sometimes called the portable bo.

The rope is used to ensnare and trap a bo or an opponent's wrist, creating a painful submission hold.

The targets of attack are the same as with all striking weapons of kobudo: the hands, wrists, forearms, head, face, clavicles, ribs, groin and knees. Attacking the hands, wrist and elbows can limit the opponents ability to hold his weapon

The nunchaku swinging ninja portrayed in karate movies has diluted the history of this unique weapon. Westerners incorrectly call this weapon numchucks chaku sticks. The nunchaku, and other weapons described here, were practiced diligently by oppressed people to accomplish their own defense against life threatening attacks. In this historical context, many kobudo practitioners of today dedicate themselves to this additional practice to perpetuate the history and culture of the Okinawan people.

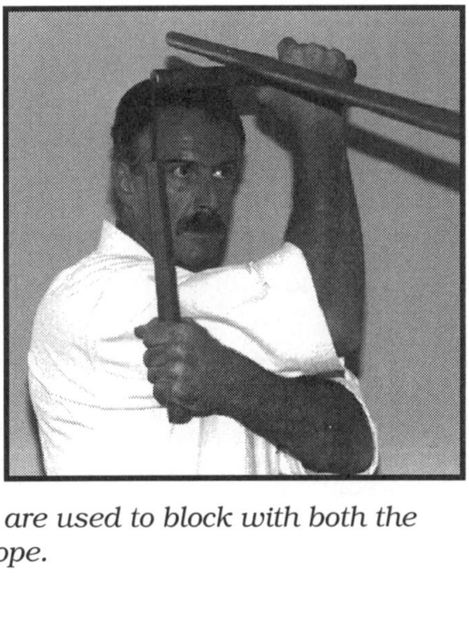

Primarily a short range weapon, nunchaku are used to block with both the wood and the rope.

Early nonchuku were connected with straw, rope, wonen's hair and horse hair

TONFA

トンファー

Tonfa (sometimes called tunfa, toifa, tuifa, tunkua or tungua) means "handle". In older times, it was the handle wedged into a hole in the side of a large milling stone used to mill beans, peas, rice and other grain. It could be easily disengaged from the millstone to make the transition from tool to martial arts weapon.

Some believe that the earliest tonfa was a tree branch in the same configuration as the mill handle. Other origins are: a hook for hanging pots over a fire and a type of short hoe in which the handle was used to dig. As it developed as a weapon, two tonfa were used, one in each hand.

Tonfa, usually made of hardwood such as oak or cherry wood, measures 15 to 20 inches in length. It has a distinctive round handle at ninety degrees to the main body, about 6 inches from one end.

The millstone handles that were the source of origin for the modern weapon included a bamboo sleeve around the insertion of the handle. The sleeve served as a bushing allowing for faster and easier movement of the handle. The configuration of ancient tonfa remains consistent, while the main body may differ in style from square to round, or half round.

Tonfa techniques, similar to the sai, are based on karate techniques. They are used for blocking and parrying by placing the main body of the weapon along the arm. From this position the end is used to punch or strike. The swinging motion of using the handle in the millstone evolved into the attacking methods of the tonfa. Power is generated by centrifugal force.

The tonfa is swung forward in a half circle to strike designated targets on the opponent's body. A snap of the wrist at the end of the swing, very similar to the snap at the final instant of a punch, gives the tonfa devastating power.

Tonfa practice is excellent for strengthening the wrists, forearms and grip. It is a very difficult weapon to control and use effectively. The tonfa is therefore reserved for advanced black belts. Masters who practice tonfa are diminishing and there is concern that this weapon will fade from existence.

American police forces have added the Okinawa tonfa to their defensive arsenal. The PR-24, or sidearm baton, offers more versatility than the standard baton and is a modern replica of this ancient Okinawan weapon.

One piece tonfa made by Master Takashi Kinjo.

EKU

櫂(かい)

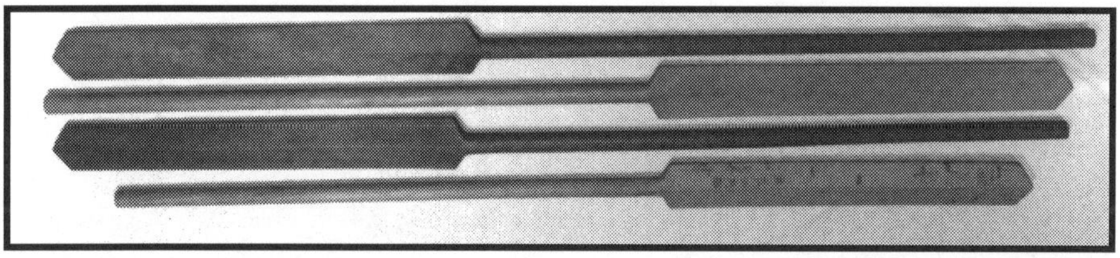

Eku (called *kai* In Japan) is commonly called an oar. More precisely, it is also used as a tiller, not only propelling a small boat but controlling the course as well. After securing a fishing boat on the beach the eku was taken with the owner, both for self defense and to discourage the borrowing, or theft of a boat that would be difficult to propel or navigate.

The oar, sometimes called eku bo, is manipulated much like a standard bo for blocking, parrying, striking and thrusting. The balance point is where the blade meets the handle. The blade of the oar offers a sharper striking surface than the bo. Edges of the wooden blade were rough from constant exposure to salt water. The result was a devastating cutting surface applied most often to the neck. The primary attacking methods of the eku emulate karate techniques such as shuto (chopping) and nukite (fingertip thrusting).

The paddle is used to throw sand or water in the eyes of attackers to the front or rear. The blade offsets the weight of the weapon, increasing the centrifugal force in swinging attacks. However, that also makes this a difficult weapon to balance.

Only two authentic katas, Tsuken Akachu no Eku (believed to be over six hundred years old), and Tsuken Sunakaki no Eku, have survived to the present.

There is an interesting myth about the tiny Tsuken Island, off Okinawa in Nakagusuku Bay, and the exile of Tsuken Ekata, a defeated prince of the sixteenth century.

After losing a fight, it was ordered that Tsuken Ekata be bound to a three hundred pound stone and thrown into the ocean near Tsuken Island. The officer charged with carrying out the sentence felt it was a terrible waste to lose such a reputable kobudo master. He asked his friend, Mr. Asato, to hide Ekata and lied to the Emperor about fulfilling his task.

Living in a cave called Pee Ku Gama, he secretly taught bo jutsu to Asato at night. Asato became a great kobudo master. In time a Japanese samurai swept through Okinawa, defeating many weapons masters, according to legend. The samurai, hearing of Asato's reputation, went to the island and challenged him. After two hours of fighting the sword wielding samurai, Asato cracked him on the head. News of Asato's victory brought praise and recognition from the King of the Ryukyus, who gave Asato the new name Akachu Bushi of Tsuken Island. (The family name was later changed to Akamine)

TEKKO

鉄 甲

Variations of the tekko (claw) are found in many Asian countries. The Okinawan version is more a form of fortified knuckles, with protruding pegs, rather than claws found in other countries.

The forerunner of this weapon was a pair of stirrups used by the mounted police of Okinawa. The pair of stirrups, joined by a strap and tied to the saddle, could be easily removed when needed as a weapon. The pegs or spikes located on the stirrup were used as spurs, unlike horseman of America who wear their spurs on their own feet.

A variation of the tekko was introduced to Okinawa by Shinko Matayoshi who learned horsemanship during his stay with Manchurian bandits. Another predecessor of the tekko was the standard horseshoe, held in the hand to intensify a punch. Use of tekko is based on karate moves and techniques. Punches against armed opponents are fortified by the pegs or spikes at the front of the weapon.

Another functional implement of daily life converted to a weapon of self defense is the traditional wooden sandal called getta. It is mentioned here because it is used in the same manner as the tekko. A pair of getta can be placed on the hands and used to block against other weapons, to intensify a punch, or to squeeze or smash an opponent's joints between the two (*hasamu*).

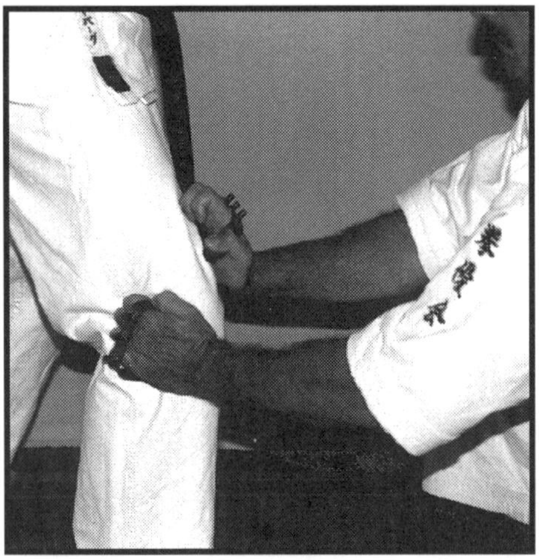

Tekko are also used to attack the joints of the body and to block attacks from a variety of weapons

KAMA

鎌

Indigenous to many farming countries of Asia, the kama is a sickle used in harvesting. Long and medium versions were used to cut fruit from papaya trees. The short version is used to harvest rice and cut grain.

Kama are used individually, with a spare kept in the belt in case of breakage. It is made of a hardwood handle that is larger at the end to aid in gripping. A curved blade, sharpened on the inside curve, extends from one end, creating a deadly close range weapon. In times when metal was scarce or forbidden, sea shells were used as the cutting edge.

The sharp edges coupled with handling kama in pairs, make this weapon dangerous to the handler. They are reserved for the highest level practitioners. The kama is preserved primarily by the practice of specific techniques developed in the last few generations.

Kama attacks include stabbing, hooking, slicing and cutting. Sometimes the handle is reversed and laid along the arm so the blade acts as an extension of the elbow. The handle of the kama is also used to block from this position. Blocking is also accomplished by trapping the opponent's weapon at the junction of the blade and handle.

SURUCHIN

スルチン(スルチン術)

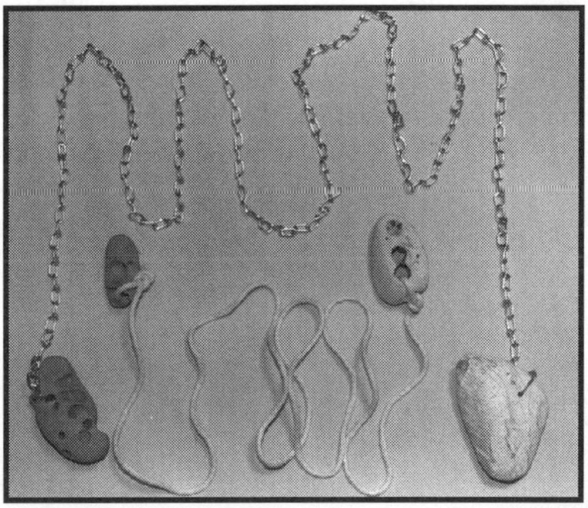

Suruchin, meaning weighted chain, is believed by some to have been introduced to Okinawa from Japan where it is called *manriki*. Others believe it was a form of a hunting device (similar to a bolo) previously used in Okinawa.

Older masters explain that in ancient times the large trading ships that frequented Okinawa had large ropes to tie them to the docks in Naha port. Tied to these huge ropes was a smaller rope with a stone tied to the other end. The small weighted ropes were thrown to dock where they were grabbed up to pull in the larger docking ropes. This, some say, is the source of suruchin.

One kobudo master expressed his belief that the origin of this centrifugal weapon dates to the time of community baths in Okinawa. Individual homes did not contain baths so everyone used the village bath. Fights often started outside the bath. Men would roll soap up in a towel and swing it in an attempt to hit their opponent in the head.

Original versions of suruchin made of rope have since been replaced with chain of varying lengths. A weight of about one pound is secured at one or both ends.

Suruchin are used to strike, immobilize, hobble or choke an opponent, and to hook his weapon. It is effective in blocking attacks from bladed weapons by stretching the chain tight to intercept the blades, then strike the opponent with the weighted end of the chain. When whirled in erratic circles around the head, suruchin increases the area of protection around the user.

TINBE

ティンベー

Tinbe is an ancient shield. Early tinbe were made of woven straw that served as carrying baskets and hats that protected farmers from the sun. When used as a shield, the angle of the hat would effectively deflect a strike from a weapon. Tinbe could also be used to scoop and throw sand or dirt into an opponent's face.

The straw hat version of tinbe was frail and could only be used once so stronger versions of wood, and sometimes metal, were developed. Tinbe is used in conjunction with a short root ax called rochin. Modern day practice with tinbe and rochin is limited to one or two modern katas. Demonstrations of tinbe are often part of traditional dances performed during Obon and other celebrations.

Many undocumented kobudo styles have historically existed, in dance, kata, and combat, from village to village. Two major systems have emerged to dominate the presentation of kobudo in the world.

The strongest version of ancient tinbe is the giant tortoise shell, native to the waters of Okinawa

They are shown in the kobudo lineage chart later in this chapter. The system attributed to Shinken Taira is by far the most practiced of all kobudo systems in the world today.

SHINKEN TAIRA

Shinken Taira (1897-1970) learned karate in Japan from Gichin Funakoshi and Kenwa Mabuni. Kobudo instruction came from Moden Yabiku. Taira taught kobujutsu in Okinawa since about 1940, and is remembered for bridging the gap between karate and kobudo by applying weapons movements to karate techniques. The Taira family name was Maezato. All the Maezato katas were created by Shinken Taira.

Shinken Taira founded the *Ryukyu Kobudo Hozon Shinko Kai*, the Society for the Promotion and Preservation of Ryukyuan Kobudo. Before his death in 1970, he named Eisuke Akamine the successor to his system.

Sensei Akamine, who began training under Shinken Taira in 1959, supports the theory that weapons were developed from farming tools. He re-organized the association into the present day *Ryukyu Kobudo Renmei*.

KATSUKIHO MINOWA

A prominent student of Shinken Taira, who became a kobudo sensei is Katsukiho Minowa, from the Uechi ryu system. I began the study of kobudo under Sensei Minowa in 1975, after receiving my Shodan in Uechi ryu karate from Kanei Uechi.

MASAKAZU KINJO

Sensei Minowa's most prominent student is Masakazu Kinjo (shown previously with tinbe), an outstanding weapons expert and historian. He holds the rank of seventh dan in Uechi ryu and Okinawan kobudo. The tenacious dedication and ability of Masakazu Kinjo and his oldest son Satoshi, give promise to a continued strong line of Okinawan kobudo for future generations. His Uechi ryu/kobudo dojo, and Ryukyu Kobudo Hozonkai headquarters are located in Kubagawa, Okinawa.

SHINPO MATAYOSHI

Historically equal to Shinken Taira's kobudo system is Matayoshi ryu kobudo. Shinko Matayoshi (1888-1947) traveled throughout Japan, Manchuria, and China, studying martial arts and weapons. While in China he learned the chuan fa style Kingai-noon, sister style to Pangai-noon.

Shinpo Matayoshi (1921-) learned kobu-jutsu from his father. His karate training also included training under Chotoku Kyan, in Kadena village. He later learned White Crane from Gokenki, a friend of Kanbun Uechi. Matayoshi reportedly trained briefly with Shinken Taira.

One of the fundamental changes from the past that Sensei Matayoshi made in his system was the positioning of the bo when striking. Under Taira's system the back hand holding the bo is locked at the side of the body near the belt when striking. Matayoshi felt that new students to kobudo lacked the proficiency to chamber accurately in this position.

Newer students would repeatedly hit themselves in the body, particularly the spleen, with the back portion of the bo. This caused many injuries and illnesses. Matayoshi changed the bo position to rest along side the arm, rather than at the side of the body near the belt. Proponents of this system feel the hold on the bo is stronger from this position.

Shimpo Matayoshi established and maintains the *Zen Okinawa Kobudo Renmei.*

YOSHITSUNE SENAGA

Among Sensei Matayoshi's students was Yoshitsune Senaga, currently an eighth dan in Uechi ryu and seventh dan in Okinawan kobudo. His grandfather was taught bo techniques by Sensei Akamine who created the kata Seijun no bo, in the late 1800's. This kata, also taught by Shinyu Gushi, is not well known. Akamine kept his karate and kobudo instruction very secret in the small village of Uebara, where his family name was Seijun. Sensei Senaga's karate and kobudo dojo is located in Nakagusuku.

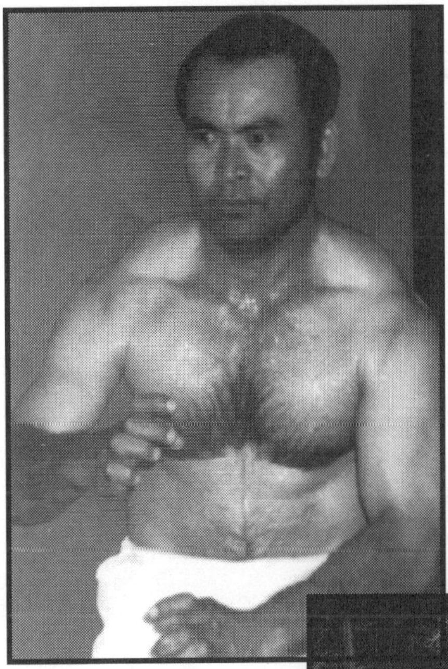

TAKASHI KINJO

Sensei Matayoshi also taught a handful of Pangai-noon ryu sensei, most notably, Seiki Itokazu, and Takashi Kinjo. Kinjo celebrated the thirtieth anniversary of his dojo, the *Konan Ryu Karate Kobudo Kobukai*, in 1995. Lesser known but renowned weapons systems of Okinawa are:

Honshin ryu - founded by Masakazu Miyagi from the Motobu Peninsula. Sensei Miyagi started his karate training in the Uechi ryu system at Koza and Futenma dojos and later went on to learn other styles of Okinawan karate.

Uchuchiku kobudo - handed down from Sanda Kangusuku (1841-1921), former bodyguard to King Sho Tai, in the late nineteenth century.

Yamani ryu - founded by Masami Chinen (1898-1976) means side of the mountain. The name represents the mountain village where the style was developed. This form of kobudo is taught and demonstrated by Toshihiro Oshiro, an outstanding kobudo and Shorin ryu sensei currently living in Northern California.

No disrespect is intended to any past or current masters of kobudo in Okinawa who were not included in this partial presentation.

SHINYU GUSHI

Itokazu passed his kobudo teachings on to Shinyu Gushi of Uechi ryu, shown previously in this chapter. Sensei Gushi is the highest ranking Okinawan Uechi ryu practitioner living in the western world. He holds the ranks of eighth dan in Uechi ryu karate and seventh dan in Okinawan kobudo. He currently resides and teaches at the headquarters of the *Ryu-ko-ka-ku-ken Karate Kobudo Association* in California.

TETSUHIRO HOKAMA

A world of thanks is extended to Goju ryu stylist and kobudo master Tetsuhiro Hokama, for his relentless efforts to preserve the history of Okinawan karate and kobudo. Sensei Hokama individually maintains the only karate and kobudo museum in Okinawa. It houses a tremendous amount of information about the karate and kobudo of Okinawa's past.

The book *Okinawan Kobudo and Tanden*, by Tetsuhiro Hokama and Masakazu Kinjo of Uechi ryu, is an authoritative presentation of the weapons and body conditioning practices of Okinawa.

The practice of kobudo fortifies karate. It develops body strength, dexterity and overall defensive ability in a different way than karate. Attaining proficiency with hand manipulated weapons enhances defensive skills. The dedicated practice of traditional Okinawa Kobudo is a deeply satisfying way of contributing to the understanding and preservation of a truly unique part of martial arts history.

OKINAWA KOBODO BO KATAS

TOKUMINE NO KUN
SHUSHI NO KUN
URASHI NO KUN
YONEGAWA NO KUN
SESOKO NO KUN
SHIROTARU NO KUN
SHUKIMINE NO KUN
CHIKIN NO KUN
SHIROMATSU NO KUN
SHIROTAROU NO KUN
KATIN NO KUN
HASSONO KUN
CHINEN SHIKYANAKA NO KUN
SAKUGAWA NO KUN
SHOSHI NO KUN
CHIKIN BO
CHATAN YARA NO KUN
SHISHI NO KUN
RUFA NO KUN
UFUGUSHIKU NO KUN
CHIKIN SUNAKA NO KUN
CHIKIN DAI KUN
KOBO NO KUN
CHOUN NO KUN
UFUTUN BO

OKINAWA KOBODO SAI KATAS

CHATAN YARA NO SAI
CHIKIN SHITAKU NO SAI
SAI 1
SAI 2
KUGUSOKU NO SAI
UFUCHIKU NO SAI
ISHIKAWAGUWA NO SAI
NICHO NO SAI
HANTAGAWA KURAGURA NO SAI
HANAGIGA NO SAI
TAWATA NO SAI
SAI 3
YAKA NO SAI
TOKUYAMA NO SAI
SHINBARU NO SAI
SANCHO SAI

While claiming no great ability in kobudo, the author is proud to have received weapons training so close to the roots of the lineage of both Shinken Taira and Shinpo Matayoshi.

KUBODO LINEAGE

Ryukyu Kobudo Renmei

Moden Yabiku
Shinken Taira
Katsukiho Minowa
Masakazu Kinjo

Zen Okinawa Kobudo Renmei

Shinko Matayoshi
Shinpo Matayoshi
Seiki Itokazu
Yoshitsune Senaga
Shinyu Gushi

Alan Dollar

Ancient Kobudo Kanji

THE
HISTORY AND CULTURE
OF
RYUKYU

琉球

守禮之邦

RYUKYU ARCHIPELAGO

The Ryukyu Islands stretch from below the southern tip of Japan (Kyushu), along the Asian Continent, to within visual sight of Taiwan, spanning a distance of about eight hundred miles. One hundred forty islands comprise the chain. The majority of islands and reefs will not support human life so only forty of the islands are inhabited. They are surrounded by the Pacific Ocean on the eastern coast and the East China Sea on the opposing shores.

The characters shown here are pronounced "Ryukyu" in Japanese and "Liu Chiu" in Chinese. Westerners pronounce the latter "Lewchew". The name of the largest and most inhabited island in the chain is Okinawa. The name means: "Rope in the making" and describes the rough appearance from the air of the stressed coral island. A note of interest about this western interpretation is that the island was called Okinawa long before the invention of the airplane.

Okinawa is about sixty five miles long and varies in width from three to fourteen miles. The northern third is mountainous while the middle and southern portions are flat with little vegetation.

Okinawa island hosts ten cities, fifteen towns and twenty-eight villages. Ninety percent of the current population of 1.22 million people live in the central and southern regions. The capital city of Naha is home to 310,000 people.

Okinawa lies between twenty-two and twenty-seven degrees north latitude (the resort belt), the same as Miami and Nassau. An ocean current originating in the Philippines called *Kuroshio* (Black Current), warms the waters around these islands adding to the humid, sub-tropical environment. It is the home of 3,000 varieties of sub-tropical plants.

Okinawa is home to 260 species of coral. The rich coral reefs support 2,000 varieties of marine life.

INTRODUCTION TO OKINAWA

KARATE, a world phenomenon today, originated on the diminutive island of Okinawa. Okinawa's karate history is presented in previous chapters. To fully appreciate the phenomena of karate it is important to first understand the history and cultural uniqueness of these island people.

With little resources or geographical importance, Okinawa experienced centuries of isolation. As trade developed between Okinawa and many countries of Asia, Okinawa had to balance its culture between the influences of Japan and China. The assimilation of alien cultures into the established society of the Ryukyu Islands resulted in a tenacious yet easy going, friendly people who rarely experienced war. The society of Okinawa is built upon respect for one another and placing the good of the group ahead of individuals.

The origins of Okinawa's people are historically unknown. Most of the archives and artifacts were destroyed during World War II in the Battle of Okinawa. There was no study of archeology by Okinawan scholars until the twentieth century Japanese scholars were preoccupied with details of mainland Japan. After Okinawa became a prefecture the focus was to assimilate the Okinawan people, their culture and history into that of Japan's. There was little concern for the history or culture of ancient Ryukyu. Historical records of Japan and China do offer some insight into Okinawa's past.

THE ORIGINS OF THE RYUKYU ISLANDS

A popular legend about the beginning of Okinawa contends that two divine beings, a male named Shineri-kyu and a female named Amami-kyu lived in huts side by side. Amami-kyu became pregnant from a passing wind and gave birth to a son who became the first King. Two children that followed, a daughter and son, became the first priestess (noro) and the first of the common people, respectively. Fire was obtained from the Dragon Palace at the bottom of the ocean. This myth personifies a virgin birth with the offspring becoming the cornerstones of society. It also appears that fire was brought to Okinawa from across the ocean.

A second version of the same myth explains that after the arrival of the heavenly beings, generations of people began populating Okinawa. They lived in fields and caves. Eventually a grandchild was born named Tenteishi. His eldest son, Tenson, became the first ruler of Okinawa. The Tenson dynasty is said to have lasted seventeen thousand years. This version of the legend first appeared in 1650 in the *History of Chuzan.*

Today scholars believe this story was created in the seventeenth century to establish a connection between the ruling family and divinity and to explain a past that had not been recorded. Between the tenth and thirteenth century there were many small domains ruled by local chieftains called *anji.* It is speculated that one of these chieftains was chosen to create the Tenson Dynasty legend.

The Okinawans emulated the Chinese belief that the succession of the ruling family received its authority from divine intervention. However, if a ruler was not worthy the divine mandate was rescinded and the ruler deserved to be overthrown. This is a departure from the Japanese system of monarchy that contends that successive members of the divine family held the exclusive right to reign regardless of the deeds or virtue of the ruler.

The end of the Tenson dynasty is attributed to this belief. The corrupt twenty-fourth overlord was assassinated by one of his retainers named Riyu.

There were three major pathways by which people inhabited Okinawa during the primitive centuries of Okinawa's development. The easiest access was from northern Asia by migrating south through Japan. It was relatively easy to paddle a small boat southward through the Ryukyu Islands without losing sight of land from one island to the next.

People migrating from Southeast Asia or the Indies arrived by way of the Philippines or along the coast of Southern China, first reaching the southern Ryukyu Islands of Miyako or Yaeyama. Stronger seaworthy crafts and skillful sailors were needed for this southern approach. It is about 175 miles from the northern most island of the Miyako group and Okinawa The ocean crossing to these islands, then north to Okinawa was an arduous journey plagued by typhoons. The larger storms of that time had winds of more than 150 miles an hour. They sometimes measured two-hundred miles in diameter.

The third direction of migration from Manchuria or Mongolia probably traveled through Korea, then southern Japan, before arriving in Okinawa.

Evidence shows the development of Okinawa's culture was influenced from both the north and south by civilizations throughout Asia. How many centuries this influx took, or to what degree Okinawa was influenced is unknown. It is speculated that the population of the Ryukyus, in ancient times, never exceeded thirty to fifty thousand people.

One example of the influence of other cultures is the method by which Okinawan women previously carried their daily cargo. Women of northern Okinawa and outlying islands carried their load on their back with the help of a band placed around their forehead and over the shoulders. This method was used by the Tayal people of Formosa. The women of southern Okinawa carried their burden on top of the head as the Korean women did.

Coins, called mei-to-sen, found in shell mounds in Okinawa indicate a connection with the Chinese continent as early as the third century. The knife shaped coins are similar to those of the Kingdom of Yen in Northern China that ended in 265 B.C. The Kingdom of Yen maintained relations with the dwarf people (Wa) living on islands southeast of Korea. In Okinawa a *koku* (5.11 bushels) of rice was the basis for the monetary unit, *yen*.

All islands between Japan and the Philippines were called Liu Chiu by the Chinese, and could have included Formosa (Taiwan) and other islands. Later in history the distinction was made between Great Liu-chiu, the islands of Okinawa and Small Liu-chiu, Formosa.

Inspired by stories of gold and silver, a Chinese expedition traveled, in 608, to the land of the Happy Immortals. The people they found were not immortals, nor was there any gold or silver to be found. Chinese officials insisted that the inhabitants of the islands yield to Chinese rule. They refused and a battle ensued in which over a thousand of the Wa people were captured and taken back to China.

In 616, the first official record of the "Southern Island people" was recorded in Japan's history annals. In 698, a Japanese force was sent to Ryukyu to claim the islands for Japan. It was a moderate success.

The first use of the name *Okinawa* is found in the records of a shipwrecked Chinese mission in 753. Official missions were also conducted between China and Japan from 607 until 894. They were discontinued because of the treacherous nature of the journey and internal problems within China.

THE SHUNTEN DYNASTY

The Shunten dynasty succeeded the Tenson Dynasty and ruled for three reigns (about seventy years). Shunten is presumed to have been born in 1166. His mother was the daughter of a local chieftain. His father, Tametomo Minamoto, was a traveling adventurer from Japan. The first Okinawa Kingdom is said to have been founded by Shunten, although his history was not recorded until six hundred years after his reign, in the *History of Chuzan*.

There is truth in the existence of the Shunten dynasty of the twelfth century. However, much is believed to be legend, created in the seventeenth century to establish the authority of Okinawa's ruling family with ties to the Japanese Tokugawa shoguns, who were from the Minamoto aristocracy.

Shunten's father left Okinawa in the pursuit of further military adventures. He found himself trapped on Oshima Island in Sagami Bay, Japan. Rather than be captured he committed suicide in ceremonial fashion. This is believed to be the first instance of *seppuku*, also known as *hara-kiri*.

Shunten and his mother, abandoned in Okinawa, moved to Urasoe near the small inlet where Minamoto had left Okinawa and waited for his return. Today this inlet is called Machi-minato, or Waiting Harbor.

Shunten rose to power when he was twenty-two years old by defeating Lord Riyu, who had ended the Tenson dynasty by assassination. His reign was marked with political and economic improvement for the island people. When he died in 1237, the throne was passed to his son Shumba-Junki. The new King built a castle in the hills of Shuri, believed to be the forerunner of the Shuri Castle known today. It was during his reign that writing was introduced, over a thousand years after the forty-seven phonetic kana symbols were developed in Japan.

When Shumba-Junki died in 1248, his oldest son, Gihon, assumed the throne. Gihon's reign was plagued by typhoons, famine and a plague that killed half the population of Okinawa. History reveals that during that period calamities such as earthquakes, storms, floods, famine and disease plagued Japan and medieval Europe.

During the remainder of the thirteenth century Okinawa began to control the outer islands and taxes were established throughout the Kingdom. Buddhism was introduced to Okinawa during this time by a shipwrecked monk named Zenkan. He built a temple named Gokuraku-ji at Urasoe.

The Mongol leader Kubla Khan, in his preparation to invade Japan by way of Korea, sent notice to then King Eiso in 1272, ordering Okinawa to submit to his rule. The Okinawans refused resulting in a skirmish in which the invaders were driven away.

The thirteenth century is viewed as a time of innovation. During this time Okinawa made the transition from a prehistoric existence to a developing social and political society.

THE THREE KINGDOM PERIOD

The fourteenth century is known as the Three Kingdom Period (Sanzan) in Okinawa. The small domains of Okinawa were united into three principalities: Hokuzan (Northern Mountain) in the North, Chuzan the central and most powerful region, and Nanzan to the South. *Zan* means mountain top and refers to the location on which the castles were built.

The ruling regional kings lived in Nakijin Castle in Hokuzan (present day Motobu Peninsula), Urasoe Castle in Chuzan (believed to be the forerunner of Shuri Castle), and Nakagusuku Castle in the southern Nanzan region. These rulers were self declared kings who controlled the area in proximity to their castle.

The northern region was the most isolated area consisting of fishermen and scattered small farms. The people of central Okinawa referred to the northern people as *yambara*, the equivalent of hillbilly.

Nakijin Castle (called Nakijinjo, Hokuzanjo, or Sanhokunakijinjo) sits on top of an isolated mountain surrounded by a deep gorge on one side and the treacherous mountains of Motobu on the other. The castle grounds cover about fourteen acres and were built as a center of religion, not as a fortress. It did not include facilities such as turrets or a donjon (prison).

Nakijin Castle Park, Motobu Peninsula

Recent excavations have uncovered coins and artifacts indicating trade with the Ming and Geng dynasties of China, and with the northern most Ryukyu island of Amami.

Shuri Castle before its destruction during World War II.

King Tomagusuku controlled the territory of Chuzan (Central Mountain). This was the most prominent kingdom of the time. It included the best harbor facilities and most highly developed castle towns of the three kingdoms.

Tomagusuku died in 1336. The throne was passed to a young son who died in 1349. The Governor of Urasoe, a man named Satto, declared himself ruler of Chuzan.

The Lord of Ozato declared himself King of Nanzan during that period. He controlled the southern portion of Okinawa, an area of few resources. The small ports of the area encouraged seagoing merchants, creating a source of income for the Nanzan region.

Nakagusuku Castle Park known for its commanding view of Okinawa.

CHINA AND OKINAWA ESTABLISH TRADE RELATIONS

During the Ming dynasty, which began in 1368, overland trade within China dwindled due to the breakup of the Mongol empire. Sea transport became the focus of China's trade. Coastal trading had existed in China for some time but China was essentially a land power and not accustomed to ocean voyages of long distances. It was now beneficial to China to establish trade links with countries accustomed to ocean trade.

The Lords of Okinawa competed for official recognition and trade rights from China. King Satto of the Chuzan kingdom secured that recognition. Formal relations between China and the Ryukyu Islands were established for the first time in 1372.

Emperor Hung Wu Ti of the newly formed Ming court sent diplomat Yo Sai to Chuzan with a seal of investiture granting license for trade with China. Okinawa would also become a vassal of China. The payment of tribute was required. Accompanying the seal were documents declaring Satto the King of Chuzan, a position he took for himself in 1349.

The new arrangement declared Okinawa a subservient satellite of China and required that King Satto send representatives and tribute to the court at Nanking. Okinawa took its place along with Vietnam, Cambodia, Korea, Siam, Tibet and others as "barbarian countries" willing to send missions and conduct business on Chinese terms.

China recognized the kings and anji of Okinawa and sent delegations there for the succession of kings. Likewise, Okinawa sent emissaries to China for the installation of each new emperor.

Tribute good for the emperor and supplementary good for open trade accompanied these missions. The first few missions conducted business at Nanking but after that the envoys had to undergo the arduous journey all the way to Peking.

Chinese rules stipulated only goods produced in the satellite country could be offered as tribute or trade but an exception was made for Okinawa because of its lack of worthy resources. In return China offered exclusive trade rights and promised to protect the satellite countries in the event of war.

Okinawan missions to China were sometimes as large as three hundred people. Only about twenty were allowed to travel to Peking. The majority were housed, under constant surveillance, at the port city of Chuang-chou. Eventually an Okinawan settlement was established there. Sailors, traders, guards and so forth from Okinawa learned much about the ways of China during the long idle wait for the envoys return from Peking. The knowledge of Chinese ways brought back to Okinawa by these missions began influencing the lives of the Okinawa gentry and government as well as the common people of the waterfront areas.

All aspects of trade and business were strictly controlled by China whose worldwide view was that no country was their equal. Okinawan envoys were required to perform ritualized ceremonies associated with doing business, especially the kowtow, formal bowing. China felt that it had nothing to learn from barbarians, while all non-Chinese could learn much from China.

Okinawans became adept at the formalized rituals of China. The Japanese on the other hand would not place themselves in a position subservient to any other country. As a result Japan did not establish formal relations but did trade with China, through Okinawa.

By the end of the fourteenth century Okinawa was actively trading with Japan, China, Korea and countries of Southeast Asia, creating a period of prosperity that lasted two centuries. The port of Naha grew and was continually bustling with foreigners. The growing strength and wealth of Chuzan increased the rivalry with Hokuzan and Nanzan. Eventually all three kingdoms received investiture from the Ming Emperor and accepted the client-kingdom relationship, creating a diplomatic bond with China that would last for five hundred years.

THE FOUNDING OF KUME MURA

In 1393, a delegation of Chinese settled in Okinawa. The "Thirty-six Families," *sanju roku sei*, settled in Kume Village, *Kume-mura*, near Naha. The term thirty-six families should not be taken literally as it is a Chinese way of describing a representative group of people.

The group consisted of artists, craftsmen, navigators and so forth. They were common people of China who were treated as dignitaries in Okinawa. They taught Chinese writing, art and the ways of government and culture. At the same time the immigrants reported to China the activities of Okinawa.

Kume Mura Park Fukushuen

No show of force was necessary to secure Okinawa's subservience. As long as tribute and formalities of trade were observed, China showed no interest in involving itself in the daily administration of Okinawan affairs.

Young men with the potential for learning the Chinese language were given national scholarships and sent to China. After two or three years of study they would return to Okinawa. Upon returning these scholars secured positions designed to advance trade and educate the Okinawan people in the ways of China.

King Satto expanded Chuzan Castle to properly house and entertain the growing number of Chinese diplomats and dignitaries and to demonstrate Okinawa's worthiness. Satto's success in securing formal relations with China established a new direction for the future of Okinawa. The country, poor in resources, now had the opportunity to develop as a prosperous society. Economic security, a new government system and a refining of their education, art and overall culture resulted from their continuing relationship with China.

King Satto died in 1395, at the age of seventy-five. His oldest son, Bunei, assumed the throne and continued developing the bond between Okinawa and China.

During that time the Japanese religion of Shinto was introduced to Okinawa. Unlike Buddhism that required philosophic and intellectual effort, Shintoism stressed the worship of natural deities and forces. Shinto practices fit easily into the belief system indigenous to Okinawa at that time.

THE SHO DYNASTY

The Japanese name system of family name first will be used to describe the Sho dynasty.

A man named *Sho Hashi*, the son of *Sho Shi* an anji of Sashiki in the South, had aspirations of uniting and controlling Okinawa. He took Chuzan from Bunei in 1406, and installed his own father as King of the central region. He conquered Hokuzan in 1416 and by 1429 had taken Nanzan, while both kingdoms were experiencing internal political turmoil. The three principalities of Okinawa and the surrounding islands became one kingdom for the first time in its history.

The principalities became regions known, from north to south, as Kunigami, Nakagami and Shimajiri. Today they are known as Hokubu, Chubu and Nanbu. *Bu* means area or region.

Sho Hashi assumed the throne when his father died in 1421. He was soon recognized by China as King of Ryukyu (Liu Chiu Wang).

King Sho (*Sho Hashi*) moved the capital from Urasoe to Shuri and embellished the castle and its grounds. He implemented the Chinese Court system and further developed Naha port to improve trade. Okinawans became prolific sailors and the island prospered as a trans-shipment point for trade with Asia, the Indies and Africa.

Staples such as foodstuffs, tea and ceramics as well as luxury items such as silk screens, spices, lacquerware and exotic animals came through the large warehouses of Naha on their way to other countries. It is estimated that merchants sometimes made one thousand percent profit on luxury items. Developing the meager resources of Okinawa became secondary to trade. Naha became one of the most bustling and international ports of the world.

The music, poetry and dance that was an important part of Okinawan social life was influenced by the many countries with which it had contact. The result is a diverse culture rich in the tradition of communal dance, song and festivals. Departures and arrivals of local village sailors, bringing stories and prizes from other lands, were occasions for festive celebrations.

Sho Hashi had a large bell cast and installed at Shuri Castle. The Bankoku Shinryo no Kane (Bell Bridging the Nations) celebrated Ryukyu's seafaring ability and international trade relations. The bell is now a part of the Okinawa Prefectural Museum.

The proximity of the Ryukyu Islands to Southern China dictated that trade be conducted with the ports of Fukein Province, particularly the capital of Fuchou. An Okinawan office, the Ryukyuan Jueneki, and a trading center were established there in 1439 to handle commercial relations between the two countries.

Sho Hashi, one of the greatest leaders in his country's history, died the same year at sixty-eight years old. He unified the government and administration of Okinawa and brought the country to a position of prominence in the Pacific.

The throne passed through three successive sons, all who died in short order. During a riot over control of the throne both claimants died and Shuri Castle was burned. The seals of investiture previously presented to Okinawa by Emperor Hung Wu were destroyed in the fire.

One of the younger kings of the Sho dynasty, *Sho Taku*, adopted the symbol of the Japanese God of War, Hachiman. The symbol, called mistu-domoe, consists of three commas in a circle.

The first Sho dynasty included seven kings with an average reign of eight years. The dynasty ended after sixty-four years by a political coup.

Kanamaro, who had served under two kings, took the name *Sho En* and in 1469 became the founder of the second Sho dynasty. He was a successful ruler whose reign marked a change from individual rule to a more social form of government.

He is known for improving the system of roads and methods of irrigation. When he died in 1477, his fourteen year old son became the king who is most noted in Okinawa's history.

Sho Shin's fifty year reign from 1477 to 1526, is know as the "Golden Age of the Ryukyu Kingdom". It was a period of peace and prosperity that included many social and economic reforms at a time when war, political turmoil and intrusion by European Christians plagued the rest of Asia.

Sho Shin established law and order in the kingdom and stopped the tradition of suicide. He believed the system of local lords, *anji*, with large land holdings and loyal retainers, posed a large threat of insurrection. He issued an order forbidding personal weapons. He further required the *anji* to deliver all weapons to Shuri where they were stored in caves under the castle. The order to disarm the populace preceded a similar order in Japan by one hundred years.

A decisive order issued by *Sho Shin* required all *anji* to establish residence in Shuri. The move was designed to distance ancestral ties and strengthen loyalty to Shuri. *Anji* from the three regions of Okinawa were housed in different areas of the castle town to minimize resistance from past rivalries. In a matter of a few years the plan began to work. The *anji* began developing their local resources to supply their royal necessities and create products for sale in the Naha and Shuri markets. Okinawa began producing goods of its own to compete for sale in the bustling international marketplace. The population of Okinawa then did not exceed one hundred thousand people.

Sho Shin commissioned the building of many parks, bridges, temples and monuments. He is noted for rebuilding Shuri Castle and its grounds. The castle, designated a national treasure in 1925, was one of the most commanding and elaborate castles in Asia. It served as the seat of government for the kingdom and as a center for intercultural exchange for five hundred years. The magnificent gates, courtyards, ponds, tombs and buildings of the castle and its grounds were destroyed during the Battle of Okinawa in 1945. They were rebuilt and opened to the public in 1992.

View from Shuri Castle

The degree of prosperity and contentment achieved during the reign of *Sho Shin* required the establishment of institutions that would prevail into the nineteenth century. Continued contact with China and Japan influenced but did not dominate the tiny island kingdom. The Okinawan people remained independent, yet reserved, in their own culture.

Enkaku-ji, first built by Sho Shin in 1492 on the grounds of Shuri Castle

THE WEST INFILTRATES OKINAWA

By the middle to late sixteenth century Spanish and Portuguese trading ships were active in East Asia. Portuguese ships were first reported in 1542. Spanish ships from Mexico and the Philippines first appeared about 1580. The Dutch established a small trading port at Hirado, Japan in 1611, followed by the British in 1613. Russian, French and American traders soon followed.

These traders were forceful in their pursuit of Eastern trade relations. In one incident in 1637, five well-armed British ships arrived at Canton and demanded the right to off-load their cargo. Their demand to trade puzzled the Chinese. It was a departure from the Chinese attitude of selectively granting the privilege to trade to those outside its borders.

During that time China relaxed its trade restrictions, allowing Japan and China to trade directly. The result of increased competition was a decline in Okinawa's trade, and prosperity. Additionally, the first half of the nineteenth century was filled with hardships for Okinawa. Multiple typhoons, tidal waves, disease and famines diminished the meager Okinawan population and economy.

Contacts with Okinawa generated reports of the kind, generous and polite people of the island. The absence of violence, weapons and thievery was also noted. They did not possess slaves nor would they sell one of their own into slavery. There was a friendliness among social classes and toward foreigners that was not found in other countries.

Okinawans would not accept any payment for provisions or entertainment supplied to visitors. As the number of ships arriving at Naha increased, this became a costly gesture.

These characteristics were in stark contrast to the reception received at other Asian ports. The proximity of Okinawa to other countries of Asia and the kind and sharing nature of its people promoted keen interest in Western countries focused on exploration and trade.

Military ships, diplomats, Christian missionaries and traders visited Okinawa in increasing numbers. The small kingdom became a focal point from which to penetrate the shield of exclusion maintained by Japan. Some Japanese leaders supported opening a trade center for Westerners in Okinawa. Others felt an armed garrison should be maintained there to keep all ports controlled by Japan closed to Western trading.

Commodore Perry's first visit to Okinawa was on May 26, 1853. He was a stern, vain disciplinarian who had already made clear the hard line he intended to take with Okinawa. Perry believed that America had the right to trade with Japan and was willing to take action he felt necessary to enforce that right.

Perry treated Okinawan officials arrogantly. In spite of laws against Westerners setting foot in their country Perry gave his men free leave to go where they liked. Ignoring the President's order to establish a land base only with consent, he marched a company of Marines into Shuri Castle.

The Okinawans were beside themselves with bewilderment. They had never experienced this audacity and were ill prepared to handle it. It was clear that Perry intended to have the regents sign a trade agreement, at all costs.

Stern directives to that effect were delivered to Shuri. Regents politely explained that the American presence in Okinawa caused their people much trouble. They explained they were a poor country who acquired goods only by trading with China and Japan.

The ongoing struggle between the power of America and frailty of Okinawa was personified by the brashness of Perry compared to the polite, hospitable nature of the Okinawans.

Perry eventually threatened to march a force of two hundred men into Shuri and capture the castle. Faced with a forced occupation of their land, the regents gave in to all of Perry's demands. In March, 1855, The United States Congress ratified the Lew Chew Compact.

Understanding Western trade influence on three centuries of Okinawa's history, let's return to the time of the first western presence in Asian waters.

THE SATSUMA INVASION

Japan had great difficulty dealing with the ceremonial subservience demanded by the Chinese. Japanese diplomats were far from diplomatic. They demanded the right to trade freely with China and threatened piracy if they were refused.

Japanese and Chinese pirates, *wako*, plagued China during that time. The raids became so bold that a band of *wako* traveled up the Yangtse River and attacked the walls of Nanking. The Ming government closed all Chinese ports to Japanese traders.

Unable to trade directly with China, Japan looked to Okinawa. The prosperity enjoyed by the cultural and trade exchange with China was too much for the Shogun to ignore. Japan had developed a fondness for Chinese goods and luxury items. Japan could now buy these commodities only at Naha.

In 1480, the Shogun issued orders, through Lord Shimazu of the Satsuma clan, for Okinawan trade to be supervised by Japan. This unwanted interference could not be ignored by the tiny, powerless country. For one hundred years Okinawa paid tribute to, and shared trade profits with, Japan.

An Okinawan trading community was established on Tane-ga-shima, a small island off Southern Japan. Firearms were first introduced into Japan by Europeans through this Okinawan settlement.

That exposure developed a keen interest in the language and ways of Japan. The next three hundred years saw an increasing division among Okinawans. Many wanted to follow the ways of Japan while others desired to continue their cultural and educational development with China.

Emperor Hideyoshi died in 1598. Japan became embroiled in bloody disputes for supremacy. Pressure on Okinawa was relaxed for a while. Ieyasu Tokugawa assumed the title of Shogun and ended the turmoil in Japan. His method of land distribution isolated the Satsuma clan in Kogshima, Kyushu, the southernmost island of Japan.

The current Lord Shimazu, unable to acquire victories or lands to the North, turned his attentions to the islands of the South. Tokugawa feared the increasing presence of Spain and their rumored desire to conquer islands in Asia. He cherished the idea of maintaining an armed force on Okinawa to protect Japan from an attack from the South. In 1606 the Shogun granted permission for Shimazu's invasion of the Ryukyu Islands.

In February, 1609, the Satsuma Clan boldly invaded Okinawa. Three hundred war-junks landed at Uten Harbor on the Motobu Peninsula. Three thousand samurai disembarked and captured Nakajin Castle. Fighting was fierce with high casualties on both sides. The Okinawan people made a bold stand considering how ill prepared they were for war.

Sokon Nogume, From Kadena village, introduced the Chinese sweet potato to Okinawa in 1606, bringing an end to famine. Sugar cane cultivation soon followed

The untrained rural Okinawans, who were without weapons, actually threw ladles of boiling water at the enemy in a feeble attempt to dispel the attack. Children fought and died along side their fathers.

The Japanese force moved toward Shuri after conquering Nakijin Castle and securing the surrounding area. The Okinawans attempted to establish a defensive line around Shuri but were unsuccessful. Satsuma met little resistance.

The Okinawan people had not fought a battle or conflict for two centuries. The last armed conflict had been during the unification of the Kingdom under Sho Hashi. All weapons had been locked in storage under Shuri Castle for over one hundred years.

On April 5, 1609, Satsuma captured Shuri castle and declared Okinawa a vassal of Japan. They looted the palaces and temples of treasures and artifacts. King Sho Nei and one hundred officials were taken prisoner and transported to Kagoshima, Japan. Commissioner, bugyo, from Kagoshima took over the Okinawan government and began a process of determining Okinawa's economic worth.

The people were heavily taxed and socially oppressed. The new government restricted travel, marriage and population growth. The Okinawan people were placed at the bottom of the Japanese hierarchy. The restriction to bear arms was strictly enforced with the disarming of all Okinawa samurai and government officials. The manufacture of weapons for ceremonial use and the import of any weapons were prohibited in 1669.

Satsuma treated Okinawa as its personal source of income. They established the policy that the islands were dependents of Satsuma and only secondary, subjects of Japan and the Tokugawa Shogunate.

Okinawa continued its tribute to China while all trade and all profits were strictly controlled by Satsuma.

Shuri Castle after restoration, completed in 1992

King Sho Nei and the other hostages were returned to Okinawa after signing pledges of loyalty, committing them and their country to Satsuma. Okinawa continued its succession of kings while under the control of Japan and Satsuma. King Sho Nei felt he had failed his people. He refused to be buried in the Sho family tomb and is the only member of the royal family not interred there.

A small group of people loyal to the King rebelled against Satsuma. They were captured and ordered to death. A large pot of boiling water was prepared and the rebels were ordered to jump in. As they met their death with defiant dignity a swirling pattern developed in the boiling water.

This pattern inspired those watching to adopt the symbol now called *hidari gomon*. The symbol of three left swirling commas in a circle resembles the Japanese mitsu domae symbol. Hidari gomon has become the symbol of the past Kingdom of Okinawa.

In 1644, The Ming government of China was defeated and replaced by the Ch'ing dynasty, of Manchu decent. They insisted that the Chinese community at Kume Mura, Okinawa, adopt the queue hair style and address other loyalty issues. The Kume villagers refused these demands. From that time forward they fashioned their hair and attire after that of Okinawa. Cultural ties to China declined.

Japan did not want China alerted to the conquest of Okinawa for fear it would effect trade relations. When a Chinese mission came to Okinawa, the locals were forced to conceal their relationship with Japan. All troop and government officers were hidden. All evidence of Japanese presence was concealed and the people displayed ignorance toward the Japanese language. The ruse was maintained for two and a half centuries.

Conspicuous caravans were assembled when envoys from Shuri traveled through Japan to pay tribute to the Shogun an Edo. As the Okinawans were adjusting to Japanese customs, Satsuma emphasized their difference from the Japanese. Lord Shimazu flaunted that he was the only Lord in Japan receiving tribute from a foreign country. The Okinawan dignitaries were the first foreigners ever allowed to travel in Japan.

It has been suggested that China knew of the hardship that had befallen Okinawa. By ignoring it they did not have to claim any responsibility or take any action. China took the position that recent events had brought poverty to Okinawa. They required the satellite kingdom to pay tribute only once every ten years. This was completely unacceptable to Satsuma.

The primary reason for the invasion of Okinawa was to cash in on the lucrative trade. Trade ships were only allowed to accompany tribute ships, shinko-sen. The opportunity to trade with China only once every ten years defeated Satsuma's purpose in Okinawa. A tribute mission was sent back to China the following year. It was refused and forced to return to Okinawa. Satsuma arranged, through Okinawan middlemen to have trading ships, *sekko-sen*, accompany investiture missions, *kan-sen*, as well as tribute missions.

Satsuma gradually gained political strength and would eventually overthrow the Shogun. The conquest was made possible by the wealth Satsuma reaped by controlling Okinawan trade.

The situation was extremely difficult for Okinawa. They feared reprisal from Japan as Satsuma flouted the shogun's restriction on foreign trade. They were also concerned that if China found out that it was now trading with the Japanese and not Okinawa, it would close its ports to them.

The difficulty of the situation cut to the core of the Okinawan personality. To balance life in dual subordination they became adept at hesitancy, delay and passive resistance. Acceptance of the control over them eventually diminished the self assertiveness and individualism for which the Okinawans had been known.

The most long lasting change was one of a country that had thrived on international trade and was now deprived of the profits from that trade. Now the Okinawans were forced to survive on their own resources. Agriculture and farming became most important. Farmers became very efficient in order to feed their countrymen and, just as important, to meet the heavy tax burden put upon them by Satsuma.

Satsuma continued the domination of the island kingdom through the seventeenth and eighteenth centuries. Okinawa would never again experience the freedom and prosperity it had enjoyed in the past. They balanced dual sovereignty, as a possession of China and a subject of Japan, until the Meiji era began in 1868.

THE MEIJI ERA

The political structure of Japan changed radically in 1867. Forty feudal lords organized a coalition that forced the resignation of the Shogun, the military leader of Japan. The two hundred sixty-seven year old Tokugawa military government was abolished. On January 1868 the *Meiji* government (Era of Enlightened Government) was implemented.

Japan battled encroachment from Russia in the Shakalin and Kurile Islands to the North and from Western intrusion in the Ryukyus to the South.

Meiji Emperor Mutsuhito

Japan realized that if it did not claim the Ryukyu Islands Westerners would eventually claim it for themselves.

In 1871 a tribute ship from Okinawa crashed off Formosa (modern day Taiwan) and most of the crew was murdered by the local Aborigines. The Japanese government seized this opportunity to justify its possession and went to work pulling Okinawa into its realm, away from China.

By 1871 the division of land, han, was changed to one of prefectures, *ken*. On October 14, 1872, Tokyo proclaimed the Ryukyu Islands a *han* of Japan, usurping China's claim to the islands. Ryukyu lost its independence without being consulted or giving consent. From that time forward Okinawa would be a dependent territory of Japan. The population of Okinawa then did not exceed 300,000 people.

Japan ordered Okinawa to sever all ties with China and to close the trading post that had been established on the coast of Southern China. They further demanded that Okinawa cease the use of Chinese reign names and adopt Meiji era names.

Use of the Chinese calendar was forbidden. The Japanese calendar system was substituted and all Japanese holidays had to be observed. Young students and policemen were sent to Tokyo to learn the ways of Japan and return them to Okinawa.

The focus of the Meiji restoration was to modernize Japan. The days of common people groveling at passing officials were giving way to social and legal equality in efforts to be recognized by Western powers. Its efforts included ending the samurai system and the Shogunate, establishing instead, national boundaries to limit individual influence, thus the abolition of the han system and implementation of the ken system.

In 1872 the Ryukyu Shobun (Disposal of Okinawa) began and lasted eight years. This policy was directed at dissolving the old ways and forcing Okinawa to adopt the modern Japanese culture and government.

The following year mandatory military conscription was implemented (Universal Male Conscription Act) causing riots in Japan and Okinawa. Okinawa felt their young men were forced to be a part of the growing Japanese army only to fight wars of conquest for Japan. Resistance to the draft was very strong on Okinawa for twenty years. National loyalties were strong and many men fled to China rather than serve in the Meiji military regime. Others were prosecuted and imprisoned.

The Okinawan people were slow and defiant in accepting Japan's government. They delayed communications with Japan and refused to prosecute those reluctant to serve in the military. In 1873 and 1874 they even held celebrations that all the prisons in Okinawa held not one political prisoner! King Sho Tai repeatedly ignored demands that he visit Tokyo and pay his respects to the emperor, claiming ill health.

Japanese officials held little interest in the fate of the tiny han. The defiance of the Okinawan people, however, developed into a political issue. Tokyo became increasingly angry with the situation and in 1875, took a hard stand. Soldiers from the Kumumoto Division of Japan landed and established the Okinawa Garrison.

Japan feared potential war with China. China believed strongly that Okinawa was their sovereign territory because of five hundred years of tribute payments and investiture missions. They contemplated war and suggested that Ryukyu go to war against Japan. Other Chinese officials suggested diplomatic discussions with Tokyo or selling their right to Ryukyu for money.

The Chinese government made arraignment to meet with General Ulysses S. Grant to discuss their sovereignty right to Okinawa. Grant was traveling in Asia as a private citizen and was scheduled to visit Peking early in 1879.

The Japanese government took quick action to head off the effects of such a discussion. They surmised that it would be difficult for China, or Grant, to ask Japan to relinquish part of its homeland. The decision was made to remove the King of the Ryukyus and change Okinawa from a territorial han to a prefectural ken. The action was justified as punishment for Okinawa's disobedience towards Japans directives of the previous few years.

In 1879 the *Haihan Chiken* was issued, officially establishing Okinawa as a *prefecture* (state) of Japan. Japanese soldiers and police immediately occupied Okinawa. King Sho Tai abdicated and was ordered to Tokyo, regardless of his health. The King, his family and retainers withdrew from Shuri Castle on March 30. The large crowd that had gathered wept as King Sho Tai passed through the Kakugaku-mon gate, ending the four hundred year reign of the second Sho Dynasty.

Japanese soldiers moved into Shuri Castle, the most royal symbol of Okinawa's loyalty to China and the seat of authority on Okinawa for five hundred years. The Kingdom of Ryukyu was gone forever.

China continued seeking support for their cause from American and European leaders. They presented themselves as the protectors and rightful owners of Ryukyu even though they had declined to respond to previous requests from Okinawa for help.

China finally decided to follow Grant's advice and established negotiations with Japan. China, apprehensive of encroaching Russian influence on its northern border, hoped to resolve the Ryukyu problem and regain friendly relations with Japan.

Negotiations between the two countries in August, 1880, suggested splitting the Ryukyu Islands. China would gain control of the southern islands of Yaeyama and Miyako while Japan kept Okinawa and the northern islands. China agreed to reopen its ports to trade with Japan. Okinawa was not consulted about these decisions.

Officials of the Chinese government erupted in opposition to the unbalanced settlement. They refused to sign the agreement. Japanese diplomats returned to Tokyo and the government considered the issue closed. The two governments would never meet again over the Ryukyu issue. China's defeat in the Sino-Japanese war brought an end to the sovereignty issue in 1895.

Okinawans were slow to adjust to Japanese modernization. A group of elders believed the easiest path was to accept modernization. The Okinawan people had no power against the Japanese to change the inevitable future. They formed a group called Kai-ka To, that was influential in the Okinawan's acceptance of modernization policies.

The Meiji government was slow to bring improvements to Okinawa. The second governor of Okinawa was quickly relieved because his policies of education and development were too generous. By 1892, Japan had appointed its eighth governor. That era became know as the "Do nothing" era.

A nominal health and welfare program was established and the first hospital in Okinawa was opened in 1885. A number of small improvements were made into the twentieth century. Japan, however, was reluctant to extend much economic aid to a resource poor prefecture located so far from the mainland. Naha harbor and waterfront were not developed because the harbor was not suitable as a military port.

Taxes were collected in Okinawa until 1903, long after they had been discontinued in other prefectures. Gradually the old class structure was dissolved and justice administered equally. The Japanese school system was established in Naha and Shuri. Sugar cane growth became a prominent source of export. Coastal shipping between islands and mainland Japan had been developed.

The government became more representative in both Okinawa and Japan. Okinawans began playing a bigger role in their own government. Education expanded and scholars began emerging from Okinawa. As the island began to recover, the prosperity began to cause overpopulation.

The population in 1903, was about 480,000. By 1940, about 750,000 people lived in Okinawa. That equaled five hundred eighty-eight people per square mile compared to forty-four people per square in America.

The Japanese government encouraged migration to other islands, to Japan and to America and Europe. The younger generation, who identified with the Japanese culture, felt no attachment to the kingdom of the past. They looked to Japan and to the West for their future. The quality of life and health on Okinawa continued to improve. That is until the war between Japan and America.

WORLD WAR II COMES TO OKINAWA

During World War II one of the worst land battles in history was fought for three months in Okinawa between Japanese and American forces. The southern third of the island was decimated, killing one third of the Okinawan population, about 150,000 people. American fire was directed at Shuri Castle (one of twenty-three national treasures destroyed) because the Japanese army headquarters had been established in huge elaborate tunnels deep beneath the castle. Cultural assets, artifacts and government documents that had been preserved for hundreds of years were destroyed during the "typhoon of steel," the Battle of Okinawa.

Noted historian George Kerr wrote in his book *Okinawa, History Of An Island People:*

> "No prefecture contributed so little to the preparation for war and it's prosecution through the years, but none suffered as much in widespread misery, in loss of human lives and property, and in ultimate subservience to military occupation."

Shuri Castle grounds during World War II

Okinawa's strategic location in Asia made it necessary to continue military occupation after the war. American rule brought many hardships upon the Okinawan people. America's priority of establishing and maintaining military bases took a great deal of land away from farmers. Continuing difficulties are inflicted on the people by the occupying military forces.

An enormous amount of information is available elsewhere about this abomination upon these humble people.

20,000 troops came ashore at this beach in Kadena Village in the first assault on the island

In the National Archives photo of the beach landing I recognized the coral formation. This photo was taken fifty years after the one above. The formation is two miles from the Kadena Uechi Ryu Dojo.

POST WAR OKINAWA

Eventually the Okinawan people began a movement to overthrow foreign authority and revert to Japanese rule. The United States was forced to change its policies concerning Okinawa. Accords were reached during the 1960's returning administrative control of Okinawa to Japan, while allowing military bases to remain. Although the people of Okinawa objected to continued American military presence, they celebrated reversion to Japan on May 5, 1972. The agreement between Prime Minister Sato and President Nixon ended twenty-seven years of American occupation of Okinawa.

Since Reversion the Japanese government has worked to develop industry in Okinawa and break the pattern of a military base dependent economy. New construction and improvements were implemented immediately, including the World Ocean Expo in 1975. An economic recession caused by a decline in the U.S. dollar and the oil shortage crisis soon followed.

Torii Station

Hanza

Site of Japan Ocean Expo held in 1975

Manza beach Hotel

禅

The Cornerstone of Peace Memorial was built to commemorate the fiftieth_anniversary of the end of the Pacific War. The concept of the Memorial is:

Remember Those Lost in the War, Pray for Peace

Pass On the Lessons of War Learned from War

A Place for Meditation and Learning

Monuments listing the names and hamlets of origin of the casualties of the Battle of Okinawa resemble the Vietnam War Memorial in Washington

OKINAWA TODAY

Okinawa's sub-tropical climate, exceptional beaches and exotic marine life have inspired a huge increase in tourism. About 3 million tourists, mostly Asians, visit Okinawa annually. Tourism and related businesses currently comprise about 78% of the gross prefectural product.

Okinawa's primary industry (agriculture and fishing) and secondary industry (manufacturing and construction), makes up the balance. The fishing industry targets bonito and tuna, while agriculture focuses primarily on sugarcane, livestock, tropical fruit, flowers and vegetables. The Okinawan cuisine consists of an excellent balance of protein and vegetables.

The people of Okinawa are one of the longest living people in the world, a fact they attribute directly to their diet. Their diet also includes medicinal herbs, *yaku-so*. Herbs used in home remedies include sarakachi, fuchiba, guava, hibiscus, kumisukuchin and ishimachi.

The manufacturing industry produces meat and dairy products, sugar, beer, Okinawan saki, *awamori*, steel, petroleum and cement. Okinawan buildings of today are constructed primarily of concrete.

Folk crafts include lacquerware and pottery, *toki*, red design fabric, *bingata*, banana cloth, *bashofu*, geometric design, *kasuri* and high quality cloth, *Miyako jofu* clothing.

OKINAWAN CULTURAL UNIQUENESS

Mr. Kinjo, shamisen master

Throughout Okinawa's history the culture and art of this tiny island kingdom have been influenced by many countries of East and Southeast Asia. While assimilating parts of these cultures, certain aspects remain uniquely Okinawan. Among these are karate, dance and music. Okinawan karate is covered in detail in previous chapters.

The shamisen is the primary musical instrument used in Okinawan dance. It is sometimes accompanied by a bamboo flute or drum. The three stringed instrument, resembling a banjo, was originated by traveling minstrels called *Akainko*. The modern version was introduced by China. The Okinawan shamisen uses snakeskin as the sound board. This gives the instrument a very different sound than the Japanese version, that uses cat skin.

An original dance form of the Ryukyu Islands is called *eisa*. It is a dynamic, spirited folk dance accompanied by the shamisen, barrel drums and hand held smaller drums called *paranku*.

Classical dance was originally performed in the royal court to entertain Chinese ambassadors attending coronations of new Okinawan kings. This classical dance form was called *ukwanshin udui*, after the Chinese crown ship, Ukwanshin.

Traditional dances of today are divided into five categories:

1. Rojin odori - old peoples dance. Rojin odori symbolized longevity, offspring, peace and prosperity and is usually performed first.

2. Wakashu odori - young boy's dance. The youthful spirit contrasts the ancestral spirits of the first dance.

3. Nisai odori - man's dance. This brisk, energetic dance is adopted from Okinawan karate and influenced by the man dances of Japan. It was not originally included in *ukwanshin udui*.

4. Onna odori - women's dance. Considered the most important genre of classical dance It is elegant and beautiful.

5. Zo odori - miscellaneous dance. This newest addition was developed during the Meiji period. It is a dance of the common people and is not as solemn or dignified as classical dance.

Kumiodori, classical theater, combines music, dance and literature. It is derived from oral legends handed down through the generations in Okinawan villages.

Odori and karate are performed at most festivals, weddings and other social gatherings.

The *shisha* (shisa in hogen) is an image of half lion-half dog, introduced by China during the fourteenth and fifteenth centuries. Legend contends these statues bring good luck to a house while keeping evil spirits away. Traditional shisha lions are displayed in pairs. One shisha is shown with its mouth open to scare away evil spirits, while the one with a closed mouth keeps good luck in the household. This sounds like superstition until one considers the religious icons Westerners employ for the same purpose.

The ancient style tombs of Okinawa are called *kamekou baka*, turtle back tomb, and originated in Southern China. Tombs, of this and more modern design can be found throughout Okinawa, existing side by side with homes and farms.

When a family member dies the remains are cremated and the ashes placed in a small urn called *monchu*. The vessel is kept inside a family tomb. The word monchu also describes the close bond of Okinawan families.

Bullfighting is an important pastime of Okinawa. Bulls do not fight against a man as in other countries, but against other bulls. When a winner dominates the other bull the match is over and both live to fight another day. Matches are conducted every Sunday throughout the year in large arenas in the Northern and Central regions. Matches can sometimes be seen in small village clearings.

Okinawa is riddled with small and large caves.

The entire village of Yomitan hid in Yomitan cave during the American invastion of Okinawa

Nakamura House, first built with a thatched roof in 1720, is a wealthy farmers house. Uechi ryu Sensei Ken Nakamatsu's grandmother was born in this house.

The complex includes stables,
the roof of which is only five feet high.

Takakura is a raised storage house for harvested farm products native to Okinawa. Being off the ground prevents moisture in the produce and prevents rodents from contaminating them.

The Ryukyu Mura folk village is known for its presentation of the old ways of life such as this Okinawa house from the fifteenth century and the daily processing of sugar cane at the sugar house, *sataya.*

Tsuseishin Hissho Nari
A pure heart is the source of victory

IRON BODY CONDITIONING AND TAMESHIWARI

忍耐力

TAI GITAE

MASTER GUSHI

STRENGTH TRAINING IN CHINA

中国

Ancient martial arts masters sometimes told highly embellished stories about the physical prowess of their instructors. These stories became legends, inspiring subsequent generations to higher levels of karate training.

Kanbun Uechi told his students a story about a man he had seen in China climb a tree using only the muscles in his back. The man gripped the tree with his highly developed back muscles and inched his way up the trunk until he was several feet off the ground. Uechi asked his students if they believed the story. Some students said they did while others stated it was too impossible to believe.

Kanbun then told the students who believed the story that their belief would make them train harder to accomplish the feat. Through years of practice they would become much stronger and better at karate, even if the feat was impossible. Strengthening the body and maintaining increased health throughout life is as important a result as superior self defense ability.

Body conditioning has historically been a significant part of Chuan fa practice in China. Hard daily chores were a requirement of martial arts study. Coupled with designated strengthening exercises such as carrying enormous weight or maintaining demanding positions and postures, strength and stamina were developed.

The second aspect of conditioning is toughening the body weapons used in self defense. Chinese martial arts systems did not use the two knuckle fist most common in karate practice today. The fingertips, middle knuckles, ridge hand and so forth were subjected to rigorous conditioning routines such as striking hard objects repeatedly as seen in the illustrations from the *Bubishi.* Pinpoint targeting during close range fighting requires specialized body weapons. Hands and feet become an arsenal of self defense as the body and will become iron. Remember the original purpose for the development and longevity of karate is life saving self defense, not sport or hobby.

Body conditioning, *tai gitae*, is the long term process to virtually create your own body armor. It is not always possible to avoid getting hit during a serious altercation. Mental and physical preparation lessens the effect of being hit. The importance of this type of conditioning increases when facing multiple attackers.

KOTE KITAE
FOREARM CONDITIONING

小手鍛え

Kanbun Uechi taught a forearm conditioning exercise called *kote kitae* he learned in China. This formal exercise involves the systematic pounding of the forearms with the fists of a training partner. The purpose of kote kitae is the toughening of the forearms and shins. Highly developed forearms are prevalent on all the major Okinawan instructors of Uechi ryu karate, especially the older ones.

Kanbun Uechi told a story to Seiyu Shinjo about a Chinese martial artist who visited him and disclosed an interesting conditioning exercise emulating a crane. The man dumped a small bag of rice on the dojo floor. He picked the rice up, one by one, with the fingertips, much the way a bird would pick them up with its beak. As the grains of rice disappeared the strength of the man's developed fingertips became apparent. The visitor explained that in a fight he could apply his pecking and pinching techniques to the veins in the arms of his opponent, causing deadly internal bleeding.

Uechi became intrigued with this idea and stood up, directing the man to demonstrate the technique on him. Several attempts were made but none were successful because of the extreme development of Uechi's arms. Kote kitae had rendered the crane technique ineffective.

Karate techniques often attack the legs, the foundation of an opponent. Leg conditioning, *ashi kitae*, is another aspect of this type of conditioning. The thighs are hardened by repeatedly being kicked by a training partner, in the same manner as the repeated forearm strikes of kote kitae. Furthermore, the shins and feet are conditioned to match hands and forearms.

The psychological confidence and physical advantage gained from body conditioning is a unique feeling that one must experience to understand. The feeling goes beyond the gratification of practicing rigorous karate. The discipline developed with long term conditioning, pain, recovery and strengthening, forge an iron will. The confidence of knowing your karate techniques will be effective in an aggressive situation greatly increases the chances of survival and victory. Body conditioning, makiwara training and board breaking are ways of testing your karate techniques and taking them to a higher level.

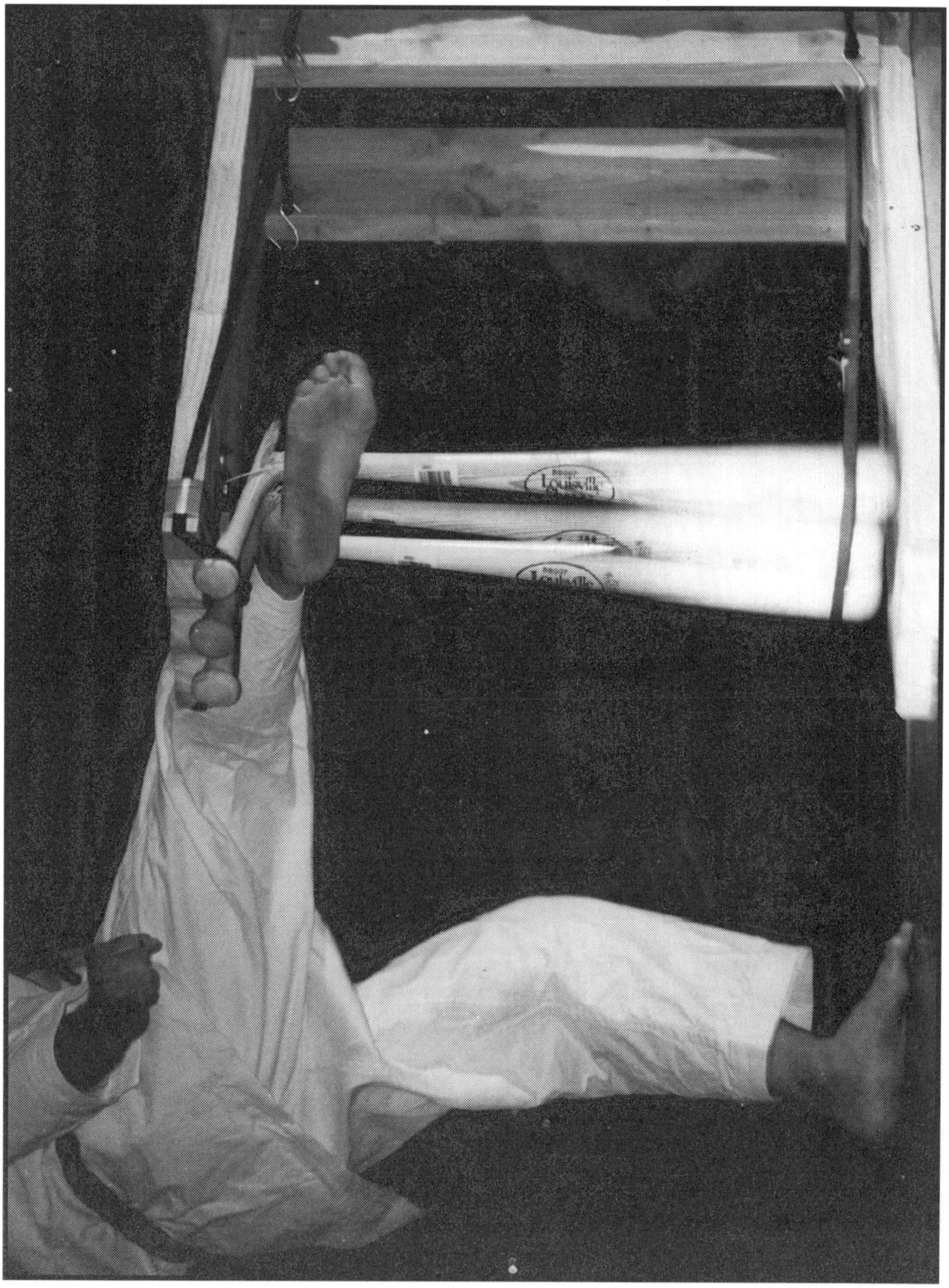

One objective of martial arts training is raising the tolerance to pain. The muscle pain of developing strong kicks or fast punches, or the emotional pain of failures or embarrassments along the way, are physically and emotionally strengthening experiences. Learning to raise the threshold of pain during body conditioning and board breaking develops a higher level of mental control.

Local pain is experienced at the point of contact or injury but the brain is where the pain registers. Control of this aspect of the brain is achieved with advanced karate training and body conditioning. You decide how much pain you will feel. Do not mistake this for masochism. The pain and discomforts of advanced physical development is positive. The pain and damage inflicted by someone hitting you is not!

TRADITIONAL STRENGTH and CONDITIONING DEVICES

壺(カーミ)

Kami, meaning jars, are held by the top in the dragons grip while stepping through the Sanchin kata. Small stones added daily increase the challenge on the strength of the body. Kami develops the trapezious muscles that help pull the shoulders down and adds power to a punch. Using the heavy jars also strengthens the hands, wrists and forearms.

One hundred year old stone bowls filled with rocks, sunabako, used for fingertip conditioning.

The Okinawan people have demonstrated ingenuity in developing training devices from their meager resources.

据石

Another device for strengthening the forearms and wrist is called *chishi.* They are made of stone, concrete, weights or metal gears. Chishi are found in virtually every dojo in Okinawa.

錠形石(サーシ)

Sashi, stone locks used on ancient wooden gates.

The use of weights, *tan*, has been a tool in body strengthening and conditioning long before its popularity in athletics. Practicing the skills particular to the physical endeavor to be performed is primary. Secondary to increased ability in that endeavor is strength training, often in the form of weight training.

The primitive weights of Okinawa are often made of concrete or transmission gears from old military vehicles.

MAKIWARA

巻わら

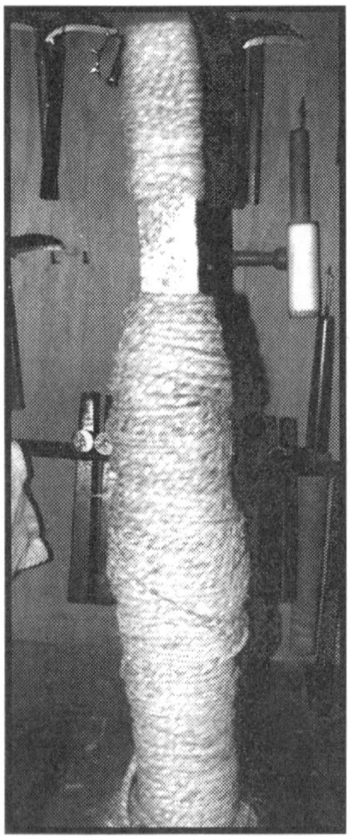

Karate at its purest is strictly defensive. Employing a solid stance, maximum body power and one explosive crushing technique, *ikyoryo*, against an attack is the emphasis of Okinawan defense systems.

This explosive power is developed from a training device called *makiwara*. It is the most prominent training tool found in the dojos of Okinawa.

Makiwara range from a conveniently located tree to long wooden planks planted in the ground. The most common makiwara are now made of spruce and taper to create a spring action. They vary in height but are usually about three feet tall, firmly mounted to the floor in a metal bracket.

Older Okinawan dojos still have makiwara that slide into a hole in the ground. Different size and shape makiwara can be installed to practice repeated punches, strikes and kicks, or arm and leg conditioning. The knuckles and parts of the hand reach an unbelievable degree of toughness from continued makiwara practice.

Huge knuckles and hideous blisters are not the goal of makiwara practice. This local toughening is secondary to developing maximum power in the strike. Repetitive strikes to the makiwara develop immense power in your body and techniques.

A goal in makiwara training is to push it back as far as possible when striking. This develops strength in the wrist, elbow and shoulder and solidifies the Sanchin stance during the strike. Through contact with the makiwara you can feel the power of Sanchin from the feet, through your foundation and into the strike. Makiwara training and Sanchin kata compliment each other in a common goal of body strengthening.

Legend contends the crushing power developed from makiwara training helped to defeat armed samurai soldiers. Some older masters feel that Sanchin kata and makiwara practice are all that is necessary to develop a strong body and formidable karate power. Practicing techniques without applying them to the makiwara leaves out an important part of karate understanding and ability.

Choki Motobu, an infamous street fighter from the past was known for makiwara training, lifting heavy stones and fighting. He preferred a low stance and would creep toward his opponent, taking a few hits until he could deliver a devastating punch or kick. Motobu's techniques were not very polished but his numerous victories are testimony to the effectiveness of body conditioning and makiwara training.

The person with the strongest weapon has a good chance of winning. In times past, a high level of body conditioning and hardened striking surface was good insurance for survival. Firearms are prevalent everywhere today, making empty handed self defense more difficult. The confidence derived from developing an iron body and mind is ever important on todays streets.

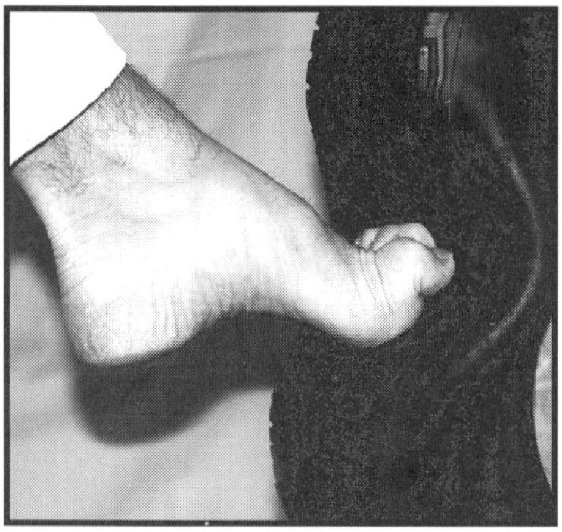

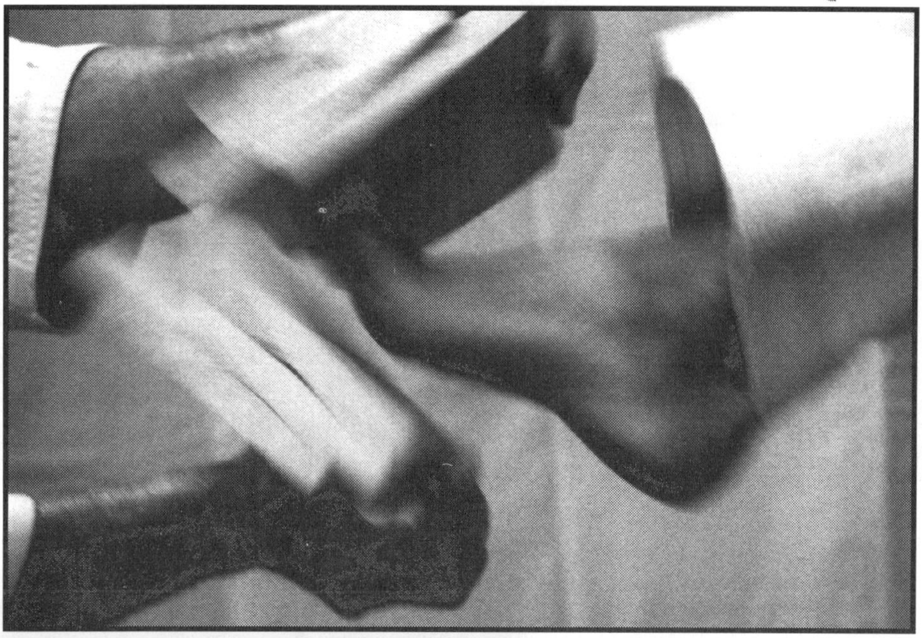

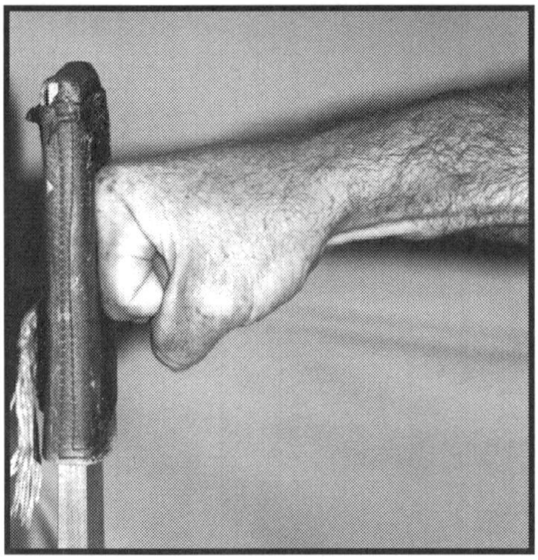

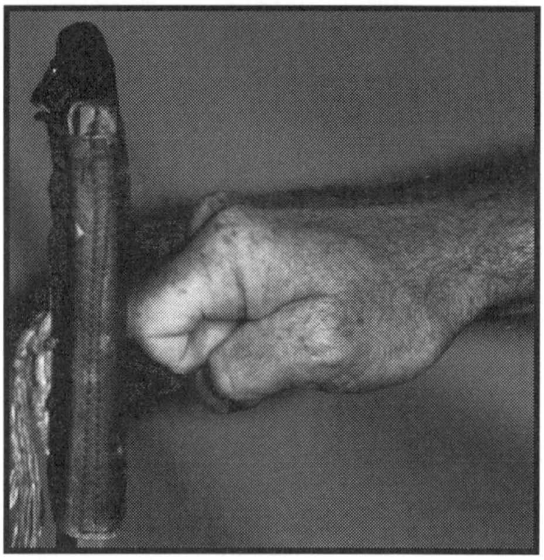

闘牛

TAMESHIWARI

試し割り

Uechi ryu masters are known for amazing breaking demonstrations. The extraordinary level of body conditioning developed over years of rigorous training is demonstrated by breaking boards, bricks, roof tiles, poles, two by fours, and baseball bats. Sorry, no fire or blocks of ice.

The wood used in demonstrations in Okinawa is dense and very tough. Often cement, stuck to wood, previously used to form concrete, must be scraped off before breaking. The poles are cut short and the boards are cut long. An enormous amount of force, focus and technique is necessary to break wood in the humid climate of Okinawa.

The large ceramic roof tiles *akarenga* used on many Okinawan houses, are another popular breaking medium. The terra cotta tiles are very stiff and dangerous to break.

The degree of body conditioning discussed here does not apply to children. Muscular and skeletal development from karate practice is good for children, makiwara training is not. Children's bones are still growing and should not be subjected to repetitive striking of hard surfaces. The sometimes bizarre body conditioning of the past is explained here to complete the unique history of Okinawan karate, and to perpetuate its practice among the more dedicated advanced karate men and women.

上地流

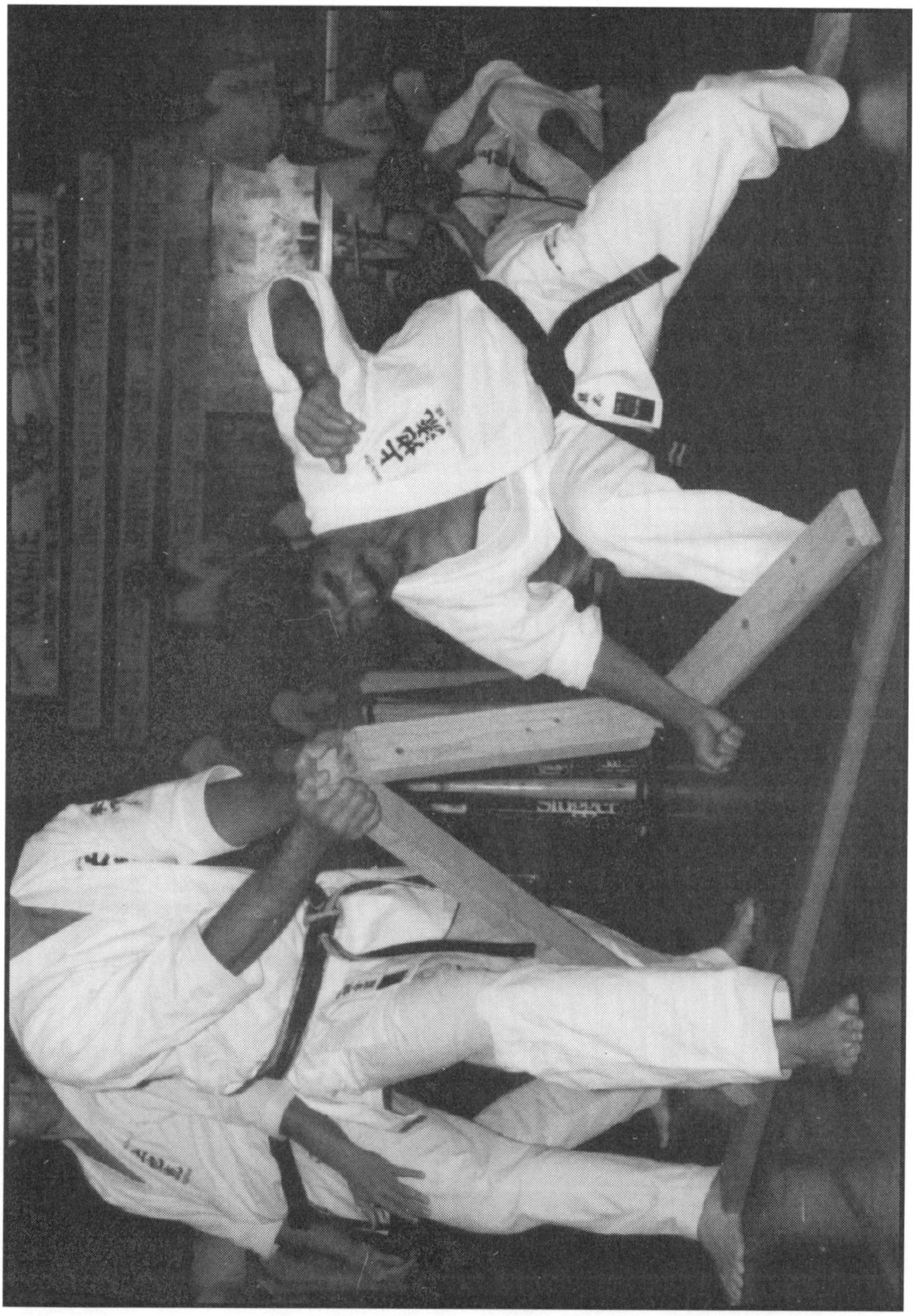

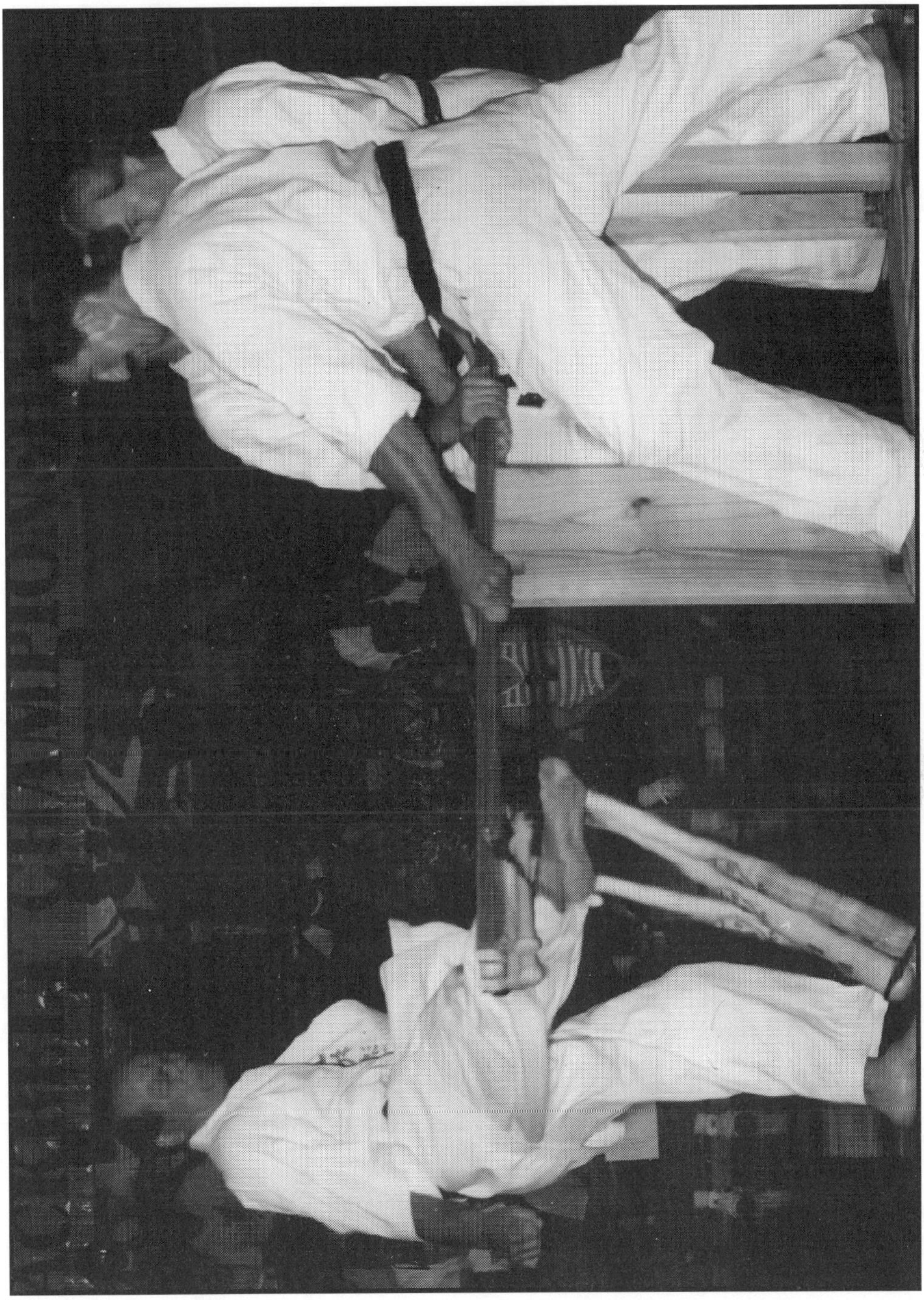

BLOCKING TECHNIQUES

受け耐

UKE WAZA

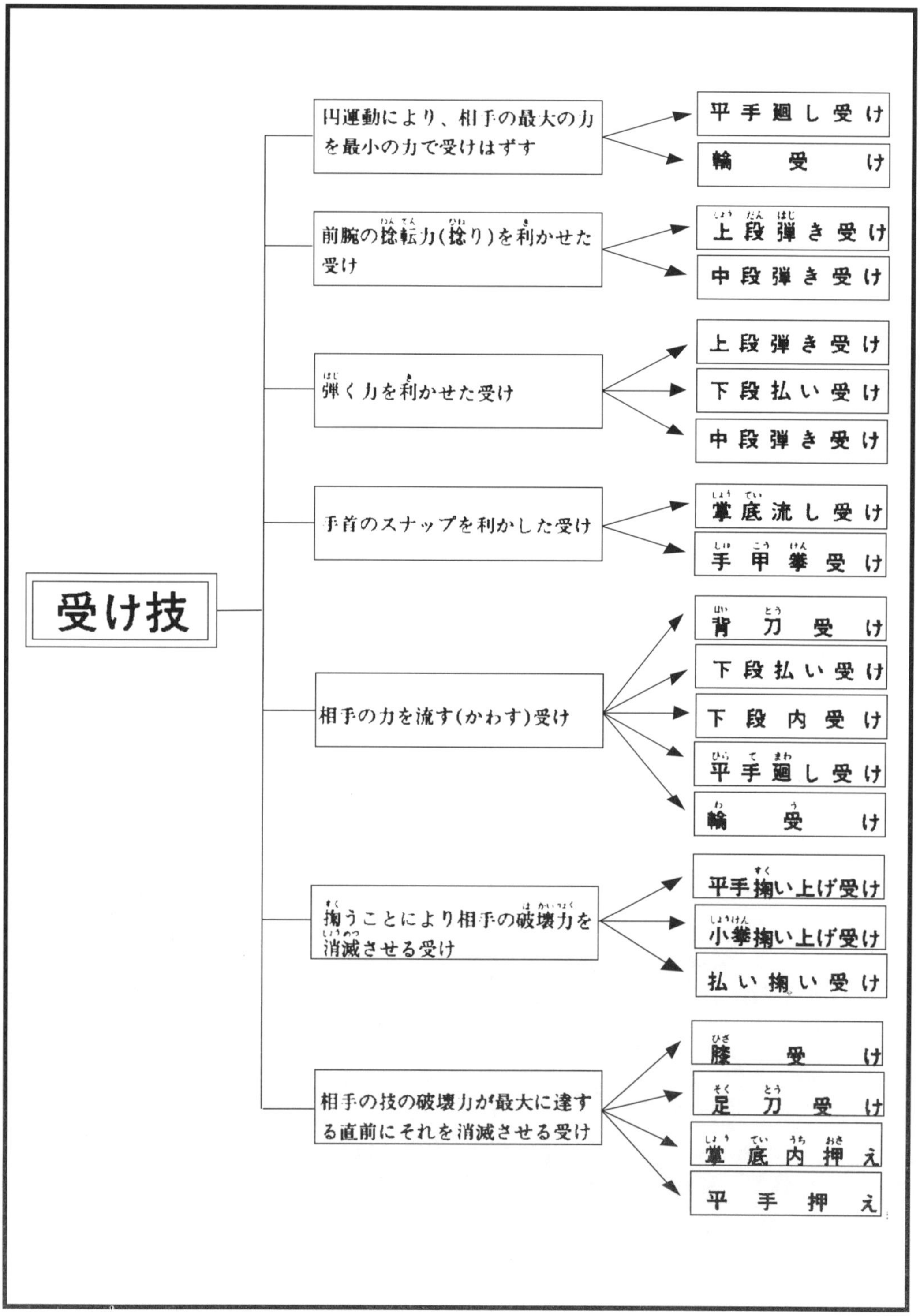
受け技
円運動により、相手の最大の力を最小の力で受けはずす
平手廻し受け
輪受け
前腕の捻転力(捻り)を利かせた受け
上段弾き受け
中段弾き受け
弾く力を利かせた受け
上段弾き受け
下段払い受け
中段弾き受け
手首のスナップを利かした受け
掌底流し受け
手甲拳受け
相手の力を流す(かわす)受け
背刀受け
下段払い受け
下段内受け
平手廻し受け
輪受け
掬うことにより相手の破壊力を消滅させる受け
平手掬い上げ受け
小拳掬い上げ受け
払い掬い受け
相手の技の破壊力が最大に達する直前にそれを消滅させる受け
膝受け
足刀受け
掌底内押え
平手押え

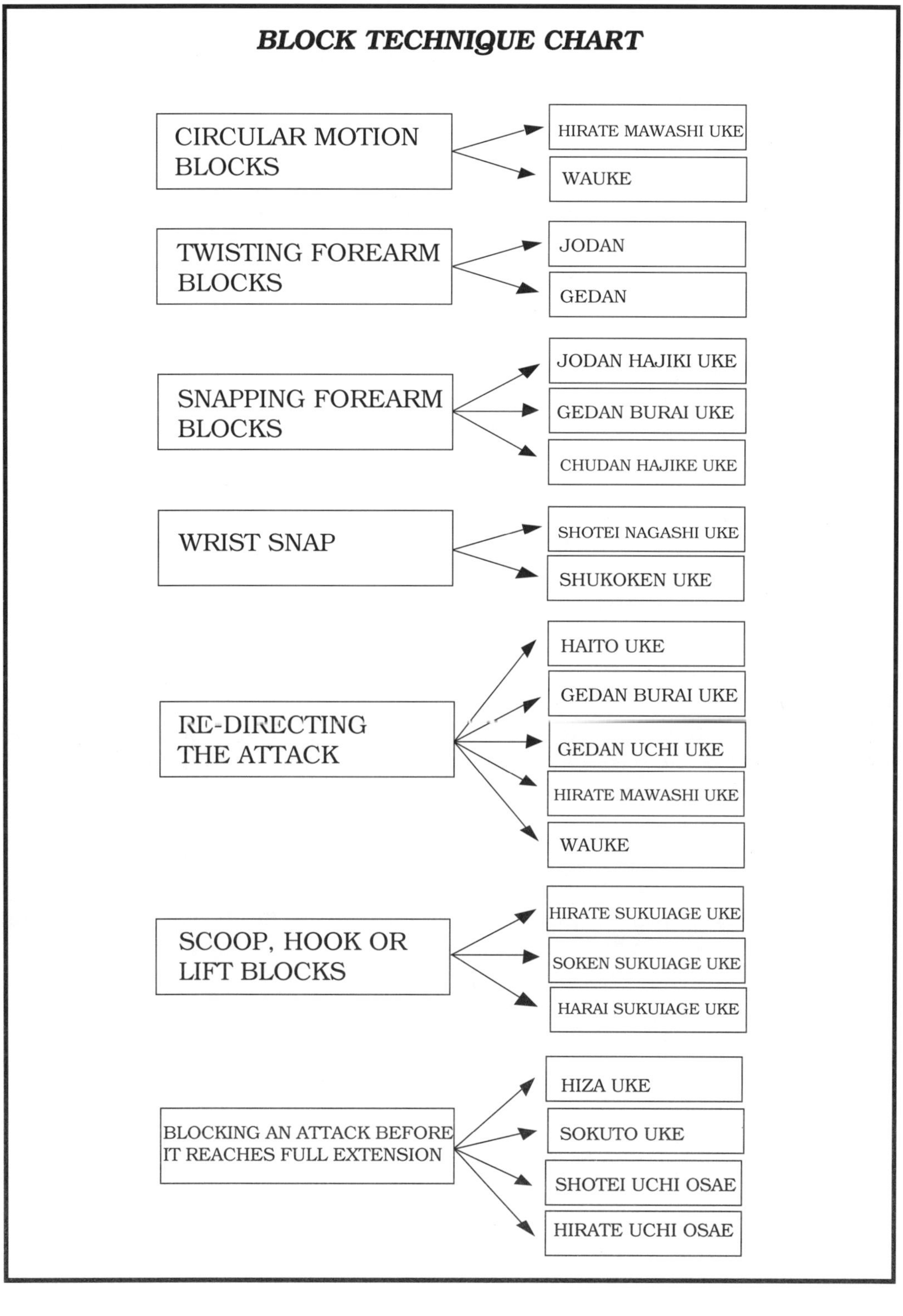
BLOCK TECHNIQUE CHART
CIRCULAR MOTION BLOCKS
HIRATE MAWASHI UKE
WAUKE
TWISTING FOREARM BLOCKS
JODAN
GEDAN
SNAPPING FOREARM BLOCKS
JODAN HAJIKI UKE
GEDAN BURAI UKE
CHUDAN HAJIKE UKE
WRIST SNAP
SHOTEI NAGASHI UKE
SHUKOKEN UKE
RE-DIRECTING THE ATTACK
HAITO UKE
GEDAN BURAI UKE
GEDAN UCHI UKE
HIRATE MAWASHI UKE
WAUKE
SCOOP, HOOK OR LIFT BLOCKS
HIRATE SUKUIAGE UKE
SOKEN SUKUIAGE UKE
HARAI SUKUIAGE UKE
BLOCKING AN ATTACK BEFORE IT REACHES FULL EXTENSION
HIZA UKE
SOKUTO UKE
SHOTEI UCHI OSAE
HIRATE UCHI OSAE

The pre-dominance of circular blocks in this Okinawan karate system is attributed to its Chinese origins. The large circular motion of the arms resembles the manner in which the crane moves its wings for defense and exercise.

Blocking is the ability to defend yourself against attack. It is the essence of karate. The proper moral use of karate dictates that your first technique will be one to protect yourself. The code "there is no first attack in karate" is an axiom to traditional stylists The second technique will be a counterattack to end the threat of danger. Effective blocking means also setting your opponent up for counterattack. A properly trained defense also becomes an excellent offense. To better understand the damage that can be inflicted to an opponent's limbs by strong, effective blocking refer to Chapter VI, Body Conditioning.

There are three ways to defend yourself: blocking (holding your ground and deflecting strikes, to counterattack), maneuvering (using mobility and distance for evasion and counterattack), and offensive attack (beating your opponent to the attack). All three require perception, reaction and proper execution. Blocking is the foundation of self defense, and the most important form to develop.

The blocking intensity discussed here refers to the intensity necessary to protect yourself from life threatening situations encountered on the street. Blocks used in the sport aspect of karate require less intensity.

There are two approaches to blocking an attack. One is opening your opponent up with your block for immediate inside counterattack. This presents more available targets to you but also leaves your opponent in position to continue the attack.

The second method is to cross your opponent up by blocking the outside of the arm or leg. This approach positions you outside his defenses and decreases his opportunity to continue attacking. Closing your opponent up in this manner places you in a good position for a controlling technique or take down.

The methods of attack and offensive styles vary from person to person. Train to be versatile in your choice of defense. As you advance, develop the ability to be selective to gain maximum control from a defensive position.

This chapter explains a variety of blocks and blocking concepts. Because of different methods of application, some blocks may be included in more than one section.

CIRCULAR MOTION BLOCKS

Circular motion blocks enable you to block an attack of maximum power by using minimum power. They re-direct power more effectively than straight-line, linear blocks, but are also more difficult to execute. Mastering circular blocks enables smaller people to re-direct the force of larger attackers easily. They also lessen the occurrence of tissue damage to the arm caused by more direct blocks. Circular blocks develop the muscles of the shoulder and enhance hand and arm coordination.

HIRATE MAWASHI UKE
Open Hand Circular Block

To execute hirate mawashi uke, begin with your extended arm and open hand (hirate), about twelve inches in front of your body. Sweep across your body as with a downward inside block. As your hand reaches shoulder height, turn the palm toward your opponent. As you continue the circle, your fingers should go no higher than your head. Return your hand and arm to the original starting position with the elbow tucked in near the ribs. The other hand remains in the on guard position, *hirate gamae*, or it can be chambered for a counter strike.

The circle created by this block should not go outside your body or above your head. The empty space on each side of you does not need to be protected. If your arms are in that void, your body is exposed.

As this large circle is being created by the hand, a smaller circle occurs at the elbow. The large circle will be centered on your body, however, the small circle will not. Since the elbow is the center of the small circle, when you block with the right hand the center of the small circle will be more to the right side of your body. The center will be more to the left when blocking with the left hand.

As your opponent punches, practice blocking close to your opponents elbow and close to the wrist. Blocking close to his elbow maximizes the effect of the block while requiring minimum strength. Blocking at the elbow also puts you in a closer position to grab and counterattack.

Blocking near the wrist can deflect a fast incoming punch, but places you slightly out of counter punching range. You may need to slide in closer to deliver a punch, or use a kick. Both methods are effective and each leaves you in a different position for counterattack.

When blocking near the opponent's elbow, do not overextend your arm. Straightening your arm in this manner decreases the strength of your block. It also positions your arm on the same plane as the incoming attack. This lowers the likelihood of the block being effective. Keep your elbows bent in the proper Sanchin (Chapter X) position during this block.

When blocking a punch meet your opponent's elbow near your own elbow rather than near your hand. When the punch is close to your elbow it is easier to move with less power. The farther from the center of the small circle that you engage the punch, the more power must be used to move it.

When executing the circular block do not let the elbow raise up or go outside your body. Keep the elbow down, and squeezed inside your body line to make the circular motion effective. That factor makes this one of the most difficult blocking techniques to master.

Avoid starting the circle outside your body. Beginning students have a tendency to "wind up" to add power to the block. Further training will develop understanding of how to apply the power of your body, not momentum, for strength in the circular block.

In the advanced stages of this block you may change the starting position to more accurately intercept the incoming punch. Hirate mawashi uke is found in Hojoundo, Yakusoku Kumite and in all katas except Sanchin.

WAUKE
Double Arm Open Hand Circle Block

The wauke block is found primarily in Sanchin. Wauke is taught in the first kata to instill correct circular blocking. A great deal of practice of the wauke block is necessary as a beginner to properly perform the hirate mawashi uke in later katas.

The blocking arm and hand follow the same pattern as described in hirate mawashi uke. The other arm assists the block. The hand of the supporting arm is placed at the elbow of the blocking arm to insure the proper position of the elbow while blocking. Remember the elbow should not move outside the body line while blocking. When performing hirate mawashi uke in the remaining katas, the supporting hand will serve as a secondary or back-up block.

Although hirate mawashi uke is performed with one arm, the remaining arm should always be prepared to aid in blocking an incoming punch. It is not necessary to post the supporting hand formally when executing hirate mawashi uke as you do in wauke.

TWISTING FOREARM BLOCKS

The power in these blocks comes from the twisting motion of the forearm.

JODAN UKE

High Area Block

Jodan uke is used to protect against a high area punch or vertical strike to the head. Prepare this block by twisting your forearm into the chambered position with your palm up. As the block rises to meet the incoming attack, twist your forearm quickly when meeting the punch. It not necessary to block any higher than your forehead. It is better to use a hiraken fist rather than a seiken fist because it allows more flexibility in the forearm. After blocking quickly lower your arm, placing your elbow close to your ribs so they are not vulnerable. Be prepared to perform another block or counterattack following all blocks. Jodan uke is found in Hojoundo, Yakusoku Kumite and Seichin kata.

CHUDAN UKE
Middle Area Block

Chudan uke is used to block the lower face and middle area of the body. To prepare the block, twist your forearm until the palm of the hand is facing you. Twist your arm outward as it moves to the outside of your body. Encounter the incoming punch with the outer part of the forearm or the hand.

Maintain the elbow close to your body. End the block with the elbow inside your body line for proper forearm alignment and maximum effectiveness. Chudan uke is found in Hojoundo and in Kanshu and Seichin katas.

SNAPPING FOREARM BLOCK

The power in these blocks comes from using the strength of your shoulder, coupled with a snapping force against the attack. The energy of the attack is deflected in the same way as a baseball being hit with a bat.

JODAN HAJIKI UKE
High Area Snapping Block

Execution of this block is very similar to jodan uke and is prepared in the same manner. Contact is made with the top of the forearm rather than the outside. Tense the shoulder and elbow at contact and add a strong snap of the arm to this block. This will re-direct the incoming energy in a more aggressive manner than the twisting forearm block.

Keep the elbow lower than the hand so your forearm is at a slight angle. This will allow vertical strikes to slide off your arm, instead of breaking it. Positioning the forearm at right angles to the attack increases the potential of damage to the forearm. As you practice insure that the forearm, not the hand, is in the proper position to meet the incoming attack. This is a common mistake among new students that will result in damage to the hand and the head when blocking attacks from solid objects. Jodan hajiki uke is found in Hojoundo, Yakusoku Kumite and in Kanshu and Seichin katas.

GEDAN BARAI UKE
Low Area Down Block

Gedan barai uke is used against the front kick (mae geri) and side kick (yoko geri) delivered to the middle area, *chudan*, and low area, *gedan*, of the body. The block is a quarter circle downward motion. Use a seiken fist with this block to accomplish maximum tightness in the forearm.

Unconsciously leaving the hand open will result in broken or dislocated fingers upon contact with the leg.

Twist your forearm outward as you block, tighten your elbow and add a strong snap at the end of the block.

Avoid bringing your fist back to the opposite shoulder to wind up for this block. This takes additional time, moves in the opposite direction desired and places the arm too close to the body creating an opening for your opponent.

Newer students can be seen rubbing their arms in pain after using this block. This is a result of blocking on top of the opponent's leg, hitting his shin. Arms are much smaller than legs and will lose frequently in a conflict of power against power. To prevent this, use more accurate timing in executing your block. Start the block a little sooner so you make contact with the outside of your opponent's leg rather than his shin. Gedan barai uke is found in Kanchin and Sanseiryu katas.

CHUDAN HAJIKI UKE
Middle Area Snapping Block

Chudan hajiki uke is executed in the same manner as chudan uke, with the added snapping power just described in jodan hajiki uke. Remember it is important that your elbow does not extend beyond the outside line of your body. This block is found in Hojoundo, Yakusoku Kumite and in Kanshu and Seichin katas.

WRIST SNAP

SHOTEI NAGASHI UKE
Palm Heel Inside Block

Use only the heel of the palm of your hand. The inside of the forearm can also be used. Avoid using the fingers or upper palm for this block. Keep the elbow down to add body power to the block and keep the wrist straight. This will decrease the possibility of damage to the wrist and allow you to use the upper part of the forearm to aid in the block.

Shotei nagashi uke is used against upper body and face attacks. It is most effective when applied slightly above the opponent's elbow, causing joint damage while deflecting the attack. This block involves more than pushing away a punch with the palm of the hand. A well-timed snap of the wrist when encountering the punch adds power to this blocking technique. This block is found in Hojoundo and Yakusoku Kumite.

SHUKOKEN UKE
Top Of The Wrist

Shukoken means the crane's head. The top of the wrist is used when applying this block vertically, against a frontal grab, or punch. The back of the wrist is used when applying the block horizontally. An immediate counterattack with the fingertips (crane's beak) usually follows. Shukoken uke is found in Hojoundo and in .Seichin and Kanchin katas.

RE-DIRECTING THE ATTACK

The following blocks are effective in changing the direction of power of an attack away from the intended target. Some of these blocks have been described in previous sections.

HAITO UKE
Ridge Hand

Haito uke, ridge hand, is applied from the outside to the inside, in the same manner as shotei nagashi uke. The hard striking area of the inside ridge hand creates an effective re-directing block. Apply this technique near the opponent's elbow to maximize the re-directing effect.

GEDAN BARAI UKE
Low Area Down Block

Gedan barai uke has been explained in the twisting forearm section. This application is slightly different. The block previously described is with a hard hitting motion to stop an incoming kick. To re-direct the kick, this block is applied more softly with a smooth follow through motion. It is most effective in re-directing the kick when it is applied to the outside of the leg. Remember to time your block so you make contact with the side of the leg, not the shin. This block is found in Yakusoku Kumite and in Kanchin and Sanseiryu katas.

GEDAN UCHI UKE
Low Area Turning Inside Block

This block moves from the outside to inside, opposite of gedan barai uke. To execute this block, lower your arm in front of your body. The forearm twists as it moves across your body, blocking the kick with the top of your arm. Use this block to open up or to close your opponent. Be sure to tighten the shoulder and elbow and include body strength.

Gedan uchi uke is effective in controlling front, side and especially, roundhouse kicks. The other arm should be used to protect the upper body against a higher kick or a double kick. Proper distancing is important in blocking your opponent's leg near the ankle, not near the knee. The further up the leg you execute the block, the more difficult it is to move the leg.

Positioning yourself too close will place you within punching range at a time when you are engaged in blocking a kick. Be sure to keep your back straight to keep your face out of attack range. Bending forward is a common mistake made by beginners until they develop leg strength in the deeper stances. Gedan uchi uke is found in Yakusoku Kumite and Kadena Yakusoku Kumite.

HIRATE MAWASHI UKE & WAUKE

These blocks were explained in the section covering circular motion blocks. They are included on the chart in this section because of their outstanding ability to re-direct an incoming attack.

SUKUI - SCOOP, HOOK or LIFT BLOCKS

These are advanced blocking techniques. They are very good for gaining control of your opponent and upsetting his stance and balance. They also have the potential for damage to the blocking hand if performed incorrectly.

HIRATE SUKUIAGE UKE
Open Hand Scooping Lift Block

The open hand scoop block is executed with an upward lifting motion. It is effective against a front kick or side kick. The block is finished by firmly pinching the Achilles tendon with your fingers. The pain caused by this technique help set your opponent up for a counterattack.

There are two important distancing factors with this block. The first factor is the proper distance between your blocking hand and your body. Keep your elbow down with the upper arm close to your body. Pull your shoulders down to employ the strength of your body instead of only the arm and shoulder.

The second factor is proper distance between you and your opponent. You must position yourself outside the range of the kick to catch it near the ankle.

Executing open hand scooping blocks without damaging your fingers requires an advanced level of accuracy. In practice, catch the kick with upward scooping motion of your inner forearm then slide your arm until your hand is in position to grab the tendon. Hirate sukuiage uke is found in Seichin kata.

SHOKEN SUKUIAGE UKE
One Knuckle Scooping Lift Block

The one knuckle lifting block is similar in effect to the open hand lifting block. It is effective against front, side and roundhouse kicks. Catching a kick with this block requires an advanced level of training. To become proficient with this block, begin the execution with gedan uchi uke. As you make contact with the kick, tuck your elbow into your body and raise your fist to catch the leg.

Two different methods of executing this block were taught by Kanei Uechi and Seiyu Shinjo. Kanei Uechi taught the method of lifting your block upward, throwing your opponent backward.

Seiyu Shinjo taught the method of continuing the circular motion of your arm to throw the opponent's leg to the side instead of backward. This allows you to attack the opening you have created on the side and back of the body.

A third possible application is to secure control of your opponent's foot with your other hand, exerting pain on the ankle and foot to gain control. Shoken sukuiage uke is found in Kanchin and Sanseiryu katas.

HARAI SUKUI UKE
Downward Scooping Block

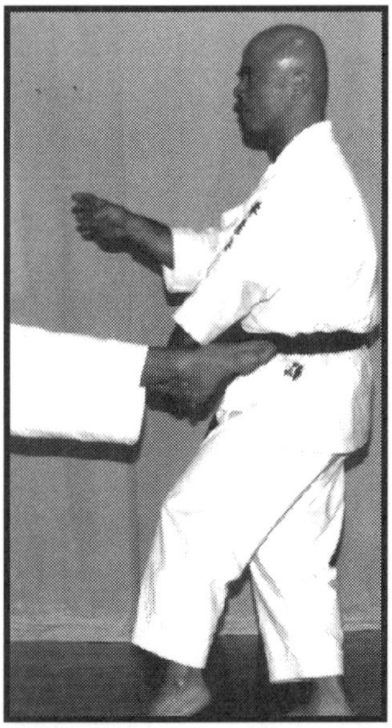

This block is executed with a circular downward motion, similar to gedan burai uke. It is completed by hooking and catching the incoming kick with your hand. Continue the circular motion until you have moved the kick to the outside of your body. This allows you to step inside your opponents range for a counterattack or to upset his stance.

If you open your opponent up by blocking his leg outward, you face his punching attack. Blocking his leg inward will gain a superior position for a counter attack.

When you begin practicing this block the timing will be difficult. Many students have damaged their fingers by making contact with the incoming kick. To avoid this, block the kick with the forearm during its circular motion. Continue this motion until you have scooped the leg up with the hand, at the end of the block. Harai sukui uke is found in Seichin, Seisan, Kanchin and Sanseiryu katas.

BLOCKING AN ATTACK BEFORE IT REACHES MAXIMUM POWER

The purpose of these blocks is to diffuse the power of an attack by blocking before the attack reaches full extension.

HIZA UKE
Knee Block

Hiza uke is not executed with the knee. Use the shin (sune) for this block by raising your knee, similar to chambering a kick. It is effective against front, side and roundhouse kicks by using the front, inside and outside of the shin. The shin is well in front of the intended target (your body) so you can jam the kick before it reaches full power.

A major advantage of this block is that it leaves your hands free for a counterpunch. After executing this block you are in a position to kick to the groin and knee, or step inside your opponents defensive line.

It is important to practice the crane stance to be strong with this type of blocking. Hiza uke is found in Yakusoku Kumite and Kadena Yakusoku Kumite and in Seichin, Seisan, Serui, Kanchin and Sanseiryu katas.

SOKUTO UKE
Side of Foot Block

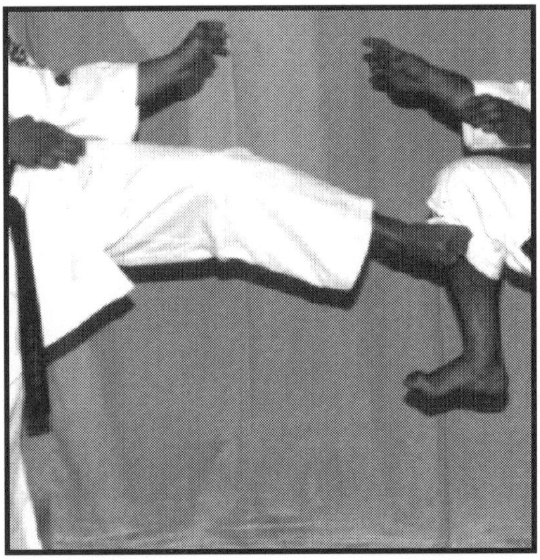

The side of the foot can be used to jam an incoming kick. Using this block leaves your hands free to follow-up. It is important to stop the kick before it nears full extension. Practicing this technique will improve your kicking reaction time.

SHOTEI UCHI OSAE
Palm Heel Inside Push Block

This technique is applied with the same principles as shotei nagashi uke, from outward to inward with the heel of your palm. Nagashi uke (previously described) is applied with a strong snap of the wrist against a punch. Shotei uchi osae is a pushing block against a punch at its inception. Practicing this blocking technique will improve your hand reaction time.

HIRATE UCHI OSAE
Open Hand Grabbing Block

Grabbing the opponent's arms or legs is a major component of Uechi ryu close range fighting. It is the vision of the dragon catching with his claws. At the advanced level, *hirate osae*, open hand grabbing, is the conclusion of many of the blocking techniques described here.

Sappu means disarming an opponent's attack. Grabbing at the conclusion of a defensive block is done to offensively gain control of an opponent after stopping the attack.

Kuzushi is the holding, pushing and pulling of an opponent to set up a counterattack. Kuzushi changes a defensive block into the first stage of an offensive attack. Sappu and kuzushi are significant factors in the blocking concepts of Uechi ryu karate.

THRUST AND STRIKE TECHNIQUES

突き耐

TSUKI WAZA

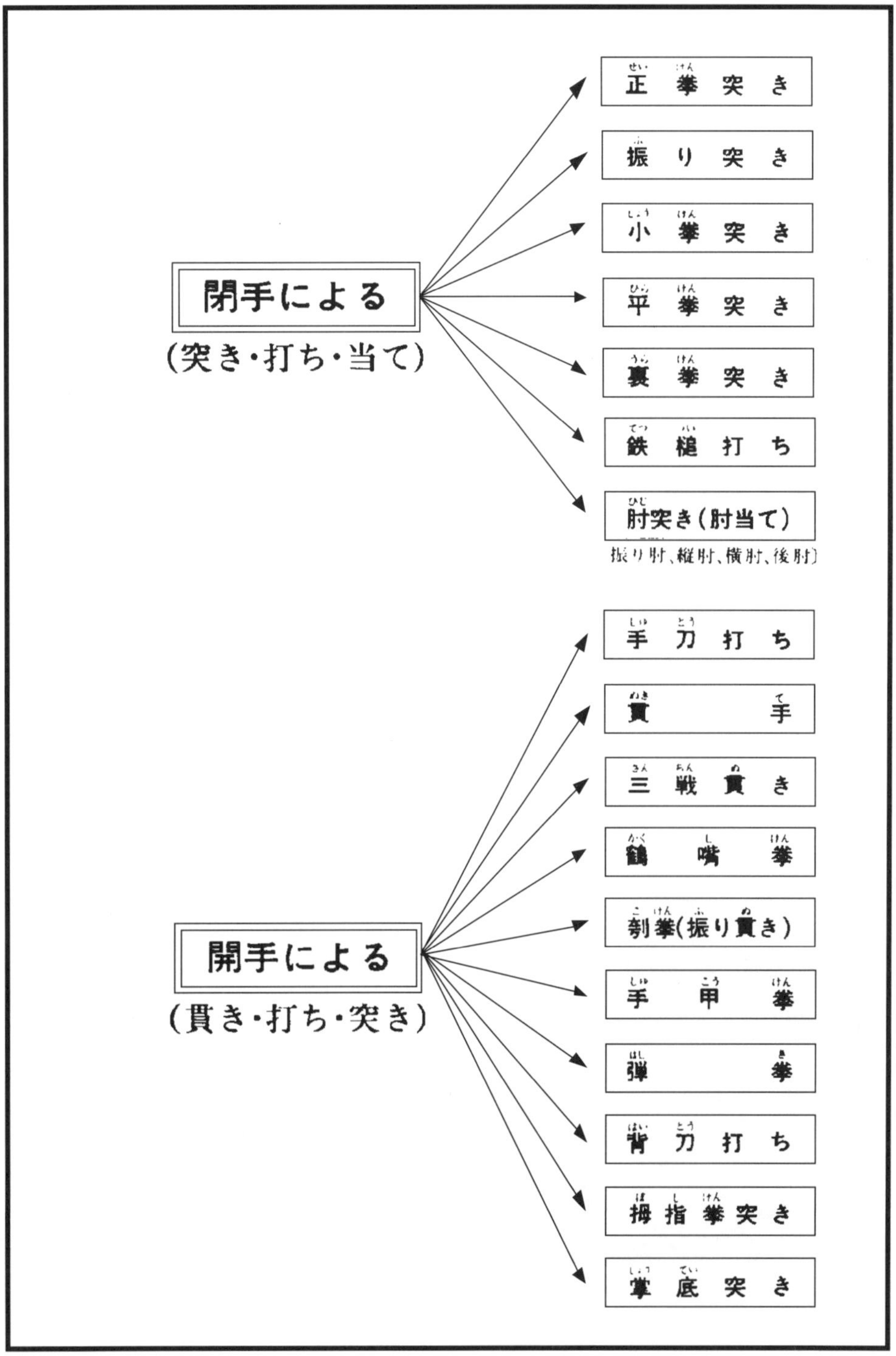
閉手による
(突き・打ち・当て)
正拳突き
振り突き
小拳突き
平拳突き
裏拳突き
鉄槌打ち
肘突き(肘当て)
振り肘、縦肘、横肘、後肘)
開手による
(貫き・打ち・突き)
手刀打ち
貫手
三戦貫き
鶴嘴拳
刳拳(振り貫き)
手甲拳
弾拳
背刀打ち
拇指拳突き
掌底突き

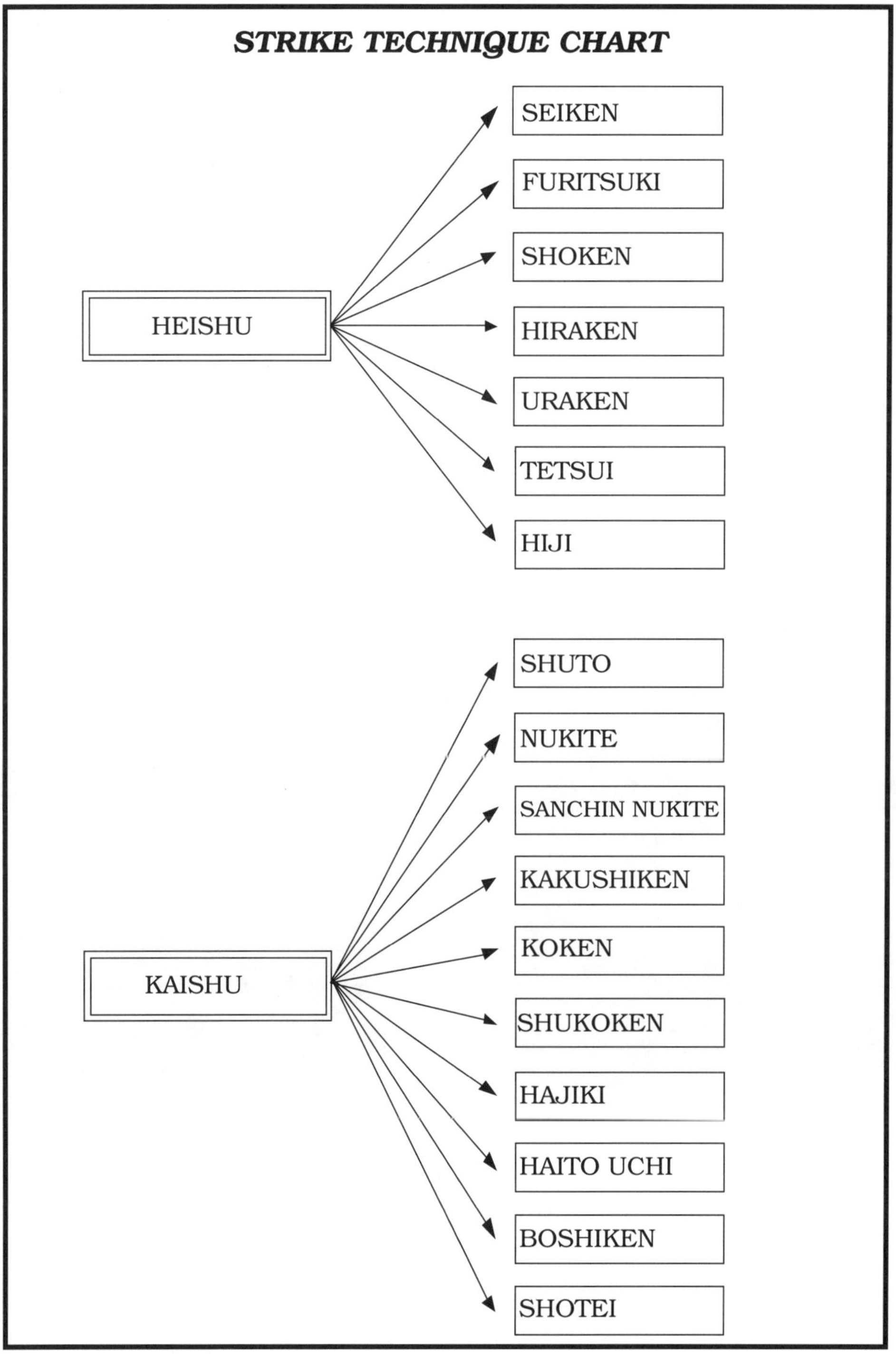
STRIKE TECHNIQUE CHART
HEISHU
SEIKEN
FURITSUKI
SHOKEN
HIRAKEN
URAKEN
TETSUI
HIJI
KAISHU
SHUTO
NUKITE
SANCHIN NUKITE
KAKUSHIKEN
KOKEN
SHUKOKEN
HAJIKI
HAITO UCHI
BOSHIKEN
SHOTEI

The effectiveness of both closed and open hand attacks in Uechi ryu karate are difficult to understand unless one has relentlessly trained on the Okinawan makiwara. When first reading about the body parts used as weapons one may have an image of pain, broken bones or joints on yourself rather than your adversary. Achieving this refinement of body weapons requires extra attention to body conditioning. (Chapter VI)

HEISHU
CLOSED HAND

There are three types of closed hand strikes in Uechi ryu karate: tsuki, uchi and ate. *Tsuki* means thrust and applies to all forward thrusting actions such as a straight punch. The word tsuki changes to zuki when used with another word, as in seiken zuki. *Uchi* strikes are roundhouse or swinging strikes. *Ate* (pronounced autay) is used to describe strikes with larger surface weapons like the knee and elbow.

The word *Ken* means knuckle. Ken has been expanded in the martial arts to mean fist and encompasses many fist or hand strikes.

SEIKEN ZUKI
Two Knuckle Fist Punch

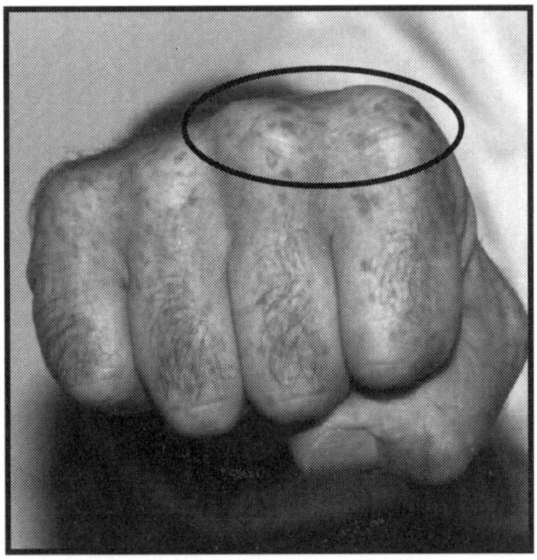

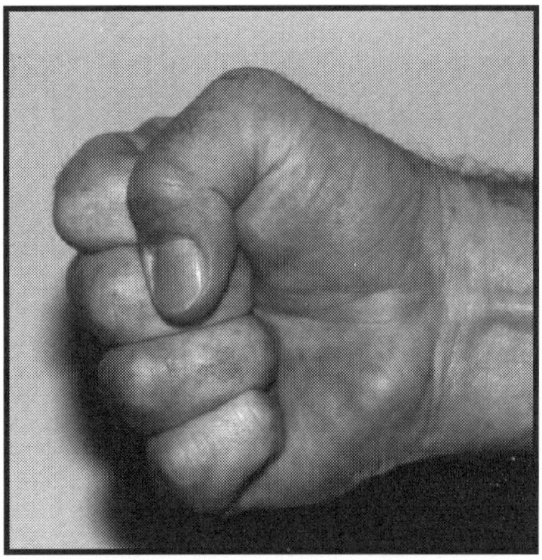

This is the most popular hand weapon in karate. It is the least difficult fist to form and the safest to use, therefore, it is good for beginners. The seiken fist is formed by folding the fingers in toward the palm starting with the first row of knuckles, followed by the second row. Curl the fingers tightly into the palm. Stretch the thumb across the fingers for stability.

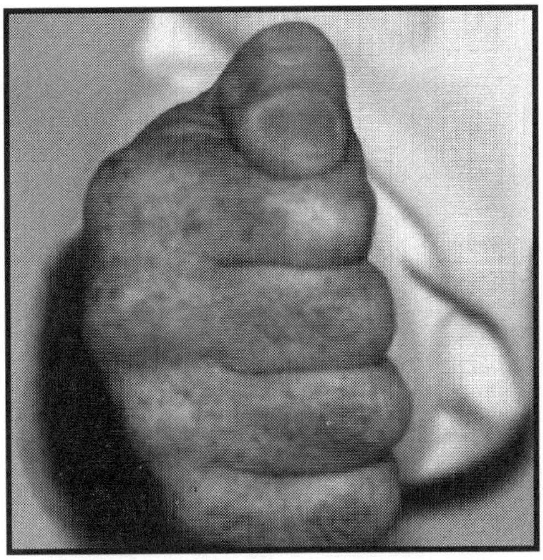

From the experience of having broken thousands of boards, it is my opinion that placing the thumb on the side of the hand makes for a weaker fist that will break down during hard contact.

There are no seiken punches in Sanchin, Seisan or Sanseiryu, the original three katas of Uechi ryu karate (Pangainoon). The Chinese origins of this system emphasized many of the other striking techniques listed, delivered to precise targets or pressure points.

Grand Master Kanei Uechi created additional katas to aid in worldwide understanding and growth of Uechi ryu karate. Seiken punches were included in Kanshiwa kata for that reason. It is the only kata in Uechi ryu that contains seiken punches.

The seiken punch gained popularity in the Uechi ryu system with the development of pre-arranged (yakusoku) and free-style sparring (jiyu kumite).

Correct punching and proper body application for maximum power are covered in more detail in the Sanchin kata section of Chapter X.

The seiken punch begins by chambering the fist beside your chest muscle near the armpit, the back of the hand facing down.

正拳

your hand like a corkscrew, at the end of the punch. The back of the hand, wrist and arm should be in a straight line to prevent wrist injury on impact.

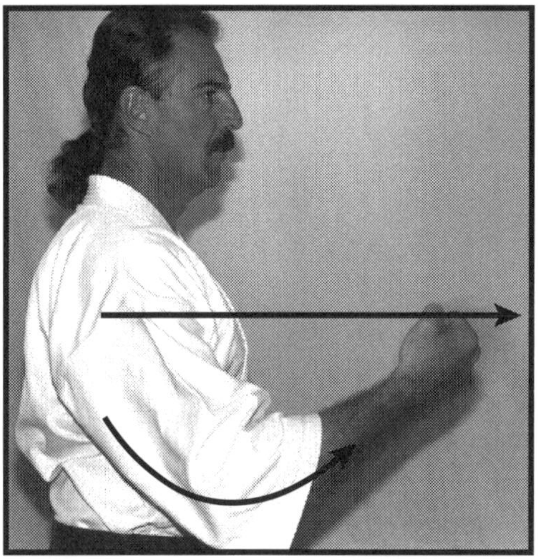

Pull your shoulder down to create a deep arc with your elbow and focus the power of the body, straight forward, through the fist.

Raising your fist as you punch will cause you to raise your shoulder. This separates the power of the body from the punch. Dropping the hand in an arc as you punch decreases power and slows the punch down, making it easier to block. This is a subconscious error executed by many beginner and intermediate students. Keep the elbow behind the fist as you punch. Do not let the elbow drift away from your body as the fist moves forward. Any part of the body is a target for a seiken punch because of the power of this fist developed through makiwara conditioning, as explained in Chapter IV.

FURI ZUKI
Roundhouse Punch

Furi zuki is chambered the same as seiken but takes an arcing path to its target, rather than a straight line. It is effective to the head, neck or upper ribs of an opponent who is attempting or completing a frontal grab. The roundhouse punch, executed with hiraken fist, is found in Hojoundo and in Kanshu, Kanchin and Sanseiryu katas.

SHOKEN ZUKI
One Knuckle Punch

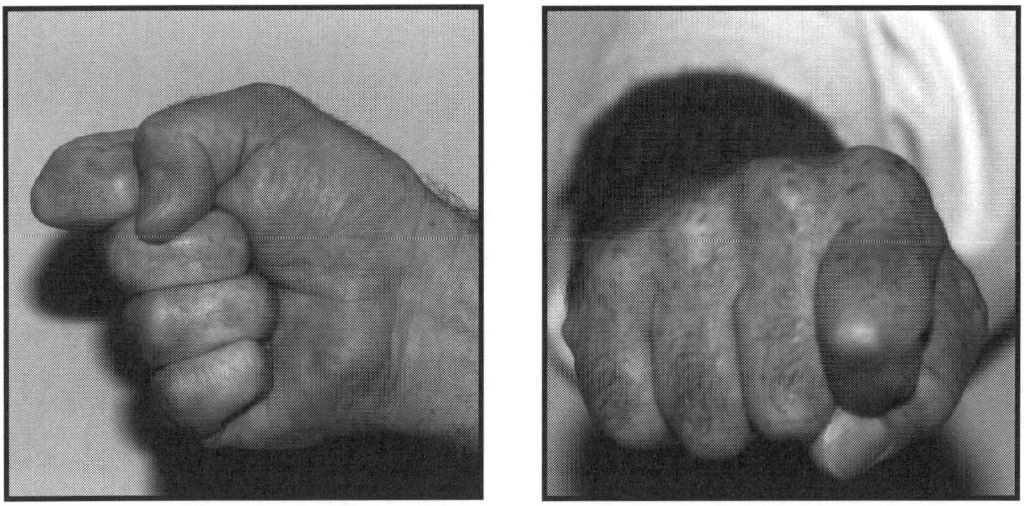

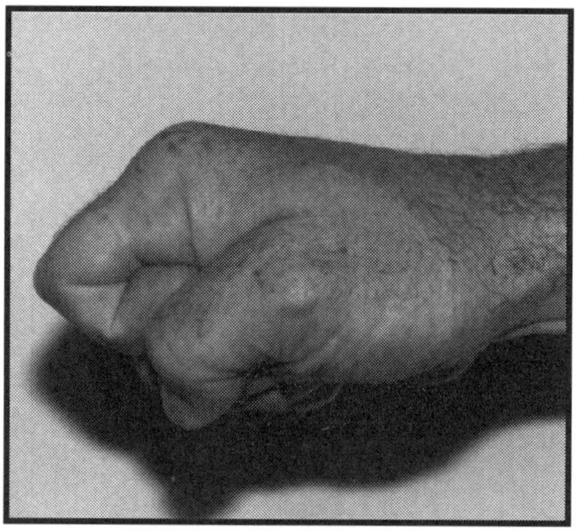

Shoken is used only to attack pressure points, *kyusho*. Shoken is called the tiger's tooth. This punch is compared to being bitten by the teeth of the tiger. The tissue damage caused by a shoken punch is more intense than the blunt result of a seiken punch. It delivers more destructive power than any other hand strike because the force of the punch is focused into a very small area. The impact penetrates deep into the body.

The literal translation of shoken means "small knuckle." This refers to the second knuckle of the index finger, the proximal joint. A shoken fist is made very similar to a seiken fist except that the forefinger is brought forward and locked against the thumb. It is chambered and delivered in the same manner as seiken zuki.

Shoken is a dominate weapon of the Uechi ryu system and is found in Hojoundo and all katas except Sanchin.

小拳

HIRAKEN ZUKI
Four Knuckle Punch

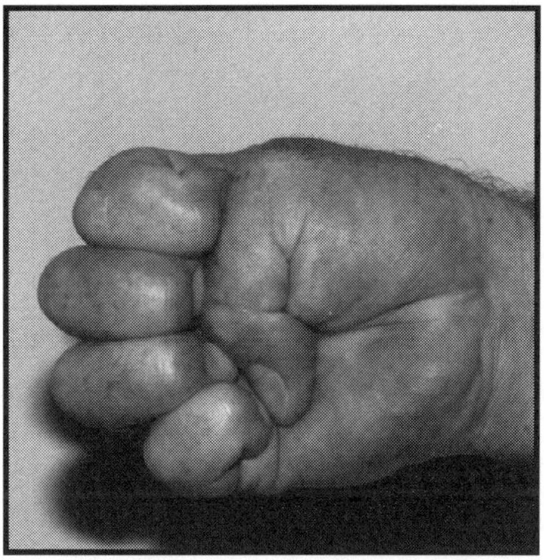

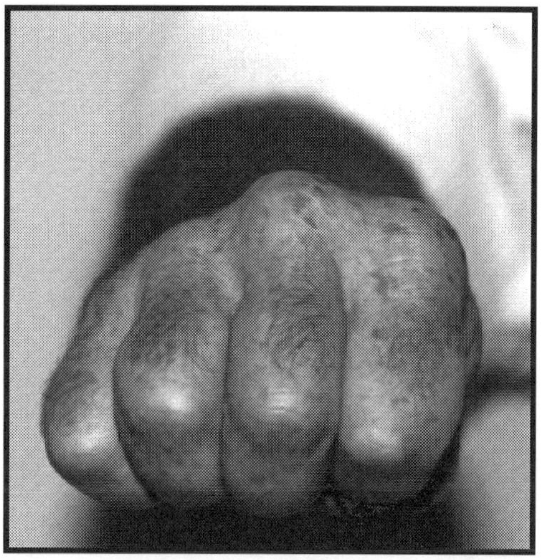

Hiraken, or four knuckle punch, is made by laying the thumb across the palm and rolling all four fingers into the thumb. Press the fingers tightly against the support thumb. Sometimes called tiger fist, this hand configuration resembles a tiger's paw.

The striking surface appears to be all four middle knuckles. However, you should strike with the middle knuckles of only the first three fingers. Targets for hiraken are the nose, upper lip, temple and throat. A shorter opponent who may be unable to reach these targets on a taller opponent can also target the ribs.

Hiraken is used for straight and roundhouse punches and is found in Hojoundo and in all katas except Sanchin and Kanshiwa.

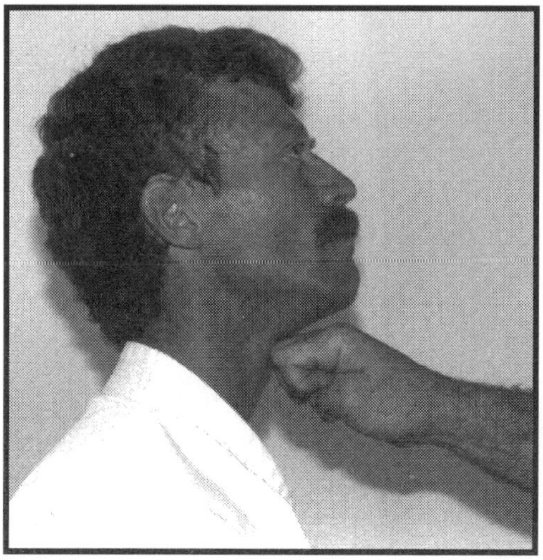

URAKEN ZUKI
Back Fist Strike

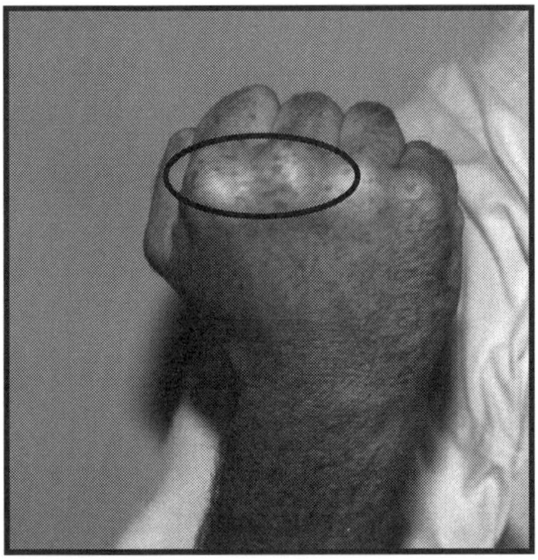

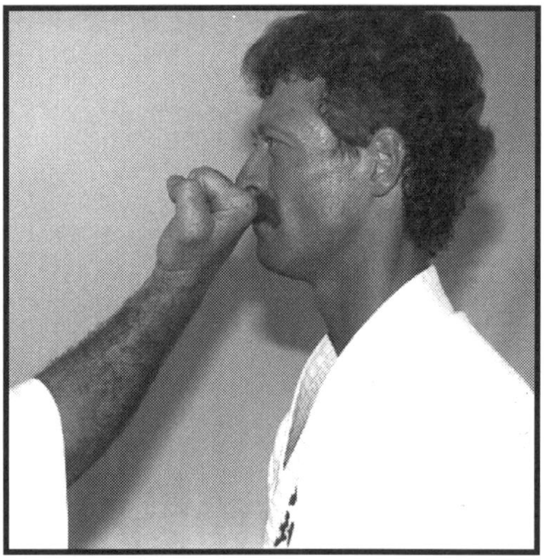

The back fist is made the same as a seiken fist but a different part of the hand is used for contact. This is a close range weapon using snapping power in the strike. It is important to quickly bring your hand back to the starting position to maximize the snapping technique and prepare yourself to execute multiple back fist strikes.

This strike is thrown vertically rather than horizontally. The vertical line of attack is more difficult to block and is a natural follow-up to the close range elbow strike. The targets are the vulnerable parts of the face and side of the head. Because of its limited power, the backfist is not suitable for attacking the hard parts of the body. This strike is found in Hojoundo, Yakusoku Kumite and all katas except Sanchin and Seichin.

肘

TESTSUI UCHI
Hammer Fist

The hammer fist is made the same as the seiken fist, but uses the side of the fist like a club or hammer. The strike is very powerful when used in a long arc. It is effective against the hard parts of the head. When executing this strike it is important to bring the fist from higher to lower level and from outward to inward at the same time. Tetsui uchi is found in Kanshu, Seichin, Seisan and Serui katas.

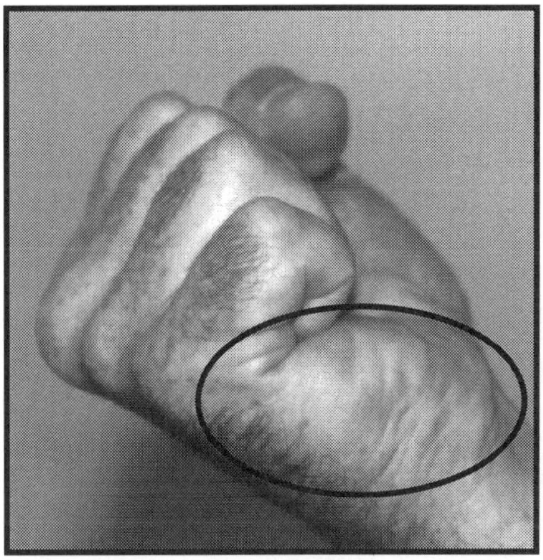

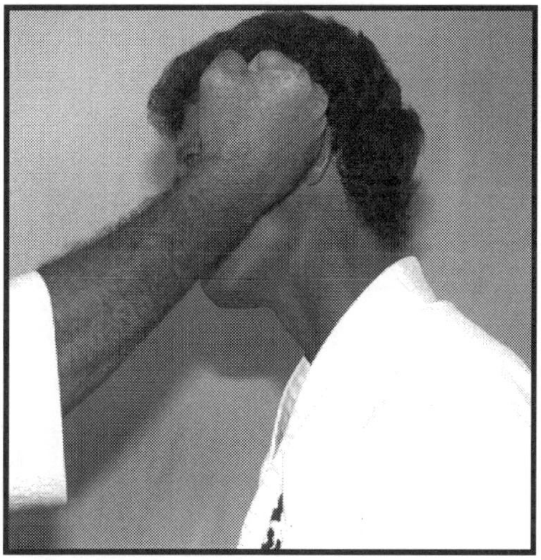

HIJI ZUKI, HIJI UCHI, HIJI ATE
Elbow Strike

Hiji is the bony part of the elbow formed when the arm is bent. When you swing your elbow the shoulder should be pulled down and held steady because it forms the fulcrum of this movement. The elbow strike is a very powerful close-range weapon.

There are four types of elbow strikes used in Uechi ryu: furi, tate (pronounced tautay), yoko and ushiro hiji. Use either a seiken fist or hiraken fist with hiji strikes, depending on which follow-up technique most suits the particular elbow attack. Elbow strikes are found in Hojoundo, Yakusoku Kumite and all katas except Sanchin.

FURI HIJI ATE
Roundhouse Elbow Strike

When executing this attack keep the forearm parallel to the upper arm in order to hit with the proper part of the elbow. If you drop your forearm lower than you upper arm, as is common with beginners, you risk dislocating your shoulder on contact with a solid object. Targets are ribs at the side of the body, neck and head.

TATE HIJI ATE
Vertical or Elbow Strike

When forming tate hiji the palm of your hand should face downward. As the vertical elbow strike makes contact, the palm of your hand should face your opponent. The primary targets for tate hiji are the solar plexus, *suigetsu*, and the jaw.

TATE HIJI ATE
Vertical or Elbow Strike

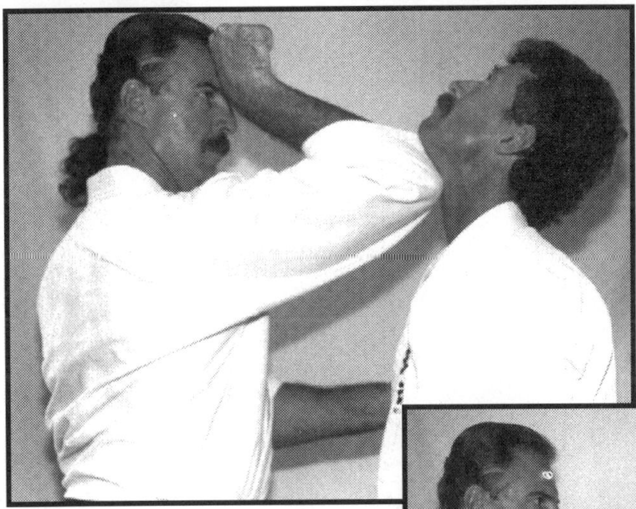

After executing the elbow strike the arm is positioned to follow-up with a hiraken strike to the face.

YOKO HIJI
Side Elbow Strike

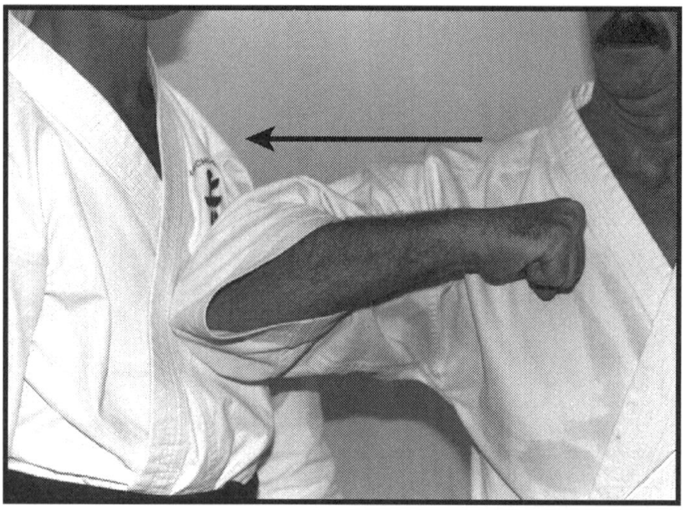

This strike is thrown horizontally to an opponent beside you. Reach across your chest to wind up for power.

USHIRO HIJI
Reverse or Back Elbow Strike

When striking behind you be sure your hand stops in the same position as when chambering for Sanchin strikes, to maintain a sharp elbow. Lowering your hand toward your belt as your elbow moves behind softens the point of the elbow, thus reducing contact power.

OTOSU HIJI
Downward or Dropping Elbow Strike

A fifth type of elbow strike, *otosu hiji* exists in many styles of karate. Although not in Uechi ryu kata, it is a powerful weapon to the back of an opponent.

KAISHU
OPEN HAND

There are three types of open hand strikes used in Uechi ryu karate: nuki, uchi and tsuki. *Nuki* means attacking with a smaller weapon in a poking motion. Uchi (circular) and Tsuki (straight) methods of striking are explained in the previous, Closed Hand, section.

SHUTO UCHI
Knife Hand Strike

Shuto uchi is commonly called the chop. *Shu* is an older translation of te, meaning hand. *To* (pronounced toe) means sword, thus "shuto" is hand sword. It is applied with the edge of the hand like the cutting edge of a sword. Shuto is a popular open hand strike in Uechi ryu karate for many reasons.

Shuto uses the soft part of the hand so is less likely to injure the hand of the attacker. With practice, shuto can be delivered from a variety of

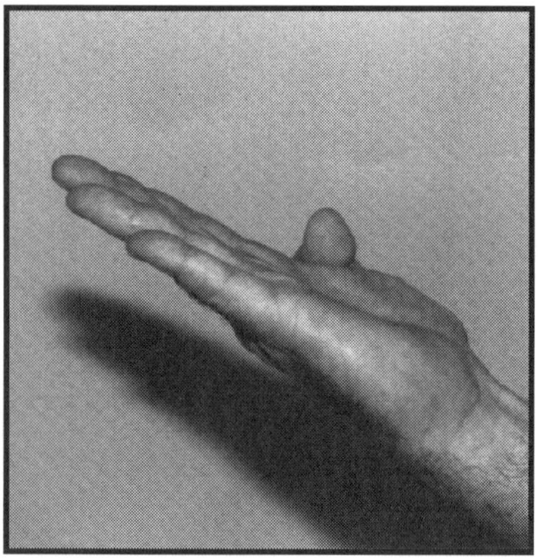

angles. The sides of the head, neck, upper shoulders, collar bone, groin and abdomen are primary targets. It can be used against both hard and soft targets, making it a very versatile weapon.

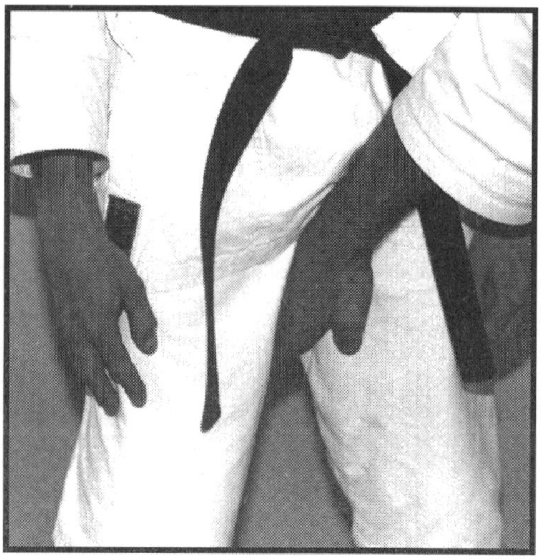

Shuto can be used effectively in both offensive and defensive movements. One example of this technique's versatility, is blocking an incoming punch with a circular block at the opponents elbow, and with the other hand, deliver a shuto to the triceps of the attacking arm. This slows or eliminates subsequent punches. Shuto is found in Hojoundo, Yakusoku Kumite and Kanshiwa kata.

NUKITE
Spear Hand Thrust

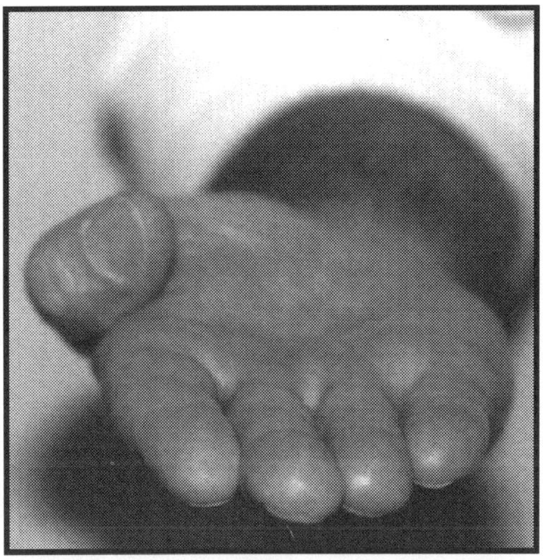

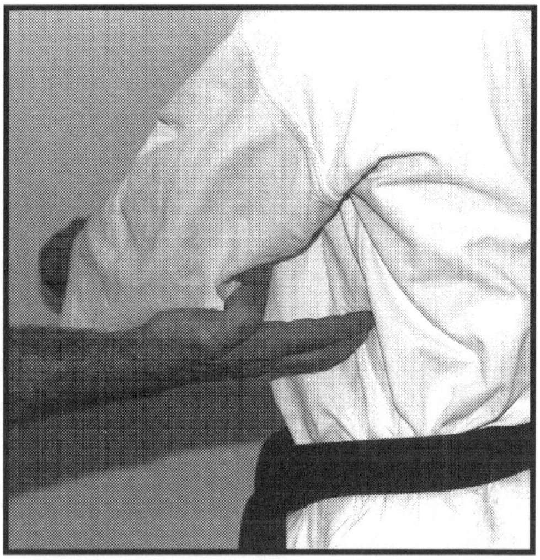

Nukite, fingertip thrusting strike, is an advanced technique that is extremely prevalent in the Uechi ryu system. It is found in all eight katas. Like a shoken, it delivers the primary point of impact to a very small area. Attacking pressure points and soft body parts with this specific strike allows you to inflict maximum damage using a small amount of motion. Therefore, body size and strength are not a factor for effectiveness.

When you form your hand for a nukite strike tighten all four fingers together and place the thumb firmly against the ridge of the hand. When you tighten your fingers they will naturally curve in slightly. It is important not to let the fingers bend backward on impact.

SANCHIN NUKITE
Sanchin Style Spear Hand

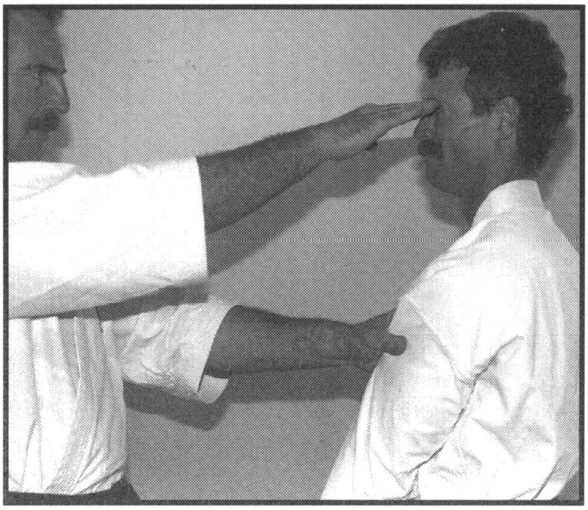

This technique combines the force of nukite strike with the twisting power of a punch, while refining your focus in pinpoint striking. Nukite or Sanchin nukite techniques are found in all eight katas.

KAKUSHIKEN
Crane's Beak Strike

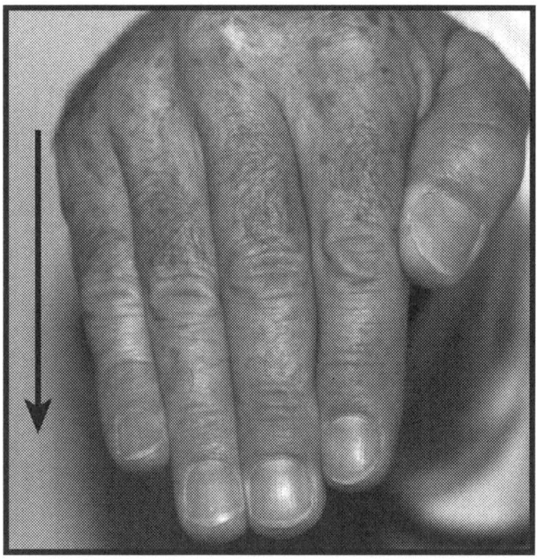

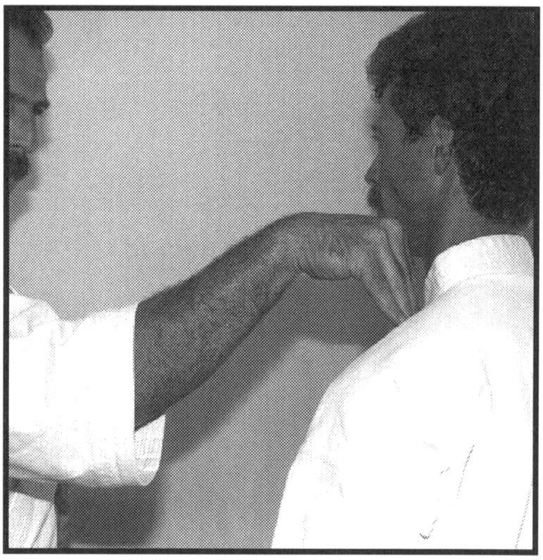

To form kakushiken bend all four fingers where they join the hand and support them by placing the thumb at the base of the forefinger. Kakushiken is executed with the fingertips, in a forceful downward strike. Snapping the elbow and wrist increase the power. The targets of the crane's beak are the neck, throat and soft area behind the collar bone. Kakushiken, an advanced and deadly technique, is found only in Sanseiryu kata.

KOKEN
Crane's Beak Strike To Groin

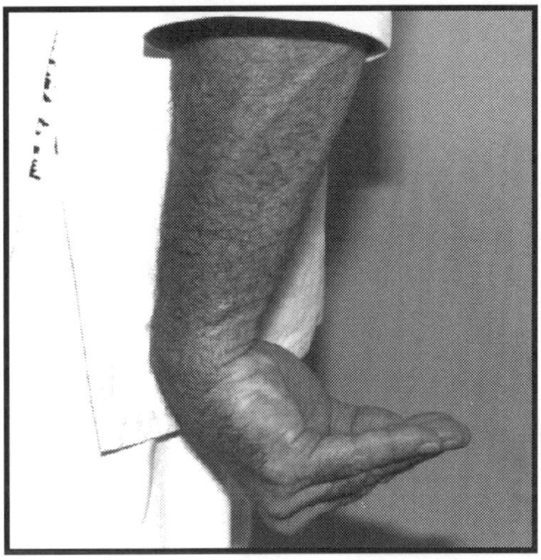

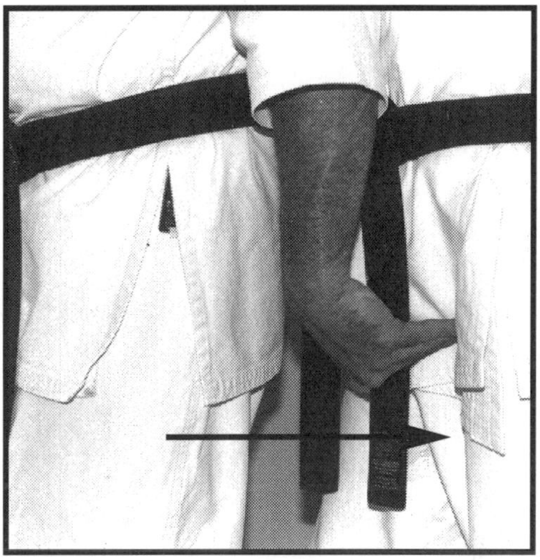

This hand weapon is formed the same as the kakushiken strike but is applied differently. A large swing motion is used to deliver this downward strike. To increase power in this technique, a scooping action is added at the point of contact. Koken is found in Seichin and Seisan katas.

SHUKOKEN
Crane's Head Strike

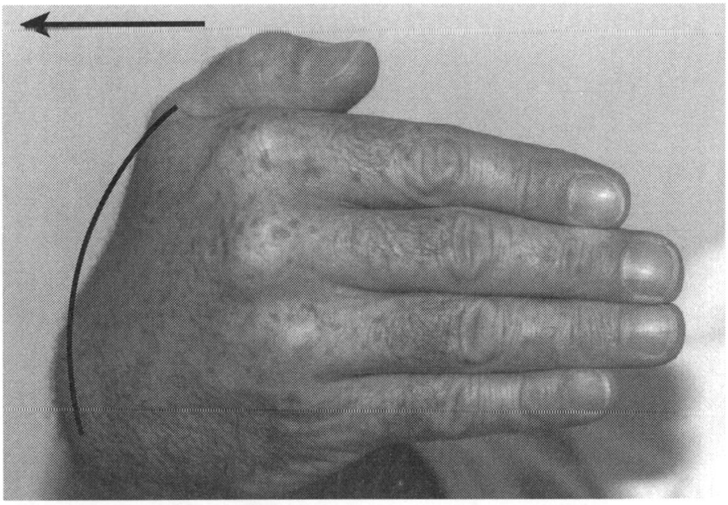

This hand technique resembles the head of a crane. It is sometimes called Kakuto. When executing this strike, bend the wrist inward and press your thumb against the second joint of the index finger. This is important to insure a tightly locked wrist. Strike with the wrist and lower part of the back of the hand. Shukoken can be delivered vertically or horizontally to targets on the face and head. The bony surface of the wrist and hand make this a devastating close-range weapon. Shukoken can also be used as a block. It is found in Hojoundo and Seichin and Kanchin katas.

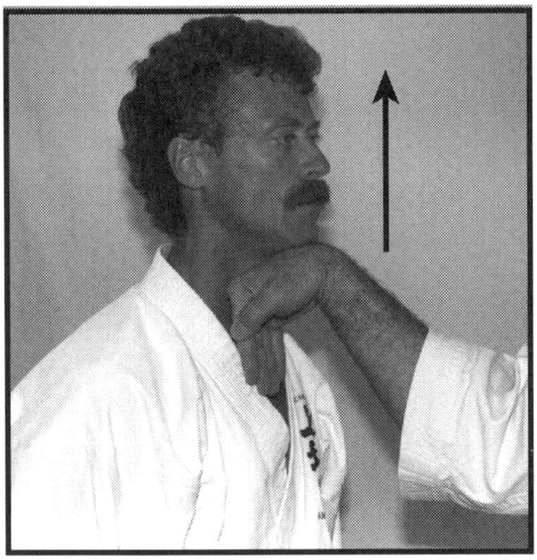

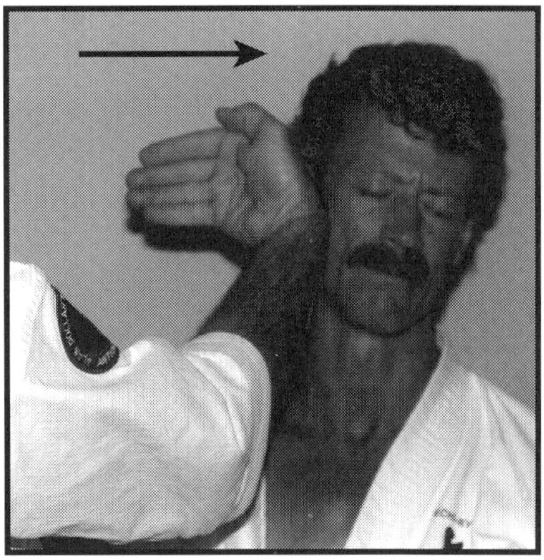

HAJIKI
Snapping Fingertip Strike

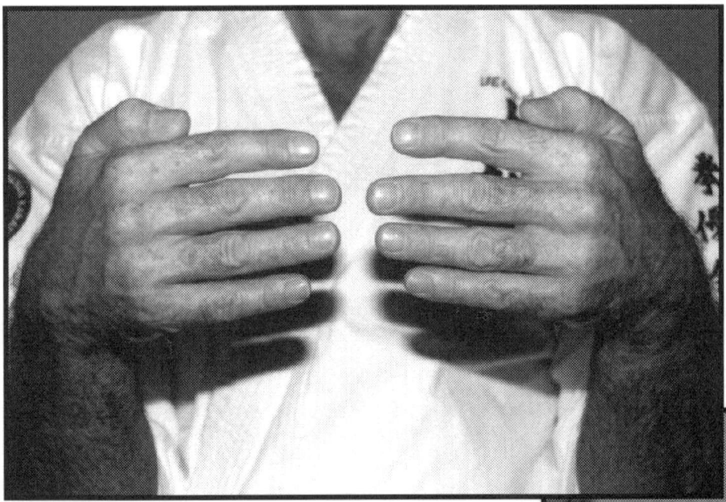

Hajiki is a snapping strike with the fingertips aimed at the eyes. To form this weapon place all four fingers and thumb together. Keep the fingers relaxed and flexible, rather than tight as with other hand techniques. Strike with the back of the fingers from the second joint to the finger tips. Apply a snapping motion in the wrist and fingers at the point of impact.

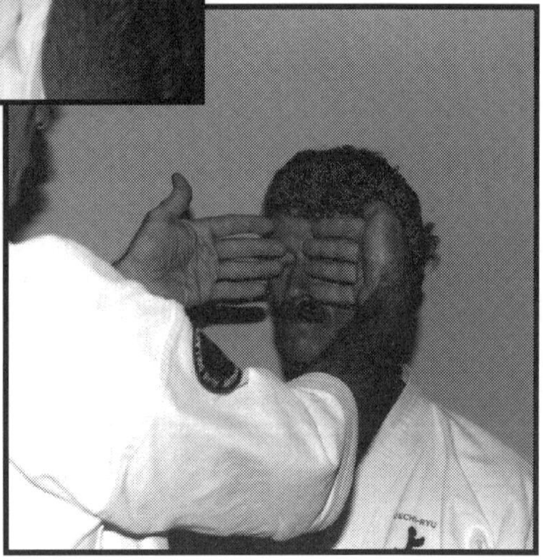

A finger jab, nukite, into the eyes is applied in a similar manner. Hajiki and nukite are excellent defensive weapons for smaller people, or those of less strength, since it requires little power and attacks a very vulnerable area. Hajiki is found in Hojoundo and Serui kata.

HAITO UCHI
Ridge Hand Strike

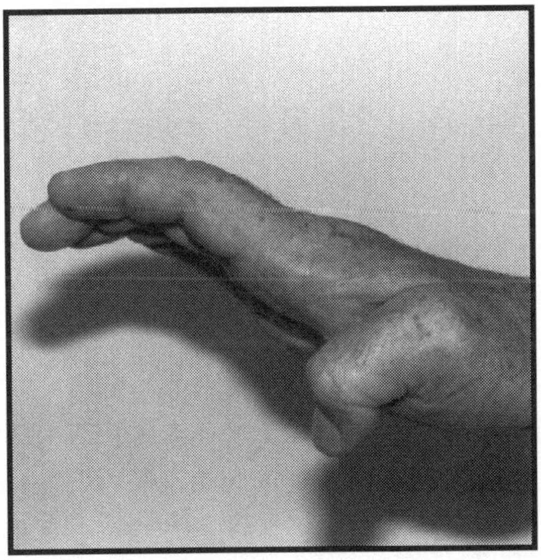

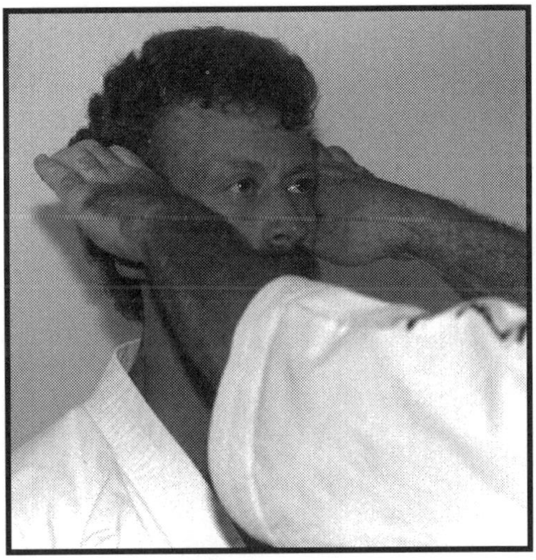

Haito uchi is a strike with the inside ridge of the hand. It is the opposite of shuto uchi, and is delivered with an inward circular motion. Haito uchi utilizes the large knuckles of the index finger and the thumb knuckle. The thumb is placed in the palm of the hand to position the large knuckle of the thumb and forefinger to strike the side of the head or neck. This technique is found in Seisan, Kanchin and Sanseiryu katas.

BOSHIKEN ZUKI
Thumb Strike

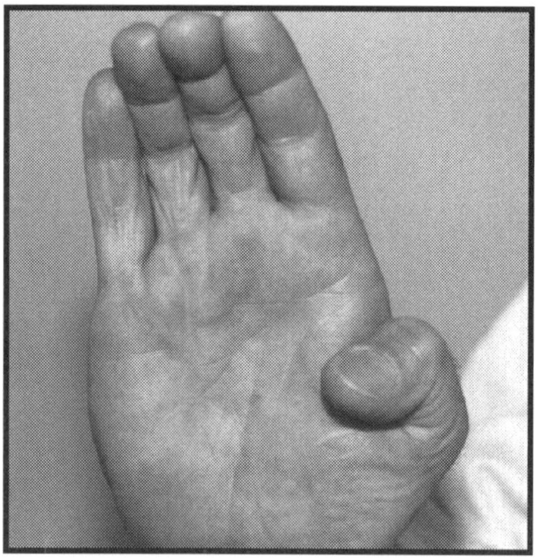

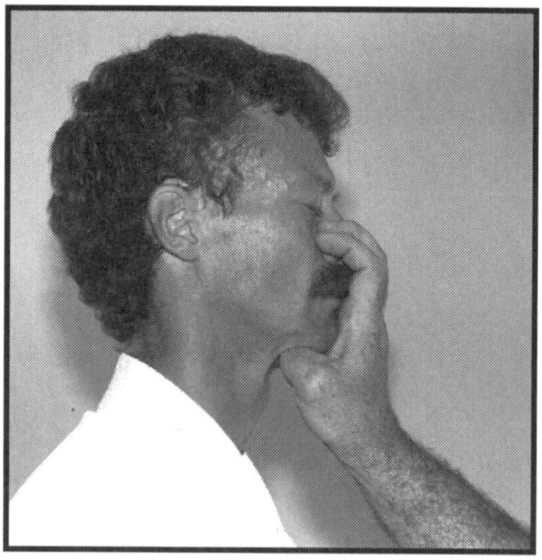

The thumb strike is very common in Uechi ryu karate. With an open hand, fold and tuck the thumb against the edge of the palm at the base of the index finger. Strike with the entire thumb, especially when striking the face. It is also effective against the soft areas of the body. Boshiken zuki and two handed thumb strike, morote boshiken zuki, are found in all Uechi ryu katas except Kanchin.

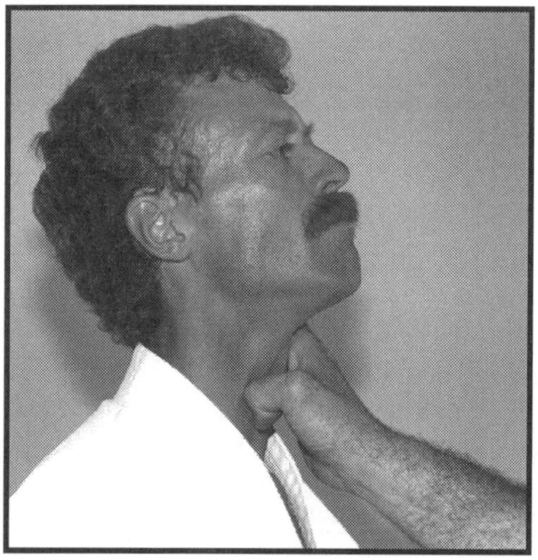

摑指拳

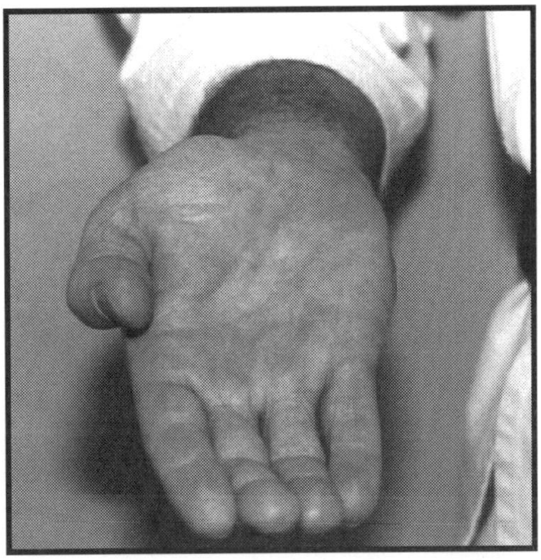

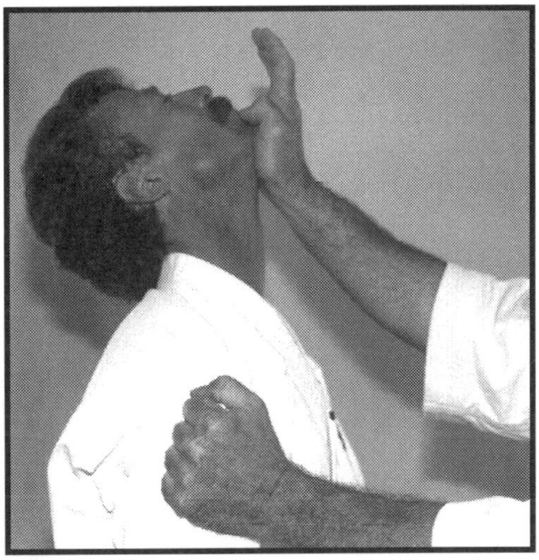

SHOTEI ZUKI
Palm Heel Strike

Shotei zuki and boshiken zuki resemble each other. They are delivered with a thrusting forward motion of the arm, however, the point of contact on the hand is different. Boshiken uses the hard knuckles of the thumb while shotei strikes with the soft heel of the palm against hard targets. The palm heel can also be used as a block. This technique targets the head and face. Shotei zuki is found in Kanchin and Sanseiryu katas.

KICKING TECHNIQUES

蹴り耐

KERI WAZA

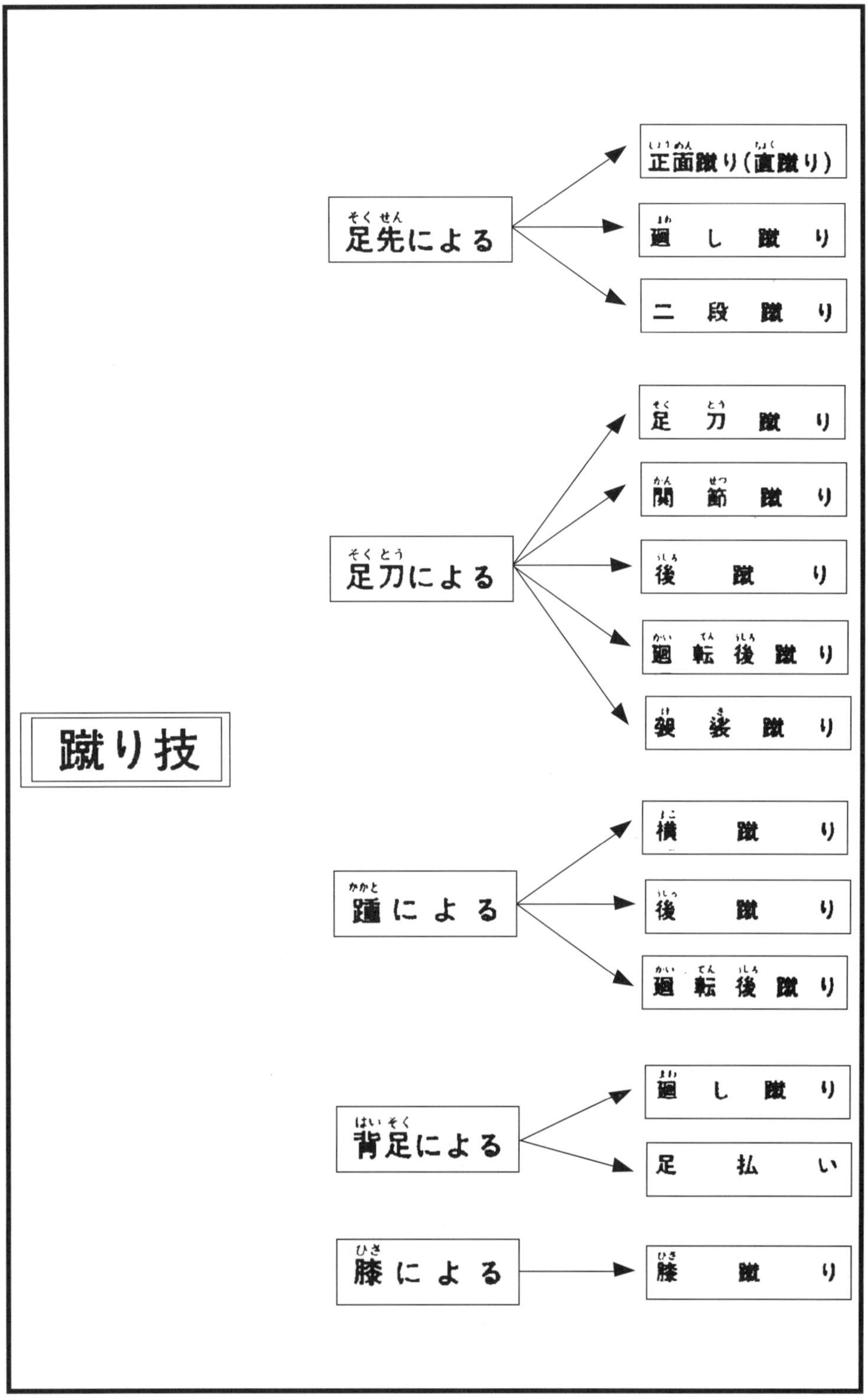
蹴り技
足先による
正面蹴り(直蹴り)
廻し蹴り
二段蹴り
足刀による
足刀蹴り
関節蹴り
後蹴り
廻転後蹴り
袈裟蹴り
踵による
横蹴り
後蹴り
廻転後蹴り
背足による
廻し蹴り
足払い
膝による
膝蹴り

KICK TECHNIQUE CHART

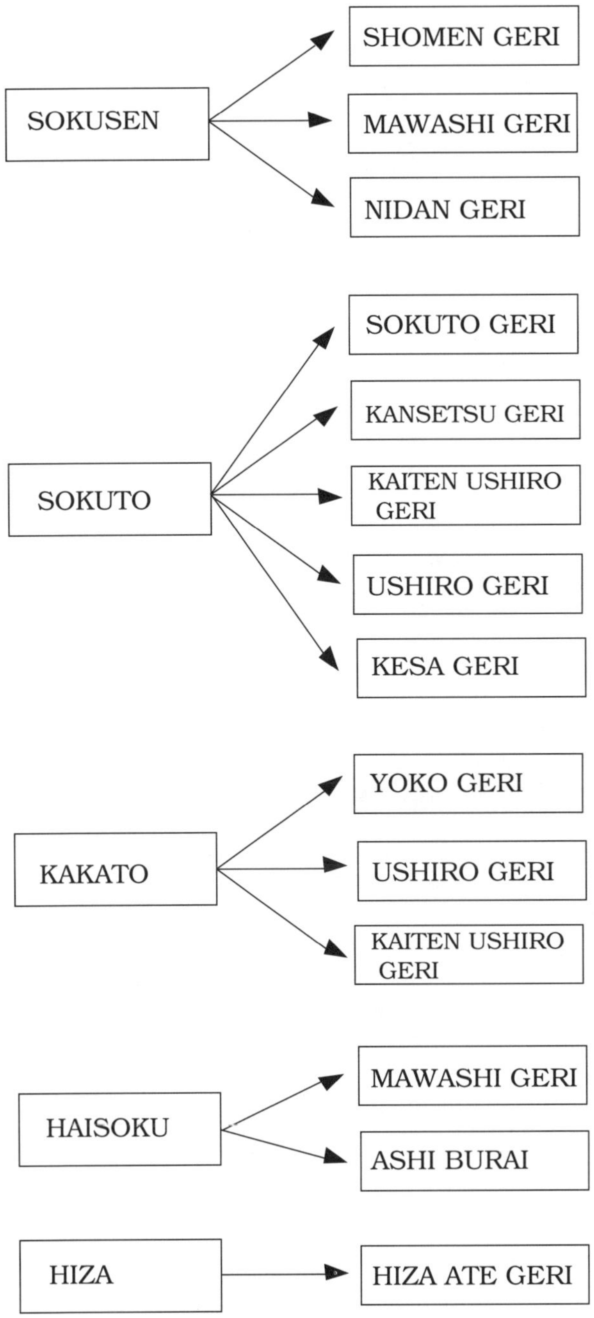

SOKUSEN
Toe Kick

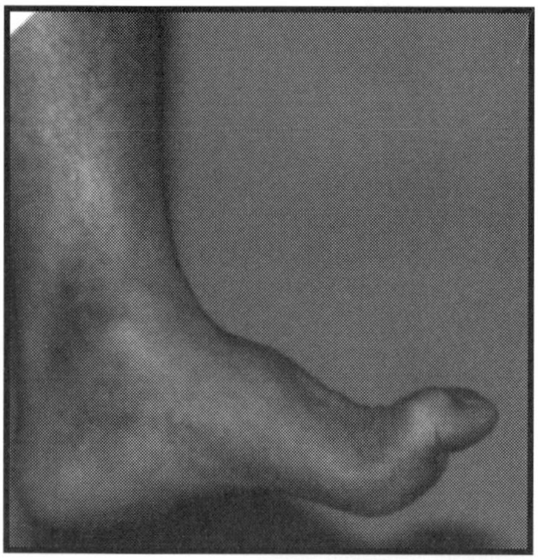

足先

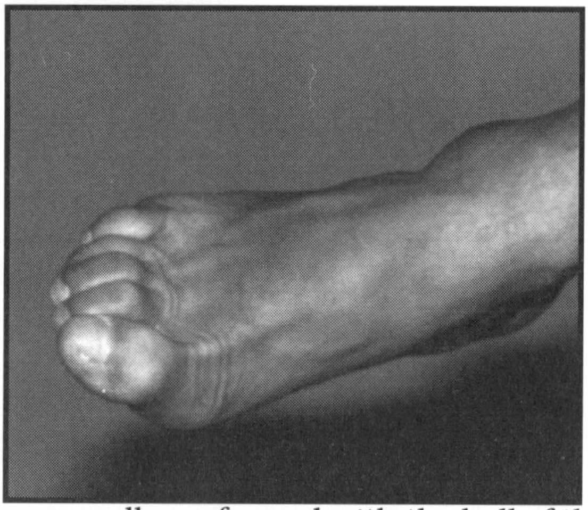

Kicks that are normally performed with the ball of the foot, *sokutei*, are executed, in Uechi ryu karate, with the tip of the big toe (sokusen). Kicks with the ball of the foot do not exist in this system. Sokusen geri is the only kick in the original three katas brought from China. The shoken (one knuckle punch) and sokusen (toe kick) emulate the tiger's teeth and their destructive effect. These techniques deliver an enormous amount of power to a small area. Deeper body penetration, and more damage to the area attacked, are the results. Any part of the body is a potential target for sokusen.

Newer students should practice kicking with the ball of the foot for their own safety. Preparing the toes for kicking is an arduous process. First the muscles in the toes must be developed so they can be flexed into the proper position. This can take several months. Second, the tip of the toe must be conditioned to take hard contact. This takes several years.

When kicking with the ball of the foot, point your foot forward into the target just as you would if using the toe. Avoid angling your foot upward. This will cause your kick to skip up your opponent's body and prevent any penetration into the target.

To form sokusen, pull your toes back toward your foot, tightening all toes together.

Here are six methods for strengthening sokusen technique:

1. Make a tight sokusen foot and walk on the tips of the toes.
2. Jump up and down on sokusen toes.
3. Kick in the air with a tight sokusen foot.
4. Kick the makiwara, tire, and sandbag with sokusen.
5. Keep a tight sokusen foot when you do Sanchin kata.
6. Use sokusen when practicing all kicks.

SHOMEN GERI
Front Kick

There are two types of front direction kicks: the front leg snap kick and the rear leg thrust kick. The front leg snap kick is the only kick used in the katas brought from China. It is found in every kata of Uechi ryu except Sanchin, which contains no kicks. The front leg kick, like the lead hand punch is the first line of defense, as it is the closest technique to the opponent. It can be executed quickly against an incoming attacker.

The front leg snap kick is executed in four movements. The first movement is raising the knee to prepare the kick to be launched. This is called chambering the kick. You should raise your knee at least as high as your belt. The higher you chamber the kick, the more effectively you can kick at close range.

The second movement is extending the leg to deliver the power of the kick. The effect of this is increased by delivering with the big toe rather than the ball of the foot. The third, and very important movement, is quickly retracting the kick to its original chambered position. The snapping of the kick is an important source of power since the hips cannot be used in the front leg kick as effectively as with a rear leg kick.

Immediately retracting the leg prevents the kick from being caught allowing you to execute repeated kicks. Pulling the leg back quickly also aids in regaining balance more quickly. The fourth movement is returning the foot to the floor in a stable stance.

There is a tendency among beginners to drop the foot and leg after hitting the target. Have you felt a beginner's foot slide down your gi after a kick? This incorrect form takes the power out of the kick, increases the chances of the leg being caught, and eliminates the option of throwing multiple kicks. These reasons make it important to practice all four counts of all kicks.

The rear leg thrust kick is slower but delivers a lot more power. The four count kicking method is also important for this kick. Drive this kick deep into your opponent by adding forward hip movement and full extension of the leg.

Compare the front and rear leg kicks to the hand techniques of the jab and reverse punch. The lead technique is a fast defensive or offensive weapon. The back hand and leg techniques produce more power by adding the hips and body to the attack.

When executing shomen geri keep the supporting foot flat on the ground for stability. Avoid the tendency to raise your center of gravity and stand on the ball of the foot. Keep the supporting leg slightly bent and spring-like. Do not bend the support leg too much as this will slow down the kick.

Keep your body upright as you kick. Do not bend backward to counterbalance the weight of your leg. This decreases power in the kick and makes your balance weak. To prevent this, develop the muscles of the quadriceps (front of the legs) and the abdomen (stomach).

Shomen geri, in traditional Okinawan kata, are aimed at the *gedan* area which is the mid-section or lower. High area, *jodan*, kicks are less preferred because they create the longest line between weapon and target, requiring more time to deliver. High kicks also leave the kicker vulnerable. It is also more difficult to maintain or recover balance when executing a high kick.

The growth in popularity of free style sparring (jiyu kumite) has increased the use of high kicks in sport karate. In movies and television, kicks to the head are a common method of good guys taking out bad guys. In spite of media glamour, high kicks are the least desirable choice for street self defense.

Kicks are five times more powerful than punches. They are also more difficult to deliver. A great deal of practice is required to insure that your kicks are an asset, not a hindrance, to your chances for success.

MAWASHI GERI
Roundhouse Kick

The roundhouse kick can be delivered with the rear leg or as a front leg snap kick. Chambering is the same as for the front kick. The third count of the kick, extending the lower leg into the target, is executed using a circular path rather than a straight one. Roundhouse kicks executed with the rear leg, increase power by pivoting the hips, supporting leg and foot into the kick.

Beginners often incorrectly chamber the kick with the knee open wide, to set up this circular motion. This has three negative results:

1. It telegraphs the technique to your opponent.
2. It is easier to block because of its wide arc.
3. The kick lacks power. Without proper chambering the muscles are not contracted to create dynamic force in the kick.

Chamber the roundhouse kick with the knee inside your body line, then extend your hip while pivoting on the stationary foot. Targets include the abdomen, head, back, and entire side of the body and legs. Mawashi geri is found in Yakusoku Kumite and Sanseiryu Bunkai.

NIDAN GERI
Double Kick

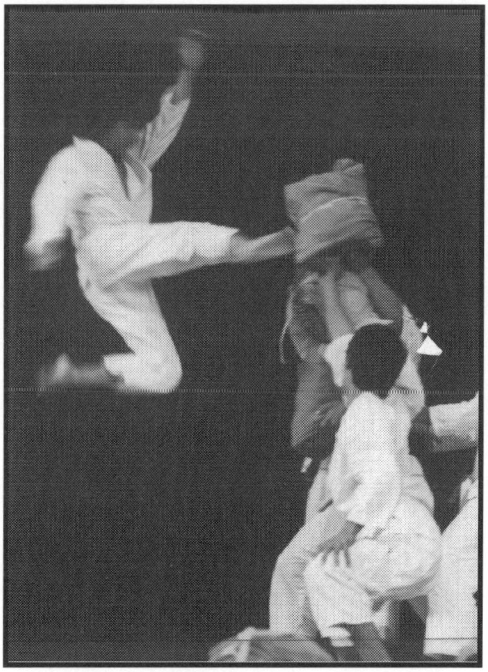

The double kick is also known as a jumping double front kick, or jumping scissors kick. Legend contends that jumping kicks were used long ago to dismount soldiers on horseback, or to snap the neck of armored samurai. Weaknesses in the jump kick are incorrect landing, losing balance, or being caught in the air.

To execute the double kick, the first one should be a small kick, or a fake kick. With this action lift your body and begin your assent. Lifting the second knee adds to the elevation desired for the kick. The second kick should be a powerful and fully extended front or side kick.

There are two ways to deliver nidan geri:

Chudan - jodan (middle then high area kick), executed with a high jump.

Gedan - chudan (low then middle area kick), executed with a low jump.

SOKUTO
Knife Edge

Sokuto (foot sword)is the side of the foot, from the heel to the beginning of the toe. It is commonly referred to as knife edge, rather than sword edge.

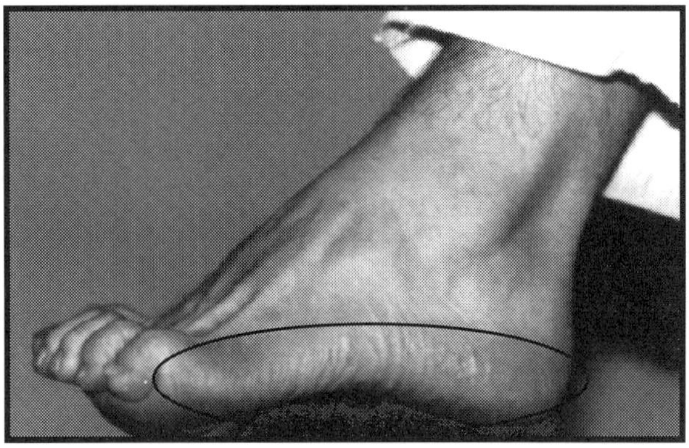

SOKUTO GERI
Knife Edge Kick

It is easier to hit the target using sokuto geri because of the large area of the foot that is used. You can also make contact at a variety of angles. Pull the toes back toward you and extend the heel as you kick. Kicking posture is the same as described for shomen geri, but is more difficult to achieve because of bending the foot. To maintain body balance and have power in your kick, avoid leaning backward as previously described.

Power is added with a strong snap of the knee, and a fast retraction of the kick. Proper distancing is important because the moment of full extension is the moment of maximum power for this kick. Momentarily lock you hips into the kick at this time. Targets of sokuto geri are the legs, abdomen, chest, throat, chin, face and back.

KANSETSU GERI
Knee Joint Kick

There are two types of knee joint kicks. One is done with sokuto geri; the other with mawashi geri. When executing kansetsu geri with sokuto, strike diagonally downward as if stepping or stomping on the knee. This technique is highly effective against opponents who take a side stance. This dangerous technique should never be used in sport karate. A technique such a this or many others described here, with potential for damage to the opponent, were developed for self defense in life threatening situations. They should never be used in sport karate. Kansetsu geri is found in Kadena Yakusoku Kumite.

足刀

USHIRO GERI
Back Kick

The back kick is used against someone attacking you from behind. Chamber the kick as you would a front kick. Create a long arc with your knee as you extend the foot in a straight line toward the target. This resembles the same action of your arm during a front punch. Look over your shoulder to focus the kick. Use sokuto with this kick because the wide area of the weapon increases the chance of hitting the target.

KAITEN USHIRO GERI
Spinning or Turning Back Kick

Kaiten ushiro geri is a back kick to an opponent standing in front of you. The kick is executed by spinning away from your opponent, then chambering and delivering a back kick as described in ushiro geri. This is a deceptive kick. The knee is pointed toward the floor rather than upward as in a front kick. This allows the kick to slip past blocks more easily than front kicks.

The second way of delivering this kick is called kaiten ushiro mawashi geri. It is delivered in the same manner but utilizes a roundhouse kick. As you initially spin to set up your kick, you are vulnerable for a moment, with your back to your opponent. This technique must be practiced with great speed.

KESA GERI
Jumping Side Kick

The jumping side kick utilizes sokuto, executed diagonally downward. Jumping, and a strong snap of the knee, increases the power in the kick. Unlike nidan geri, the first leg off the ground does not perform a small kick but initiates a strong upward thrust for elevation. Kesa geri is found in Yakusoku Kumite.

嘉手納

KAKATO
Heel

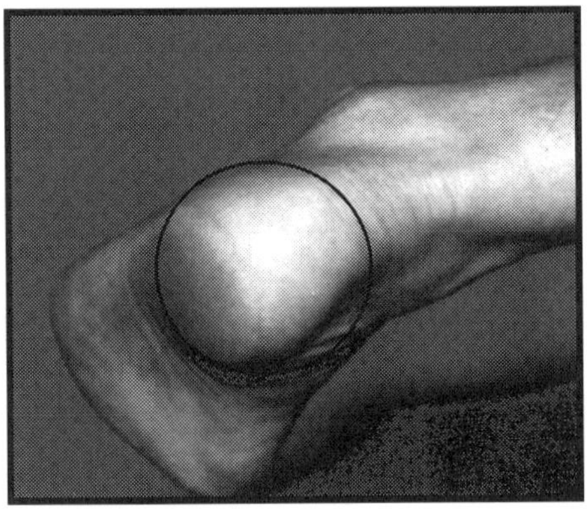

YOKO GERI
Side Kick

Yoko geri is delivered to an opponent standing at your side. Maximum power for this kick is reached at full extension of the leg. Chamber the kick high to create explosive power.

When practicing the side kick, add a step in the direction of the kick. Also practice continuous low (gedan), middle (chudan), and high (jodan) yoko geri, each with a step, to increase your kicking ability.

There are two weaknesses of yoko geri to be aware of. One is that people tend to lean their upper bodies away from the kick to maintain balance. Optimum balance is achieved when the shoulders are directly over the hips. The further the shoulders are moved out of line with the hips, the more unbalanced the stance becomes. This makes the kicker more vulnerable to being overtaken. Second, people who use a lot of side kicks develop a side fighting posture, vulnerable to leg kicks and sweeps.

USHIRO GERI and KAITEN USHIRO GERI
Back kick and Spinning Back Kick

These kicks, previously explained as being executed with sokuto, can also be executed with kakato. Using the heel in kicks focuses the power in a smaller area than sokuto but requires more focus to deliver. Remember one advantage of sokuto is the wide target area it covers. For beginners who do not yet have sufficient strength and control of their ankles, the heel is safer for practice.

HAISOKU
Top of Foot

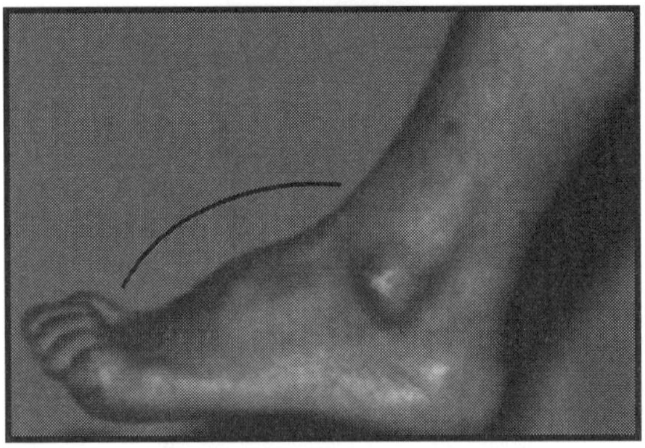

MAWASHI GERI
Roundhouse Kick

The roundhouse kick, described in the sokusen section, can also be performed with the top of the foot and lower shin. Avoid using the top of the foot near the toes as this can stretch and damage the ligaments of the ankle upon contact.

ASHI BURAI
Leg Sweep

決め

This is a devastating leg sweep, using a large motion, delivered to the ankle or calf of one or both your opponent's legs. The purpose of ashi burai using haisoku is the obvious upsetting of your opponent's balance, while causing local damage to the leg. A smaller motion judo sweep, using the instep to contact the opponent's ankle with a controlled takedown, is more common for practice and tournament competition.

HIZA ATE
Knee Lift Kick

This is an excellent close range weapon against a frontal grab, or close range grappling. As your opponent grabs you, grip his hands or arms and

pull him toward you forcefully. If you are already in the grasp, grab his clothing or neck. At the same time lift your knee strongly into the target. Pull your opponent into the knee attack to increase the power at impact. Point the toes of your foot toward the ground and pull your foot back to prepare the sharpest, strongest knee possible. Targets are the groin, abdomen, chest and face.

Maintain a strong stance with the stationary leg. Use the muscles in your abdomen, back and leg to execute this technique. Avoid rising up on the ball of your foot, or using upward motion of your body to create power. It is better to pull your opponent into your strong Sanchin stance.

Remember with all kicks, balance and speed are essential. Although kicks are stronger than hand techniques, they require more skill to execute. Leaning forward or backward breaks your balance, diminishing power in your kick. Keep your upper body vertical and the support leg slightly bent. Slow kicks, or kicks that are not retracted immediately, can be caught by your opponent.

Uechi ryu's emphasis on the crane stance greatly helps the development of balance and strength while standing on one leg. To develop dynamic kicks always work on balance, speed, flexibility and proper technique.

THE KATAS OF

型

UECHI RYU KARATE DO

WHAT IS A KATA?

A kata is a pre-arranged pattern of defensive and offensive techniques. Multiple attackers approaching from different directions are visualized. It is imagined combat that is challenging and rigorous. Katas contain combinations of techniques emphasizing both speed and slowness, strength and weakness, hardness and softness.

Traditional katas are strictly defensive. They start and finish with a block and all offensive techniques are preceded by a block. They contain no music, no somersaults and little jumping through the air.

Martial arts practice of the past stressed the repetitious execution of a particular technique or set of techniques. *Ikyoryo* is the practice of one explosive technique at a time. Ikyoryo combined with body conditioning and actual fighting experience made up the basic self defense systems of ancient Okinawa.

Chuan fa systems from China that influenced Okinawa te contained more formalized patterns of practice. These katas were designed after the fighting styles of animals in combat with each other. Humans developed a method of defending themselves by emulating the fighting tactics of animals.

The individual techniques of Okinawa te, when combined with Chinese kata, began to blend to include footwork and defenses against multiple opponents.

Creating new katas and restructuring existing ones became necessary when karate was first taught in Okinawan public schools and later at colleges in Japan.

Kata practice is the foundation of traditional karate. It is the challenge that never relents. There is always more to learn and accomplish within kata and within yourself. Every individuals kata is their personal work of art.

Traditional katas generally derive their names from the creator of the kata or the area where they were originally practiced. Chinese numbers are used to name some katas from China. Discrepancy surrounds the names of some katas. Kusanku, for example, is a kata reportedly named after a person of the same name. According to Master Tetsuhiro Hokama's (Okinawa Karate and Kobudo Museum) research of ancient Chinese documents, kusanku was rank or title. Bassai (Passai) was named after a Chinese man who taught martial arts and calligraphy when he lived in Okinawa.

KATA AS MOVING MEDITATION

Kata is a total body workout. The speed and dynamics of the katas can be adjusted to fit the particular workout. The advanced level practitioner who knows many katas can develop an excellent aerobic workout by doing a few repetitions of each kata while progressing from the basic to the advanced katas. The speed and intensity can vary from slow to fast and soft to hard as you progress through multiple repetitions of each kata.

No equipment or partner is needed and a kata can be adjusted for small spaces if necessary. Including a few minutes of brisk kata practice at selected times in the daily routine can be an effective stress reducer.

Sometimes called "moving meditation," kata develops self discipline and mental tranquility. It is also an excellent tool by which an instructor can measure the progress of a student. Organized sets of defensive and countermovements of varying difficulty afford a student a formalized method of learning the physical aspects of karate.

Kata has traditionally been a method of documentation and quality control as karate styles have been handed down to subsequent generations of students. Degrees of change occur with each new generation of karate practitioner. Limited understanding of kata, personal interpretations, self indulgence and too little time spent under a qualified instructor are some factors that alter katas or even complete systems over the years.

Intentional and unintentional changing of kata techniques or patterns have altered some systems more than others. Some styles remain true to the katas of the past, however, cultural evolution lends itself to a certain degree of erosion. It is the responsibility of traditional stylists to maintain the accuracy, dignity and artistry of authentic katas.

禪

TRAINING STRUCTURE OF UECHI RYU KARATE

Uechi ryu practice is founded on the principle of reason before skill, *Risen Gyogo.* A person can approach karate training from either direction first, reason or skill.

Ri - reason or principle
Sen - first
Gyo - skill or technique
Go - later

The person who chooses reason first will develop faster because he is attempting to understand each move and technique as it is being taught. Traditional dojo training enhances and expedites this growth.

On the other hand, consider street fighting training, *yakuza*, or karate schools who focus only on attaining physical ability. Without reasoning it is a trial and error method of winning and losing. Without a concept of principles and standards, *kihan*, karate practice becomes a matter of survival of the fittest and lacks the character building aspects of the art.

When sparring or fighting you will possess a higher level of skill if you understand the structure and reason of the skill. Reason is skill and skill is reason, balance the two for the most well rounded results.

In Uechi ryu karate, reason is interpreted as kata because kata comes first! Sanchin is the foundation of reason because it is the first of the three main katas. Skill is interpreted as application of kata and free sparring. Therefore, Uechi ryu begins with Sanchin kata and ends with kumite.

上地流空手道の理念構造

道	精神修養	受動の精神 能動の精神	一 心練
	理論研究	歴史的な面 生理的な面 物理的な面	一 理練
術	規範としての空手	準備運動 補助運動 中間補助運動 諸型 型の分解 約束組手	一 技練
	運用としての空手	小手鍛え 当て身の実験 自由組手	一 体練

PHILOSOPHICAL PRINCIPLES and TECHNICAL ORGANIZATION of UECHI RYU KARATE

- WAY / DO
  - Mind cultivation
    - Passive spirit
    - Active spirit
    - → I Mental training
  - Theoretical study
    - Historical
    - Physiological
    - Physical
    - → II Theoretical training
- SKILL / JUTSU
  - Kata standard
    - Warm up exercises
    - Supplementary exercises
    - Kata practice
    - Kata analysis
    - Pre-arranged sparring
    - → III Theoretical training (Skill)
  - Karate application
    - Body conditioning
    - Striking experiments
    - Free sparring
    - → IV Physical training

The study of Uechi ryu karate is incomplete without all four principles of training.

PERSONAL BENEFITS FROM KATA TRAINING

- Increased upper body strength of muscles and tendons from dynamic karate techniques such as blocking, striking and punching.
- Increased lower body strength from kicking and alternating between high and low stances.
- Improved agility from explosive foot movement and abrupt direction changes.
- Improved hand-eye coordination from visually focusing on accurate targeting.
- Improved balance from kicking and weight distribution in various stances.
- Understanding the use of the hips for centering and power.
- Increased cardiovascular fitness from aerobic workout.
- Excellent for developing motor skills in children.
- Provides a systematic pattern for development by progressive increases in difficulty.
- Intensity can be lessened for older practitioners.
- Increased health from structured daily exercise.

THE KATAS OF PANGAINOON

半硬軟

Kanbun Uechi returned to Okinawa after learning three Southern Chinese katas: Sanchin, Seisan and Sanseiryu (which he called Sandairyu). These three katas are purely Chinese chuan fa forms. The patterns and techniques of these katas are practiced today as they were in China during Kanbun Uechi's time. The methods of body movement differ between the Chinese, Okinawans and Americans. The result is a subtle evolutionary change in the appearance of the original katas.

This book is not a "how-to" manual of karate by which you can learn katas from photographs and foot charts. The three katas of Pangainoon are included here as part of the historical and technical documentation of Pangainoon and Uechi ryu karate.

The sequential presentation of each kata is deliberately incomplete. They are presented to illustrate the techniques defined in the blocking, striking and kicking chapters of this book.

No individual or book can present the "one and only way" to perform a technique or kata. I have learned a different method of executing the same kata moves and applications from four of Kanbun Uechi's students, under whom I have studied. This book does not claim to be the authority about the way Uechi ryu karate should be practiced by everyone. It is an informed and thoroughly researched historical and technical point of view.

SANCHIN KATA

三戦

The practice of Sanchin is called *Shi-Go-Ki*. This means to condition your body against pain and your mind against fear.

The Chinese characters for Sanchin would be pronounced either as Sanchian, or Sanshin or Sanchi and can be found in Confucius literature dating as far back as 350 B.C. where it refers to having fought three times.

The kanji for Sanchin in Buddhism means the Three War Gods: Marishiten, Daikokuten and Konnyamonten. References to Sanchin in Chinese history describe three fights, three wars, three wins or three losses.

Sanchin today means three conflicts or three tactics. The conflicts can be interpreted as the self conflict of mind, body and spirit. Three tactics can mean focus, stance and timing, the three most important aspects of karate according to Master Seiyu Shinjo.

Sanchin is a body conditioning and hardening kata. It is considered a beginner kata because of its fundamental essence. This is the dichotomy of Sanchin kata. It is one of the easiest katas to mimic because of its limited number of moves and monotonous appearance.

Performing a correct Sanchin kata, utilizing the maximum strength of body and mind, is difficult. Some benefits of practicing Sanchin kata are immediately apparent but years of dedicated practice and self discipline are required to achieve the ultimate results of body hardening and conditioning.

Sanchin should be practiced daily and continued through life. In formal dojo practice, Sanchin is performed three times before proceeding to any other kata.

Beginners to Sanchin should perform the kata with little power, in a relaxed form. Do not try to apply too much strength at first because it will make the kata too stiff. It is important to comprehend correct body posture, shisei, and the position of the hips, chest, shoulders, hands and head.

When understanding of the kata increases the instructor will begin testing the student's stability by applying light pushes and strikes to the body during the kata. The impact of conditioning will increase as the student becomes stronger. Five years of correct Sanchin training creates a very strong body impervious to enormous impact from attack.

"Everything is in Sanchin!" These words have been spoken by every credible instructor of Uechi ryu karate. The principals of body application learned in Sanchin are present in the other seven katas of this system. It is the definitive kata of Uechi ryu.

SANCHIN TEACHES:

Basic stance, posture and steps
Focus and position of eyes
Conditioning against dynamic impact
Zen meditation
Muscle tightness
Correct breathing

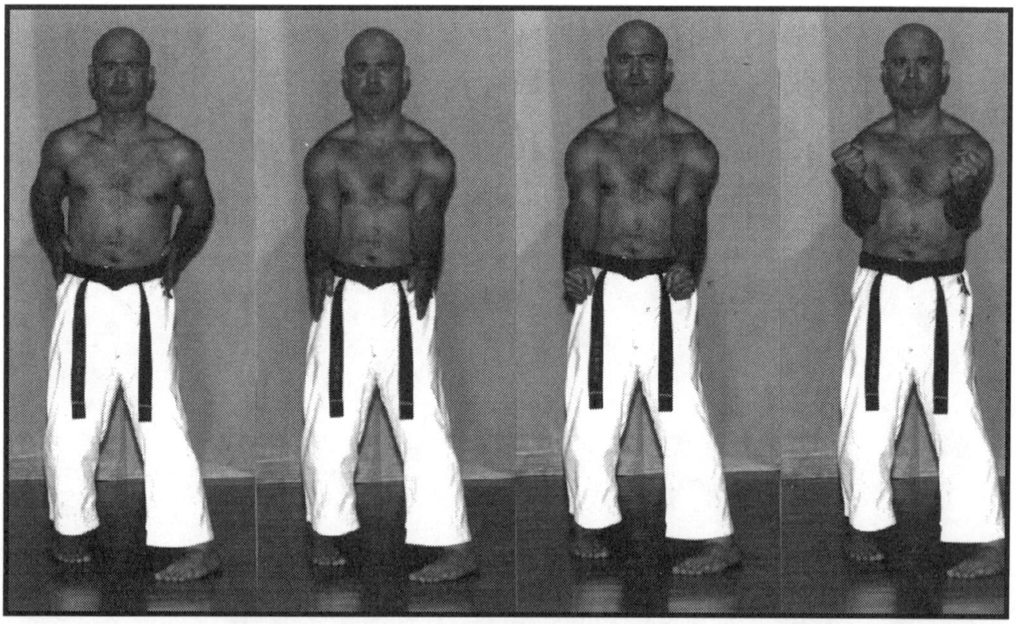

STANCE
Tachi kata

To accomplish the proper stance in Sanchin kata begin at attention *kyu tsuke* with the heels together and the feet pointed outward at forty-five degrees, *fudo dachi*. The feet are then placed shoulder width apart. One method of achieving the proper width is to place one foot perpendicular to the other, with the tip of the big toe of one foot touching the side of the other foot. Straighten the perpendicular foot. The distance between the feet should be shoulder width at this point.

Slide one foot forward so the tips of the toes of the back foot are on the same line as the heel of the front foot. Then lift the heel of the front foot and move it outward. Replace it on the floor so the front foot points inward at about thirty degrees. The rear foot remains pointed straight ahead.

After learning the proper width for the stance a student will step laterally with the left foot to establish the correct width. Okinawan people, who are much shorter than most Westerners, pivot on the balls of the feet and spread the heels apart to establish a distance the same as their shoulder width.

If the stance is too narrow it will lessen stability in the upper body. This decreases the amount of impact the stance can withstand. A stance that is too wide offers lower body stability but requires large steps when moving. This upsets proper balance as the upper body shifts back and forth when stepping.

The kinetics of Sanchin kata are hundreds of years old. The parameters of the kata were designed for the small people of China and Okinawa. The height and body proportion of Westerners differ from Asians. Extensive practice and patience is required to reach the understanding of Sanchin kata as it was originally designed. Small adjustments in width of stance may be needed to compensate for difference in body height and proportion.

The stance used in Sanchin kata is more upright than that of other styles that use this kata. The stance closely resembles a natural, straight stance with the knees only slightly bent, *choku dachi*, (also known as *Heiko dachi*). Balance, mobility and speed will be greater when working from a more natural stance.

Tighten all the muscles of the legs, especially the thighs and calves as you grip the ground with your feet and toes. Squeeze the knees inward. When correctly bent, each knee should be placed directly over the toes of the corresponding foot.

Roll the hips forward and tighten the buttocks, abdomen and lower back. When the lower body is in the correct stance, a rising kick to the groin can be caught between the thighs without changing the stance.

The body must be held in a straight posture, *shi sei.* Pull the shoulders down to tie them in with the muscles of the torso creating a strong pillar from your hips to your head.

Squeeze the upper body down while pulling the lower body up so the two halves meet in the middle, the *tanden.* Tanden, a Chinese pressure point, is the center of the body. It is located about one inch below the navel and three inches into the body.

Newer students sometimes roll the shoulders forward in an attempt to pull them down. The problem is worsened if they try to emulate the enormous trapezoid development seen in older photographs of Uechi ryu karate masters.

Rolling the shoulders forward will cause the back to curve. This loosens the tension in the muscles of the middle and lower back. It is important to keep the back and head straight. Imagine a straight line from the top of your head, down the spine through the hips and straight down to the floor between your feet.

Maintaining a straight posture and center line will minimize the effort used to turn left and right or move forward and back. Awkward, unbalanced and large movements occur when the body is bent and the vertical center line is broken. Keep the head and shoulders over the hips for smooth, effortless turns and movement.

SANCHIN STANCE IN REVIEW

Do not round your back or shoulders
Keep your back and head straight with the chin down
Distribute weight evenly on both feet
The center of mass extends to the floor between your feet
Toes touch the floor firmly, without weight on the toes

HAND POSITION
Te-No-Ichi

The upper arms and elbows are kept in front of the body at all times. Check the proper position by placing a fist sideways against the ribs, just below the pectoral muscles of the chest. Pull the opposite arm back until the elbow touches the end of the fist. Remove the fist and maintain this upper arm position.

The elbows are pulled together slightly so they are tucked in rather than straight down or protruding outward. Do not exaggerate pulling the elbows together as that will cause the back to become rounded. Hold the elbows in a tight but comfortable position and do not allow them to go outside your body line.

Bend the elbows and adjust the forearms until the fingertips reach shoulder height. Move the hands laterally until they are at shoulder width. A wider hand position creates a large opening, leaving the body vulnerable to attack. Holding the hands too close together causes the elbows to venture outward.

Turn the palms, which are now facing upward, slightly inward. Keep the wrists and fingers straight so there is one line from the elbow to the fingertip. Bend the thumb and press it against the side of the hand at the base of the index finger. Both hands are held in an equal position and distance from the body. This is the correct "on-guard" position of Sanchin kata, Sanchin *garmae*.

STRIKING
Tsuki Waza

From the Sanchin garmae position the strike is done with the hand corresponding with the back foot. The backs of the fingers of the striking hand move over to touch the palm of the other hand. As the striking arm is pulled back, the fingertips slide down the opposing forearm until they reach the bend inside the elbow. This is the height desired for chambering the striking hand.

Pull the hand across your chest and chamber it beside your body. The edge of the striking hand should touch the upper ribs when the hand is placed just below the chest muscles. The forearm of the striking hand should now be parallel to the floor with the palm facing upward.

When executing the strike, pull the shoulder and elbow down as the hand is extended forward. Keep the elbow in line with the hand. If the elbow drifts away from the side of the body the strike will be slower and weaker. Feel the elbow slide by your body during the strike to insure proper alignment.

Do not raise your shoulder or let it move forward during the strike. The shoulder muscles should be pulled down to tie in with the rest of the muscles of the upper body. To avoid raising the shoulder concentrate on creating a deep arc with the elbow of the striking arm as the hand moves straight forward. Feel the power of all the muscles of the body in your strike. Avoid swaying or rocking, attempting to add momentum to the strike.

The hand twists in a corkscrew manner as it is extended. Twist the hand more at the end of the strike than at the beginning. The resulting snap will increase the power of the strike. Turning the hand as soon as you begin the strike, a common mistake, results in a push rather than a strike.

The fingers, wrist and elbow should be straight at the extension of the strike so all the power of the technique travels from the power source straight to the target with no deflection. Recoil the strike in the same twisting manner and return the hand to the Sanchin garmae position. The opposing hand is your defensive shield when striking and should remain strongly in place.

STEPPING
Ashi-No-Hakobi

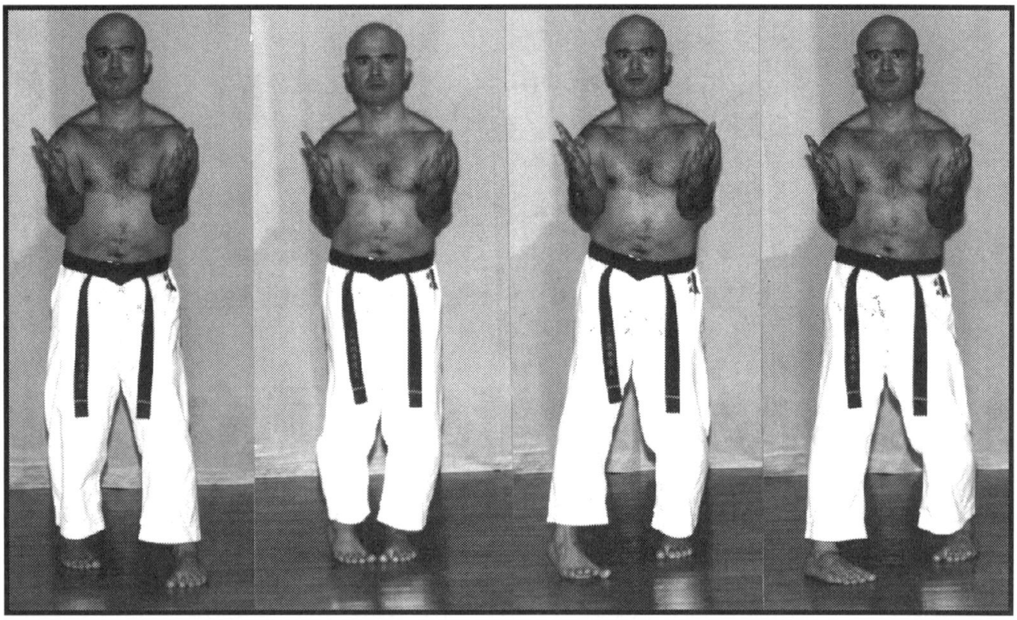

The step in Sanchin kata begins by straightening the front foot that has been pointed inward thirty degrees. Straighten the front foot by lifting the heel slightly and move it inward, pivoting on the ball and big toe of the foot. As the rear foot moves forward to become the front foot it should not be lifted very far off the floor. The step is accomplished in a sliding fashion, *suri ashi.* Imagine rolling a pencil forward on the floor with your foot as you step forward.

Replace the foot in the front position by putting the ball and big toe of the foot on the floor first. Exert pressure forward so the heel moves out into the proper position before putting the heel on the floor. This creates tension in the legs so a strong stance is accomplished when the step is finished, with no need for re-adjustment or tightening of the stance.

The rear foot does not move in a straight line forward to become the front foot. The step is done with a half circle motion as the stepping foot moves inward, close to the other foot, then outward to the correct position as the front foot. This method of stepping brings the legs close together momentarily during the step, protecting the groin while moving forward.

Maintain proper foot width and depth while stepping through the kata to prevent swaying or leaning out of the correct posture. Keep your eyes straight ahead in strong focus. Only beginning students need to look down at their feet to insure proper movement and placement.

TURNING
Tenshin

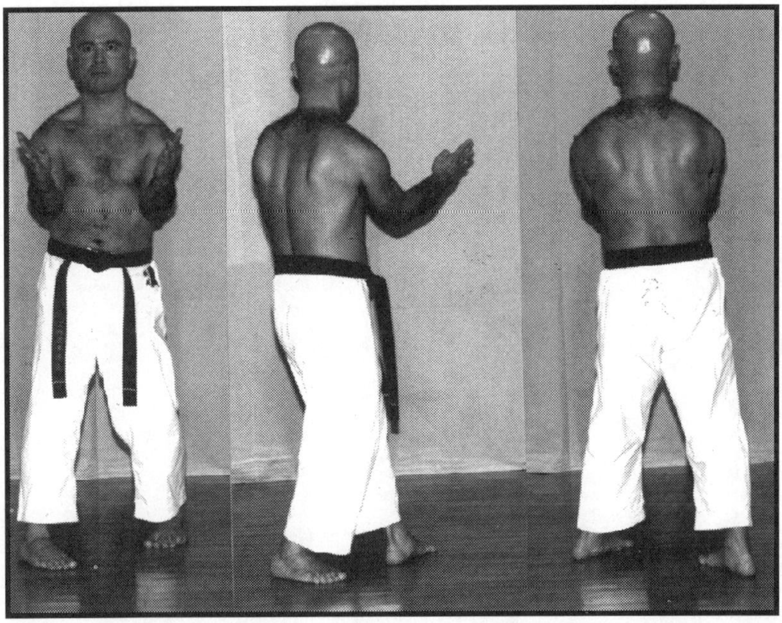

Turning 180 degrees in the opposite direction, *han ten*, is done toward the rear leg. Turning toward the rear foot requires the fewest movements and the least amount of time to execute. Pivot the rear foot on the ball and big toe, placing the heel back on the floor so that foot will be pointed inward at thirty degrees when the turn is completed.

Pivoting on the heel of the foot to turn is not desirable. Pivoting on the ball of the foot not only turns the legs but the hips as well. This is a more efficient turn than on the heel of the foot.

Turn your body from its center, the hips and abdomen, not the chest or head. Lift the back foot, turn your body 180 degrees around, then place the back foot on the floor in the correct position described earlier. Look over your shoulder as you begin the turn and keep your hands up with the arms tight to protect yourself during the turn.

REMAINING MOVES IN SANCHIN KATA

The stances, strikes and steps described to this point have been performed while stepping back and forth across the floor. The next four pages illustrate the techniques that comprise the final third of the kata.

After executing three strikes, *morote Sanchin nukite*, the practitioner will step to each side then back to the front with ninety degree turns, *tenshin*. The direction of the first turn is determined by the front leg.

A two-hand circular block, *wauke*, and a double thumb strike, *morote boshiken zuki*, is performed at each of the three directions. The upper boshiken strike is aimed at the chest, the same pressure point target as Sanchin nukite strikes. The target of the other hand is the lower ribs.

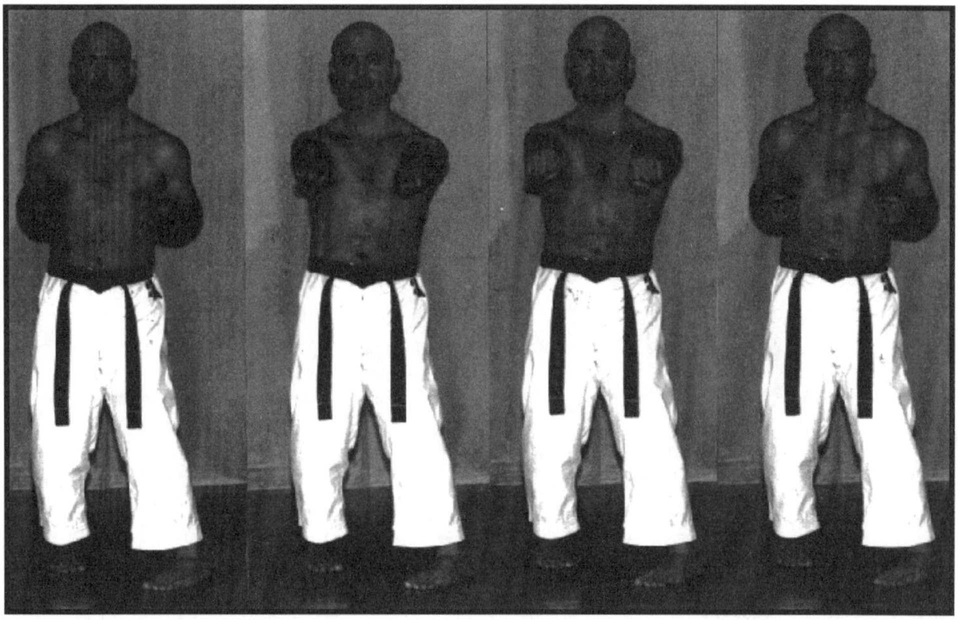

All techniques used in the katas illustrated in this chapter are described thoroughly in Chapters VII, VIII and IX.

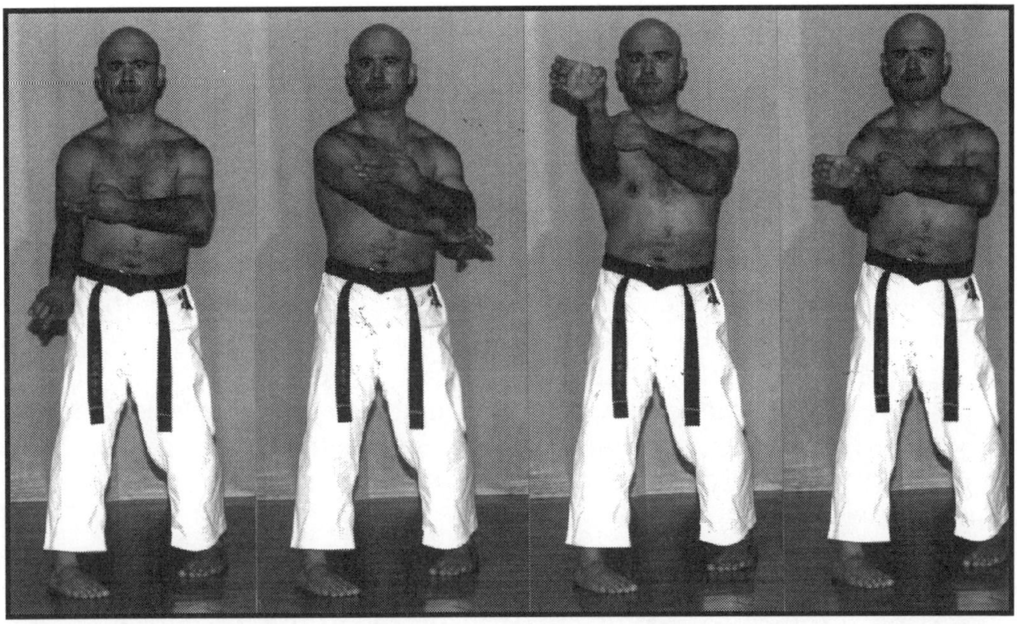

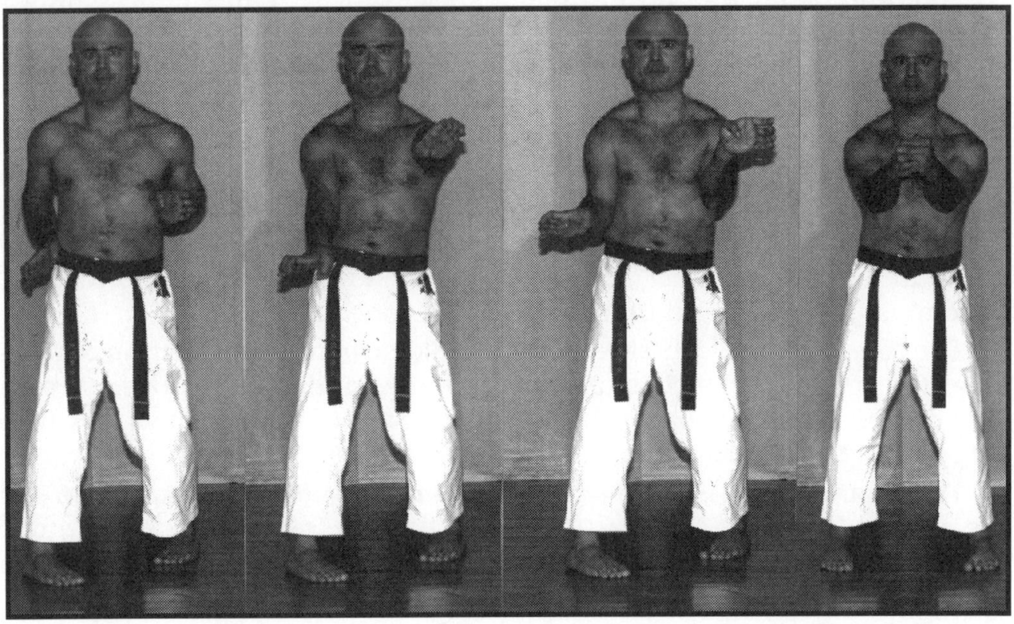

BREATHING
Ko-kyu Ho

Two very important aspects of Sanchin kata are breathing, *Ko-kyu ho* and hardening or stiffening of the body, *Tai-gatame*. These two aspects go hand-in-hand during the development and understanding of the kata. Proper breathing is essential to body hardening and stamina.

Some styles practice unnatural breathing methods for kata and a different method for sparring. Some breathing methods are good for increasing health but are not applicable for martial combat. The method of breathing in Uechi ryu is very natural.

Uechi ryu karate is practiced by holding the breath until after the completion of a strike. This aids in muscle tension and focuses all exertion into the strike. Holding the breath during a maximum effort strike is similar to a weight lifter holding his breath until the completion of the lift. This directs all energy into the execution without losing power through the exhale.

The inhale should be done through the nose, while the exhale is forced out through the mouth. Inhaling is natural and unconscious but correct exhaling requires practice. During training the tongue is pressed against the top teeth to end the exhale. This causes a short hissing sound. The sound allows the instructor to insure the student is exhaling at the proper time, in rhythm to movements.

The abrupt ending of the exhale also emphasizes the tightening of the abdomen. The rhythm of breathing in coordination with softening and hardening of the body becomes natural after learning the correct method of breathing.

Maintain about half lung capacity at all times. Moments of weakness occur when the lungs are very full of air or very empty. Make the exhale short rather than long and drawn out. Short, quick breaths are needed during the rapid movement of kata or kumite.

There is a method of checking the tightness of the abdomen while developing strong breathing. Step through Sanchin kata facing a partner. Place a six foot staff (*rokushakubo*) between the two, pressing on the abdomen. As one person steps forward the partner steps backward, maintaining pressure on the staff. This exercise teaches continuous abdominal tightness and breathing during movement.

The correct degree of body tension should be maintained during Sanchin kata. Do not remain too tight or rigid as this hinders smooth movement and makes the kata look robotic. Excessive softness, especially at an inappropriate time in the kata, makes for weak development.

The balance between proper hardness and softness, in conjunction with the appropriate movements in the kata, is the essence of understanding Sanchin kata. This understanding is achieved only from proper instruction and years of practice.

SANCHIN BODY CONDITIONING
Tai-den Ho

Vital organs such as the brain, lungs and heart are protected by strong bones like the skull, sternum and ribs. An enormous amount of outside impact is necessary to damage these organs. They are relatively safe from an empty handed attack.

Other organs such as the stomach, bladder, intestines, liver, spleen and kidneys are covered only by muscle fiber and skin. They are, therefore, more vulnerable to damage. Impact to these organs causes internal bleeding that can lead to death. When certain organs are damaged, they cannot be repaired and death is eminent.

A punch to a relaxed midsection delivers impact that penetrates through the muscles into the internal organs. When the abdominal muscles are tightened, *shime*, they absorb and disperse impact along the muscle, preventing the force from reaching internal organs. Surface damage or bruising may occur but the vital organs are not damaged.

Muscle fibers are like bands of rubber. They are flexible and resilient. Training muscles past a normal level of fitness makes them grow and become stronger. Striking a student's body during Sanchin kata is a means of testing and challenging the level of conditioning. Practicing the kata itself is the way to develop the strength needed for conditioning. Strong muscles, capable of controlled tension and deflection, are the results.

It is not necessary to be a muscle man or strength athlete to benefit from the practice of Sanchin kata. The process is gradual. The intensity is progressive. The result is a much stronger body, pound for pound, for each individual.

Sanchin kata creates body armor while increasing the mental pain threshold. The confidence resulting from conditioning helps maintain calmness and control in an altercation. This allows for greater efficiency in blocking and overall defense.

先の先

SEISAN KATA

十三

Shisan, meaning "thirteen", is a Chinese term for counting, as is sanchin. Shisan is pronounced seisan in Japanese. The number represents the opponents, conflicts or defenses in the kata. The number seisan is a kata name used by more than one karate system, although the actual katas are different.

Seisan is the second of three katas from China introduced in Okinawa by Kanbun Uechi. The kata emphasizes strength and speed. The explosive moves in Seisan vary between large, strong motions and light fast motions. The kata is performed swiftly with emphasis on speed of technique.

Seisan covers the four fundamental positions of attack: front, back, right side and left side. Seisan kata contains many effective, close range, defensive fighting techniques that are very applicable to street defense.

The hand position is established the same as in Sanchin kata. The hands are then turned over 180 degrees so the palms face downward. The wrists and hands are then bent outward but not forward or back. This is the ready position, *hirate gammae*, of Seisan kata. The method of breathing is the same as in Sanchin kata.

The position of the eyes, focused straight ahead on your opponent, is also the same as in Sanchin. In Seisan kata the eyes leave this straight ahead focus only once after the knee strike, hiza ate. You are then visualizing the opponent on the ground in front of you.

STANCE

Sanchin dachi is the stance used predominantly in Seisan kata. Other stances used are zenkutsu dachi, sue goshi dachi and tsuru dachi.

Zenkutsu dachi, a forward leaning stance, is used when executing a forward elbow strike, *tate hiji zuki.*

Sue goshi dachi is a version of the horse riding stance (kiba dachi).

Sue goshi dachi is used when executing a roundhouse elbow strike, *furi hiji zuki.*

Kiba dachi, used in practice drills, is a deep stance with feet side by side while the body is facing to the front. Sue goshi dachi is done with the left foot forward toward the opponent. The stance is not as deep as kiba dachi.

Tsuru dachi, the crane stance, is used in landing after a jump to the rear. A formidable defensive pose is then achieved. The jump forward toward the opponent is launched from this stance.

STEPPING

Stepping throughout the kata is done in the same manner as in Sanchin. A forward sliding step, *zenshin yori ashi,* is also used to advance quickly while maintaining the same lead foot. The Okinawan people describe the length of the slide in practice as the length of one of your feet. Taller people should increase the length of the slide. Yori ashi is a popular method of advancement in sport karate where more extreme distances are covered.

The slide step is used four times. First, when delivering double thumb knuckle and ridge hand strikes to the temple, *boshiken hasamu uchi.* The slide step is used a second time when delivering the first of three roundhouse blocks and fingertip strikes to the opponent's ribs. Third, it is used to move toward an opponent before picking him up and moving him to a different location.

The grab is facilitated by first using both hands to attack the abdomen with finger tip and thumb strikes. Next, firmly grab the opponent's flesh and muscle in each hand.

Finally, yori ashi is used in a different manner when grabbing an opponent and moving him to shield an attack from another direction. This slide step is used to change from a left to a right stance, without stepping, while turning ninety degrees.

The sequential presentation of Seisan and Sanseiryu katas that follow are not intended to teach these katas. Transitional steps, stances or blocks are sometimes left out. The direction of the kata is not always clear as the subject often faces forward for a clear view of the technique being performed.

TECHNIQUE NAMES and APPLICATIONS of SEISAN KATA

See Chapter VII, VIII and IX for individual explanations and illustrations

Morote gedan nuki
Two handed low area fingertip strike.
Sanchin dachi
Sanchin stance, described earlier.
Sanchin nukite
Twisting fingertip strike.
Boshiken hasamu uchi
Two handed strike to the temple. Hasamu means to squeeze together or pinch.
Boshiken tsuki age
Rising thumb strike to the face.
Morote boshiken tsuki age
Two handed thumb strike to the face.
Wari uke
Essentially a mawashi uke performed with each arm simultaneously to separate your opponents arms and break his hold on you. Wari means to cut or separate.
Hiza ate
Knee lift strike.
Koken
Swinging nukite strike to the groin area.
Hirate mawashi uke
Open hand one arm circular block.
Morote shoken kamae
Two handed shoken ready position. This is used to grab and lift an opponent.
Zenkutsu dachi
Forward leaning stance, back leg straight.
Tate hiji
Vertical elbow strike to the front.
Tetsui
Hammer fist. In this kata the target is the temple.
Shomen sokusen geri
Front direction big toe kick.
Shoken gedan zuki
Lower area one knuckle strike to an opponent on the ground.

Chudan nukite
Middle area fingertip strike usually aimed at the ribs.
Yori ashi
Sliding step.
Sue goshi dachi
Low stance with one foot forward.
Hirai sukui uke
Downward sweeping or scooping block.
Tsuru no kamae
One legged on-guard stance.
Furi hiji
Roundhouse elbow strike to the body.
Uraken
Backfist to the face.
Chudan shoken zuki
One knuckle punch to the body.

The opening for Seisan kata is the same as for Sanchin kata

Morote gedan nuki
Two handed low area fingertip strike.
Next, three sanchin strikes and steps

Boshiken hasamu uchi
Two hand strike to the temple.
Hasamu means to squeeze together or pinch.

Unguarded Method

Boshiken tsuki age
Rising thumb strike to the face performed R-L-R. Second hand protects the face.

Morote boshiken tsuki age and hiza ate
Two hand thumb strike to the face
and rising knee strike

Koken
Swinging nukite strike to the groin area.
Turn 180°

Execute three koken strikes and mawashi uke while facing the back direction

Morote gedan nuki— Two handed low area fingertip strike, facing to the back

Morote shoken kamae

Two handed shoken ready position. This is used to grab and lift an opponent, turn to the right.

Zenkutsu dachi
Forward leaning stance, back leg straight
Tate hiji
Vertical elbow strike to the front, facing sideways

Mawashi uke block precedes a boshiken strike to the face

Mawashi uke block precedes a nukite strike to the ribs

Turn to the front, block and prepare for a hammer fist strike

Tetsui and Boshiken
Hammer fist to the temple and thumb strike to the face

Turn right and perform a right mawashi uke and left nukite strike before turning to the front

Turn 180 degrees left and block

Shomen geri
Front kick

Hiza ate
Knee strike and follow-up control of opponent

Shoken gedan zuki
Lower area one knuckle strikes to an opponent on the ground, repeated three times

Chudan nukite
Sanchin fingertip strike to the ribs,
done in three directions with turns

Turn to the front,
block

Yori ashi— Sliding step
Sue goshi dachi— Low stance with one foot forward

Hirai sukui uke— Downward sweeping or scooping block done while jumping back. *Tsuru no kamae*— One legged on guard stance. *Furi hiji*— Roundhouse elbow strike to the body done after jumping forward. *Uraken*— Backfist to the face

Chudan shoken zuki
One knuckle punch to the body

Rei
Bow

Just a reminder that the sequential presentation of the three katas shown in this chapter are not intended to teach these katas. The blocks executed before each counterattack are not shown and the direction faced is not clear.

This presentation is designed to document the three katas Kanbun Uechi learned in China.

SANSEIRYU KATA

三十六

Sanseiryu, the third kata Kanbun Uechi learned in China, is the most advanced kata in the Uechi ryu system. The kata name is pronounced *San Shi Liu* in Chinese. Kanbun Uechi called this kata *Sandairyu* when teaching at his dojo in Wakayama, Japan.

The fundamentals of stance, hand position, stepping and striking are consistent with all information already presented for Sanchin and Seisan katas.

Sanseiryu involves combat with opponents from all eight attack positions: front, back, right side, left side, right forward flank (forty-five degrees), left forward flank, right back flank and left back flank.

The steps and direction changes are intended to be long and dynamic like the dragon. The techniques vary between hard and soft while stressing elasticity. The concept of stretching and returning while remaining soft is called *muchi tengwa*. The name comes from a type of rice cake that returns to its original form after being stretched. Muchi tengwa is the essence of Sanseiryu kata.

TECHNIQUES OF SANSEIRYU KATA

One aspect of foot work not found in the previous two katas is a slide step to the rear, called *koho oshiro yori ashi* or *yori ashi kotai.* In Sanseiryu it occurs after the first shoken strike. The forward sliding step, Zenshin yori ashi, is explained in the Seisan kata section.

Techniques not covered in the previous two katas are:

Watari uke

The opening circular blocks utilizing turning wrists for grabbing and deflection.

Shoken kosa no kamae

Both hands placed back to back in the on guard position, each with a one knuckle fist, shoken. This is also the closing position of Kanshiwa kata.

Morote hajiki uke

Double four knuckle strike to the eyes.

Harai sukui uke

Downward, outside direction scoop block.

Hirate sukui uke

Rising inside lifting block, concluding in a firm grip on the Achilles tendon.

Hasamu taoshi

The squeezing together of the hands against the opponent's leg to accomplish a takedown. Taoshi means takedown.

Gedan barai uke

Outward arm downblock against a kick.

Shoken sukui age uke

Upward lift block with a shoken fist, used against a kick.

Hiza ate uke

Knee lift shin block.

Boshiken gamae

Both hands open, on guard stance after the knee lift shin block

Kakushiken

Fingertip, crane's beak, strike

Opening stance

Watari uke

Shoken zuki

Shoken kosa no kamae

Both hands placed back to back in the on guard position, each with a one knuckle fist, shoken. This is also the closing position of Kanshiwa kata.

Mawashi uke while reaching for the opponent

Zenkutsu dachi and tate hiji

Boshiken and nukite

Shomen geri

Yori ashi and mawashi uke

Shoken zuki

Morote hajiki uke
Double four knuckle strike to the eyes

Harai sukui uke
Right downward, outside direction scoop block

Hirate sukui uke
Rising inside lifting block, concluding in a firm grip on the Achilles tendon.

Hasamu taoshi
The squeezing together of the hands against the opponent's leg to accomplish a takedown. Taoshi means takedown

Gedan barai uke— Outward arm downblock against a kick
Shoken sukui age uke— Upward lift block with a shoken fist, used against a kick.

Two methods of applying the counterattack

Yori ashi and shoken zuki

Side View

Yori ashi and shoken zuki
Repeated three times

Side View

Shoken sukui age uke
Upward lift block with a shoken fist, used against a kick

Tenshin and mawashi uke

Sue goshi dachi and furi hiji

Uraken and shoken

Sue goshi dachi and tate hiji

Shoken sukui age uke

Tenshin, Sanchin garmae and Sanchin nukite

Hiza ate uke
Knee lift shin block
Boshiken gamae
Both hands open, on guard stance after the knee lift shin block

Hiza ate uke
Boshiken gamae

Yori ashi and mawashi uke

Kakushen
Fingertip, crane's beak, strike

Rei
Bow

SUPAREMPE

壱百零八

A fourth kata believed to be a part of the Pangainoon system, Suparempe, was not learned by Kanbun Uechi during his stay in China. this kata can be found in other karate styles with roots in China, such as Goju ryu.

Reference to a fourth kata may be derived from the format of some chuan fa systems in that they consisted of four katas with the total number of movements equaling one hundred sixty.

Sanchin	=	3
Seisan	=	13
Sanseiryu	=	36
Suparempe	=	108
Total		160

REMAINING KATAS OF UECHI RYU

Kanei Uechi and senior members of the Uechi Ryu Karate Association developed five katas to complete the system. The additional katas are used as bridges between the original three katas of Pangainoon.

The eight katas of Uechi ryu are divided into two groups of four katas for the beginner level (kyu ranks) and four for the advanced level (dan ranks). The katas become progressively more difficult but are not related to one another, as some believe. Each kata teaches a different aspect of development.

KANSHIWA KATA

完子和

Kanshiwa, designed by Kanei Uechi in 1954, combines the names of Shushiwa and Kanbun. It was previously called *Kanshabo.* The name was changed in the early seventies when the pronunciation of Chou tsu Ho's name was changed from Shushabu to Shushiwa.

This beginner kata was originally taught using shoken punches. The first three strikes were later changed. This is the only kata in Uechi ryu containing the standard two knuckle closed fist punches prevalent in Okinawa te.

KANSHU KATA

完周

Kanshu, designed by Seiki Itokazu, also combines the names of Shushiwa and Kanbun. This kata was originally called *Dai ni Seisan*, or second Seisan. The name was changed in the late seventies. It includes many moves from Seisan kata, and was designed to aid in learning Seisan.

SEICHIN KATA

十戦

Seichin means ten conflicts. It was designed by Saburo Uehara, a student of Kanbun Uechi, in 1963. It is the most difficult of the kyu level katas. Seichin employs many techniques of Okinawan karate combined with the Chinese techniques of Pangainoon.

SEIRUI KATA

十六

Seirui means sixteen. The appearance of this kata, developed by Kanei Uechi, is different from all other katas of Uechi ryu. It emphasizes the cat stance, *nekko dachi.*

KANCHIN KATA

完戦

Kanchin, also designed by Kanei Uechi means Kanbun's tactics or conflicts. This kata closely resembles Sanseiryu kata.

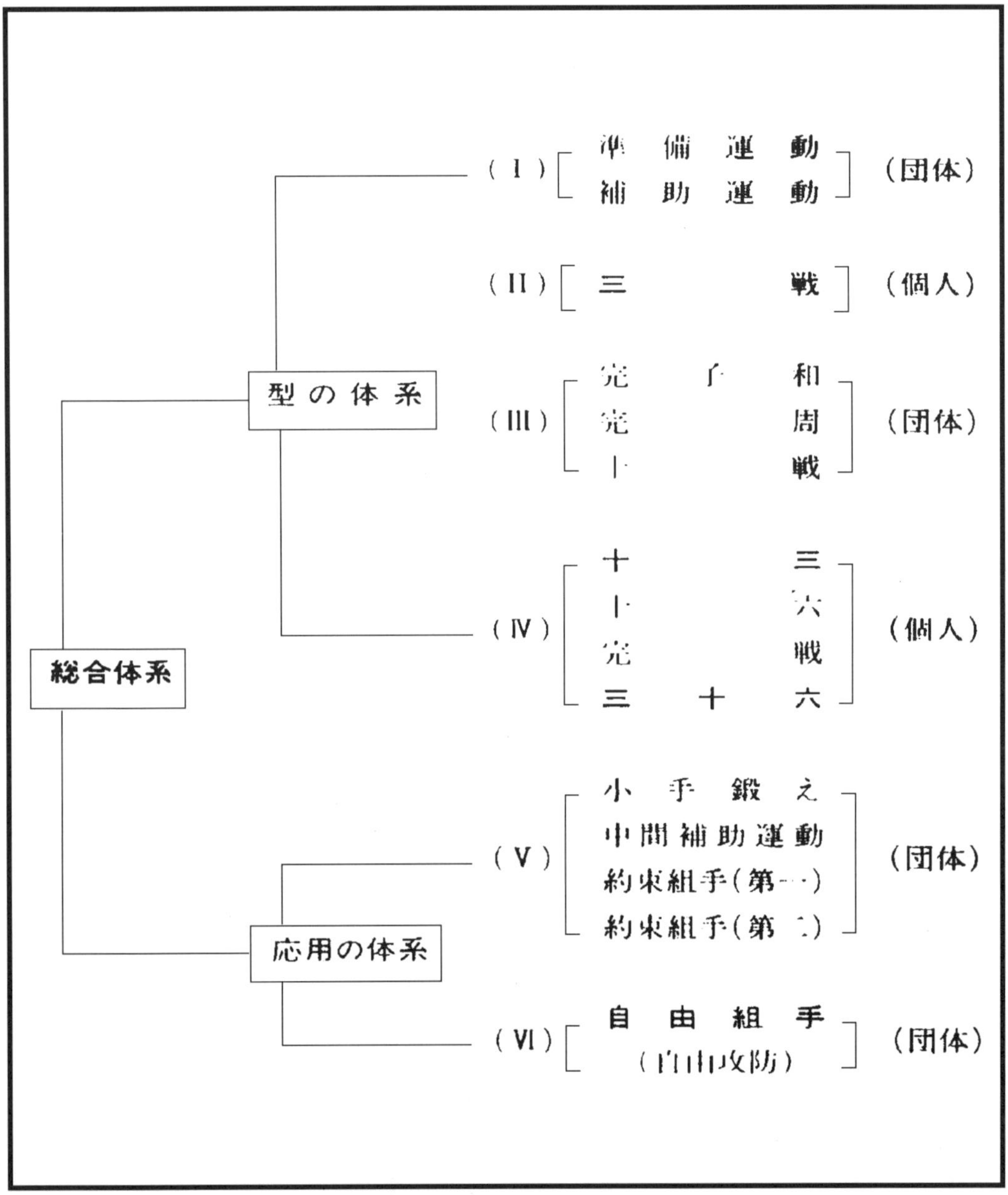
総合体系
型の体系
応用の体系
(Ⅰ) 準備運動
補助運動
(団体)
(Ⅱ) 三戦
(個人)
(Ⅲ) 完子和
完周
十戦
(団体)
(Ⅳ) 十三
十六
完戦
三十六
(個人)
(Ⅴ) 小手鍛え
中間補助運動
約束組手(第一)
約束組手(第二)
(団体)
(Ⅵ) 自由組手
(自由攻防)
(団体)

INSTRUCTIONAL SYSTEM of UECHI RYU KARATE

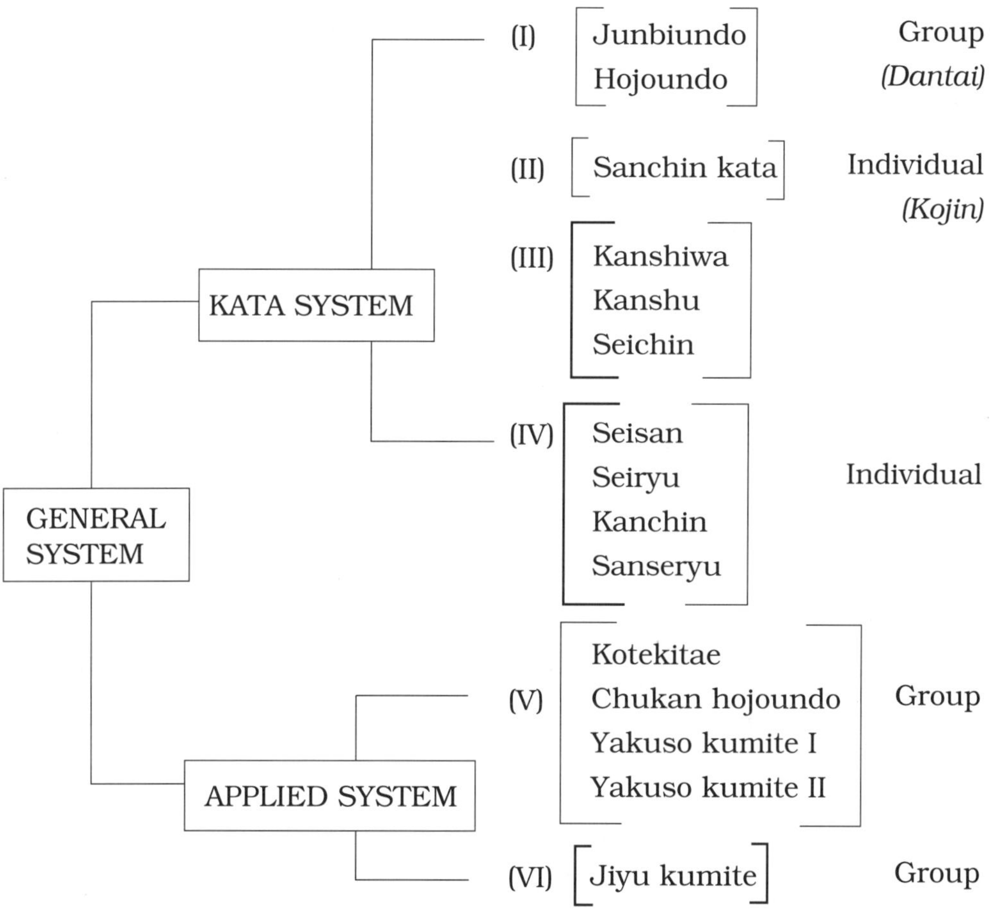

SUPPLEMENTARY EXERCISES

自由組手

Jumbiundo are a series of stretching and warm up exercises that are somewhat standardized in the Uechi ryu system. The order and inclusion of techniques vary from dojo to dojo.

Hojoundo is a set of thirteen techniques taken from kata. The various techniques are done in repetitious sets. Most of the techniques are preceded by a circle block. Hojoundo is a valuable training exercise that contains more blocks and variety of techniques than are found in all four kyu level katas. Many of the techniques are taken from the four advanced katas.

HOJOUNDO EXERCISES

補助運動

Shomen geri
Front kick
Sokuto geri
Side of the foot kick delivered forty-five degrees to the front
Hajki uke hiraken tsuki
Upward snapping block, four knuckle punch, outward forearm block, repeat the four knuckle punch
Uke, shuto, ura, chudan tsuki
Chop, backfist, one knuckle middle area punch
Seiken tsuki
Two knuckle fist punch
Hiji tsuki
Forward, side and rear elbow strikes
Mawashi tsuki
Alternating roundhouse hiraken strikes
Tenshin zensoku geri
Ninety degree turn and front leg kicks
Tenshin kosoku geri
Ninety degree turn and rear leg kicks
Tenshin shoken tsuki

Ninety degree turn and alternating shoken punches
Note:
The first turn for each of the tenshin exercises is forty-five degrees
Shomen hajiki
Stepping forward and back while executing a strike to the eyes with the backs of the fingers by snapping the wrist
Shomen nukite
Fingertips into the eyes, is practiced in the same manner
Koy no ship uchi, tate uchi
The carp tail snap block is done with the back of the wrist. Tate means forward and stands for the four direction exercise
Koy no ship uchi, yoko uchi
The same block executed from side to side

KATA BUNKAI and KUMITE
Application and Sparring

分解

Bunkai is the application or understanding of an exercise. Uechi ryu traditionally has developed two bunkai, one for Kanshiwa kata for beginners practice and one for Seisan for advanced practice. Individual instructors are encouraged to develop bunkai for the remaining katas from their own understanding.

The transition from kata to kumite is accomplished by the development of prearranged kumite. The purpose of prearranged kumite is to train beginning students in the methods of blocking and counter-attacking against a real opponent. Absent is the fear that arises from the unpredictably of free style sparring.

The two vital aspects of distancing and timing are primary areas of development in prearranged kumite. These two factors are often overlooked in this exercise.

The disadvantage of prearranged training is the loss of spontaneity. Anticipating the next move compromises reflex action and reaction time.

The offensive partner, *seme te*, must make an intense and committed attack. The defensive partner, *uke te*, should develop reflexes and reaction, without anticipation or assumption about the impending attack.

約束組手

Uechi ryu has one kyu level prearranged kumite made up of five sets of offensive and defensive moves. It was designed by Seisho Yonaha, a student of Kanbun Uechi. Originally called *Yakusoku kumite dai ichi* (number 1), the exercise is now known as kyu kumite.

Yakusoku kumite dai ni (number 2) was designed by Kanei Uechi for advanced (dan) level practice.

Seiyu Shinjo from the Kadena dojo developed a second advanced level kumite in 1980 that is now practiced worldwide. Other senseis as well have developed prearranged kumite for the benefit of their students.

Kanbun Uechi taught free style sparring as a regular part of training, as did Shushiwa. Kanbun explained that rival schools in China would challenge one another to actual fights. The school that lost would close in disgrace. Kanbun urged his students to be prepared for this possibility.

The type of sparring taught by Kanbun and perpetuated in the Uechi ryu style was derived from the moves in kata. It was an opportunity to test techniques against a spontaneous and unpredictable attacker. Free sparring in Uechi ryu karate is strong and hard because of the high level of body conditioning. Uechi ryu karate is still making the transition from sparring methods of the past to the tournament styles of today.

自由組手

Free style sparring, *jiyu kumite*, in karate is approached from many points of view. Traditional karate practice of the past involved little free sparring. It was generally felt the defensive techniques practiced in the past were too dangerous to apply to a sparring scenario.

Free style sparring is important in developing reflexes and reaction time, distancing, timing and overcoming fear. Sparring gives a person the opportunity to learn sportsmanship and respect for an opponent. At the same time all efforts are dedicated to being successful. The value of tournament competition varies with the quality of each tournament.

The popularity of sport karate is positive, however, distinctions must be made between martial sports and martial arts.

NANKO TANRENHO
SOFT AND HARD TRAINING

Yojojutsu are health oriented exercises, similar to *Doinjutsu* and *Tonoho* described in Chapter I. These exercises are aimed at increasing vigor, health, and longevity in the body.

Hard training, Renko, and soft training, Yojojutsu are important components in Chinese martial arts. *Renko* involves training methods to strengthen and harden each part of the body for martial arts skill training.

The objective in martial arts training is to understand, develop and balance both hard, *goho*, and soft, *juho*, aspects. The path to effective martial arts ability is by way of hard training, soft training, *Nanko Tanrenho* and skill training.

Uechi ryu karate practice, although a refined system, is a hard and rough style to study. The strictness of dojo practice and the pain of extensive body conditioning must be met with an unwavering spirit. This type of training eventually creates an indomitable spirit, however, the practitioner must bring a certain amount of courage to the art.

Hardness and softness alternately co-exist always. Both aspects are found within each technique, each stance, each kata, within each body part and in both offense and defense.

A stance must be hard for contact and soft for mobility.

A stance must be hard while the block is soft.

A block is soft when meeting a hard attack while a hard block is best suited against a soft attack.

A block should be soft until its conclusion when it becomes hard to control the opponent.

A punch is soft to acquire speed as it seeks its target but becomes hard upon contact.

A soft weapon is best used against a hard target and vice versa.

NAIKO

Naiko strengthens the body internally. This includes diet, herbal medicine and breathing, *kiko*.

GAIKO

Gaiko strengthens the body externally, such as developing muscle and conditioning the skin.

THE ANIMALS OF UECHI RYU KATA

Uechi ryu karate emulates three animals: the dragon, *ryu*, tiger, *tora*, and crane, *tsuru*. The correlation of the movements and fighting strategies of animals to those in a kata is vague and often elusive. Each kata does not represent only one animal. Aspects of all three animals exist in all three katas of Pangainoon, therefore all eight katas of Uechi ryu.

Dragon aspects are strong breathing, use of the dragon's claw for grabbing in conjunction with blocks and long dynamic movements and footwork.

The tiger is represented by the dynamic tension of the muscles during the kata. Muscles are tightened for strength when needed and remain supple and elastic for speed during transition and initial attack.

The one knuckle strike (shoken) and big toe kick (sokusen) are called the tiger's teeth. The destructive damage of these strikes is explained in previous chapters on specific techniques. Hiraken fist is also called tiger fist because it resembles a tiger's paw.

A system of exercises was developed in America in the 1950's that was inspired by observing tigers and other large cats in captivity. These animals maintain muscular tone and strength by tensing and relaxing their muscles as they move around a cage.

This self applied dynamic tension was developed into a system of fitness whereby one muscle is exercised by resistance supplied by another muscle. The system known as isometric exercise requires no equipment or weights. Kata practice was already achieving these results in Asia.

The crane is represented in the upright stance with the shoulders and head always over the hips. The one legged stance of the crane, tsuru dachi, teaches balance and grace.

Birds stand on one leg out of necessity. Legs and beaks are the only parts of their body that are not covered by feathers. This results in heat loss in those areas. To minimize heat loss, birds tuck one leg against their body and bury their beak in their feathers.

Marital artists stand on one leg out of necessity; to execute a kick. Martial artists of all styles use tsuru dachi while kicking although many do not emphasize the stance in training.

Uechi ryu takes one legged balance to a higher level by using the raised shin to block incoming kicks. The hands are left free to counter or take control of the opponent.

The circular block prevalent in Uechi ryu is patterned after the defensive movements of the crane's wings. The fingertip strikes used in katas of Uechi ryu are modeled after the crane's beak, kakushiken and koken.

龍虎鶴

THE PATH OF AN

亜錬拿羅

AIMLESS WANDERER

DIRECTIONLESS AND UNEXPLOITED YOUTH

Like many teenagers today I had a burning desire to learn karate. Karate schools in America were rare in the early 1960's. My family was so poor that lessons would have been out of the question even if there had been a karate school located next door.

I began learning karate from the small number of books available, much like Daniel-san in the original Karate *Kid* movie. Kicking the tops of door-ways, practicing moves pictured in the books, doing pushups and rubbing the skin off the edge of my hands with sandpaper constituted the self taught karate workout. The training proved ineffective against the alterca-tions that plagued me.

We moved a lot so I was always the new guy in school. I had the gift of running my mouth and I sometimes expressed my opinions to the wrong person, at the wrong time. When singled out by school bullies I did not have the sense to be quiet or back down. I lost far more altercations than I won.

Shortly after high school I began working the night shift in a printing plant in the industrial area of Oakland, California, while attending college during the day. I also worked as a cadet at a local police department and as a campus police officer at college.

I began boxing at night in the factory under the guidance of a former Golden Gloves champion from Oakland. I often spent the lunch break at 4:00 A.M. at the back of the warehouse fighting for my life against the large, rough looking factory workers.

At 6' 4" in height and weighing only 160 pounds, I did not possess much power. I was so skinny that co-workers called me "Allen Wrench," after a skinny metal tool used in our job. I remember sometimes finishing the nights work with a pounding headache from the repeated head blows I received during the fights.

As I developed reach, increased my pain threshold and overcame the fear of the situation I started winning more of the matches. It was not the karate training I had desired but it was a good lesson about fighting, not sport.

In the early 1970's, I boxed in the Golden Gloves circuit in Oakland, during the peak of the Mohammed Ali-Joe Frazier rivalry. I developed a keen interest in the science of fighting.

The Vietnam war was raging during that time, as were the anti-war protests in America. The hippie movement was in full swing, and attitudes in America were changing quickly and radically. It was a highly charged era in our country's history.

I was already married with children, so I was not inducted into military service during the peak of the Vietnam War. I got caught up in the turbulence of the times and dropped out of college, quit the police force, let my hair grow and bought a motorcycle. I maintained steady employment but my lifestyle and attitude began to deteriorate. When I recognized this I sought a way back to a positive productive direction. In my usual manner of opting for the extreme solution, I enlisted in the United States Marine Corps and entered boot camp in May, 1973.

In the Marine Corps each man is in constant competition with the next in every activity. I found this environment extremely exhilarating and difficult. I challenged myself to excel in every area of endeavor.

An extensive battery of intelligence tests administered in basic training placed me in the top two percent, qualifying me for communications intelligence work. I relinquished my Military Police enlistment guarantee to work in top secret communications intercept and electronic warfare.

Electronic warfare training was conducted in Pensicola, Florida. While there, I was appointed squad leader as well as receiving a second meritorious promotion in rank, less than one year into my enlistment.

Other Marines and I met daily in the gym for weight training and rounds of boxing. The afternoon training was optional, the daily three mile run at 5:00 A.M. was mandatory. The skinny kid from high school was now a fit 205 pounds with eight percent body fat.

I attended my first karate tournament, as a spectator, during that time. The tournament was held in an auditorium in Mobile, Alabama. The guest of honor was actor Robert Conrad, who had been selected because of his frequent use of martial arts in the television series "Wild Wild West". The tournament itself was not particularly impressive and certainly not very traditional.

At the conclusion of two different intelligence schools I was informed I had completed the self-paced academy faster than anyone in the history of the institution. I anxiously awaited orders, hoping they would be for somewhere in Asia. I remember the exhilaration at receiving orders to Okinawa. From the books read as a teenager, I knew I was going to the homeland of karate.

Entering the Marine Corps and being selected for top secret intelligence work were determining factors that placed me in Okinawa. The physical and mental competitiveness of the Marine Corps was responsible for me being in the most superb mental and physical shape of my life when I arrived on the "Island of Karate".

◆上地琉 カデナ 修武館 創立14周年記念◆

KARATE TRAINING IN OKINAWA

I began karate training, on base, the day after I arrived in Okinawa. Classes were taught in the gym twice a week by Shorin ryu Sensei Fuse Kise. I found the katas and structure of a karate class interesting. I dominated the other students, who were all American servicemen and women, in two-person drills and sparring.

Something was missing from the training. I longed for the traditional atmosphere of an Okinawan dojo and began my search to find one. I soon found the Uechi ryu dojo of Seiyu Shinjo in the nearby town of Kadena.

I remember vividly the night I slid open the worn door and peered into the diminutive Kadena dojo. The strength and intensity displayed in all aspects of the following three-hour workout were fascinating.

I was in the best shape of my life and had been boxing regularly, so I was not intimidated by many people. Yet the way these small, muscular people moved was daunting. Their speed and power, and their extreme level of body conditioning were unsettling. It was easy to imagine what these men could do to an adversary, with their superior ability and physical state. I knew I had found my dojo!

I approached Sensei Shinjo at the end of the night and requested admission. He nodded his head and went through the procedures of signing me up in a non-interested manner. I later realized that he probably viewed me as another American who would not stay in his dojo long because of the intense level of training there. There were times when I thought he may be right; I might not make it.

The personality and explosive teaching style of Sensei Seiyu Shinjo, of the Kadena dojo, are renowned in Okinawa. The complete history of this man and his karate family can be found in Chapter III.

Kadena dojo was the most active Uechi ryu dojo on the island. Sensei Shinjo was involved in every local or national karate demonstration that occurred. That gave us much experience performing under the pressure of an auditorium full of Okinawan people.

I was stationed at Torri Station Army base and worked at the Hanza communications intercept site in Yomitan. The site is built on the old Yontan runways used by Japanese aircraft during World War II. It offers a commanding view of the East China Sea and the Okinawa's coastline, all the way to Naha I served as a Mission Controller for top secret security missions, performing my duties underground behind cipher locked doors manned with armed guards.

Duty rotated from two day watches, two night watches and two evening watches in a four day period. Shifts alternated between eight hours of work and sixteen hours of work every other day. A three day break at the end of the cycle was used to catch up on sleep before starting the grueling routine again. The Marine Corps often conducted training during the three "off" days so we would not become too complacent around the Army and Navy. No disrespect intended, Marines are Marines.

Seiyu Shinjo taught a two hour class at 1:00 P.M. daily and a three hour class at 7:00 P.M. nightly, every day except Sunday. Day class consisted of one to six students, mostly American servicemen. The evening class included students of all ages and ranks, mostly Okinawans. Both formats offered remarkable instruction.

I would awake, often after only two hours sleep, don a gi and go to the dojo for the day or evening class. I would finish sleeping after training and report for duty. During the three days of break I trained in both the day and night classes. It was also necessary to maintain the Marine Corps physical fitness standards. Tests for pull-ups, sit-ups and a three mile run were usually administered at 7:00 A.M., after the night watch.

Day classes at the dojo were precious moments of time, often one on one, with Seiyu Shinjo. Night classes offered the challenge of training with Okinawan black belts of amazing ability.

The Okinawan black belts took advantage of my size, fitness and lack of karate ability by soundly beating me in sparring, in spite of any prior training I had. This proved to me the effectiveness of karate and increased my determination to become as proficient as my seniors.

Kiyohide Shinjo was the worst. He was winning the Uechi ryu sparring championship every year. He prepared for the championship by severely beating the rest of us in the dojo. His presence and fighting ability were remarkable. We are one year apart in age but light years apart in ability.

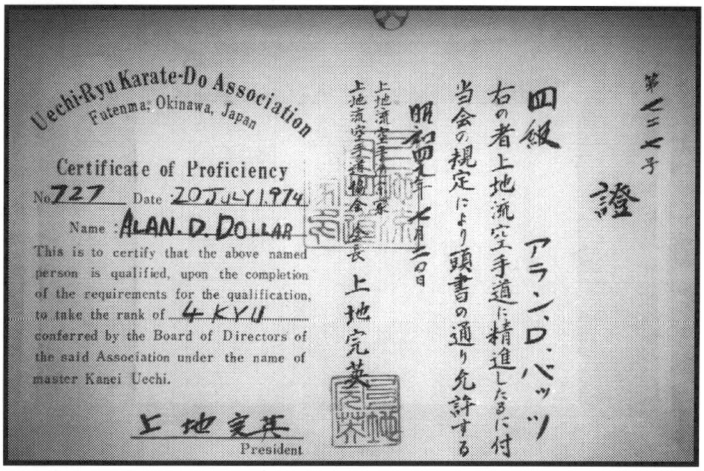

Uechi-Ryu Karate-Do Association
Futenma, Okinawa, Japan

Certificate of Proficiency
No. 727 Date 20 JULY 1974
Name : ALAN. D. DOLLAR
This is to certify that the above named person is qualified, upon the completion of the requirements for the qualification, to take the rank of 4 KYU conferred by the Board of Directors of the said Association under the name of master Kanei Uechi.

上地完英
President

第七二七号
證
四級
アラン、D、バッツ
右の者上地流空手道に精進したるに付
当会の規定により頭書の通り允許する
昭和四九年七月二〇日
上地流空手道宗家
上地流空手道協会 会長 上地完英

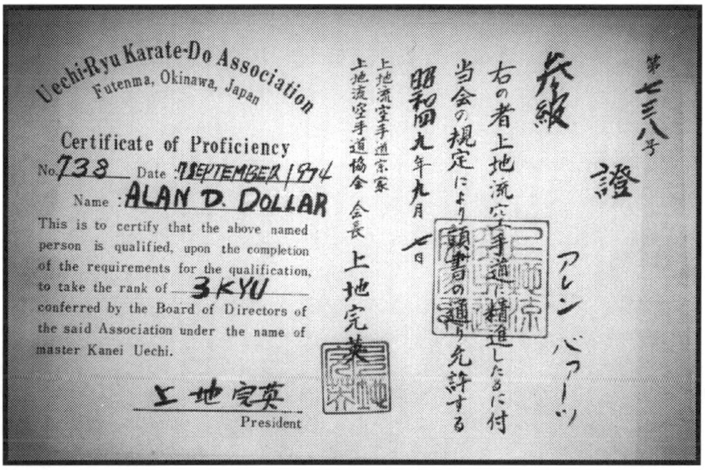

Uechi-Ryu Karate-Do Association
Futenma, Okinawa, Japan

Certificate of Proficiency
No. 738 Date 7 SEPTEMBER 1974
Name : ALAN D. DOLLAR
This is to certify that the above named person is qualified, upon the completion of the requirements for the qualification, to take the rank of 3 KYU conferred by the Board of Directors of the said Association under the name of master Kanei Uechi.

上地完英
President

第七三八号
證
参級
アレン バァーツ
右の者上地流空手道に精進したるに付
当会の規定により頭書の通り允許する
昭和四九年九月七日
上地流空手道宗家
上地流空手道協会 会長 上地完英

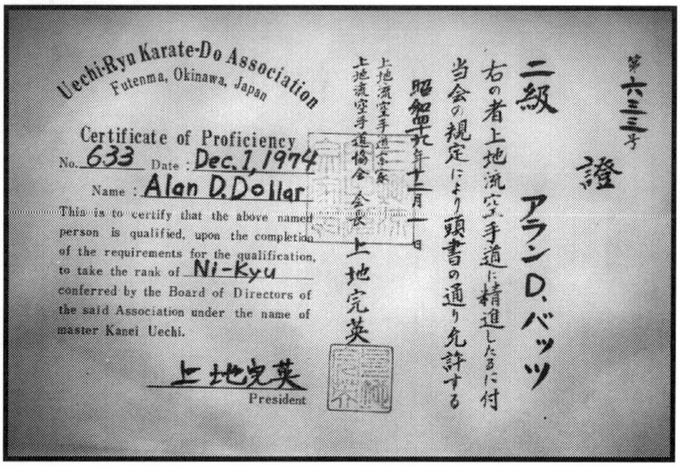

Uechi-Ryu Karate-Do Association
Futenma, Okinawa, Japan

Certificate of Proficiency
No. 633 Date Dec. 1, 1974
Name : Alan D. Dollar
This is to certify that the above named person is qualified, upon the completion of the requirements for the qualification, to take the rank of Ni-Kyu conferred by the Board of Directors of the said Association under the name of master Kanei Uechi.

上地完英
President

第六三三号
證
二級
アランD.バッツ
右の者上地流空手道に精進したるに付
当会の規定により頭書の通り允許する
昭和四九年十二月一日
上地流空手道宗家
上地流空手道協会 会長 上地完英

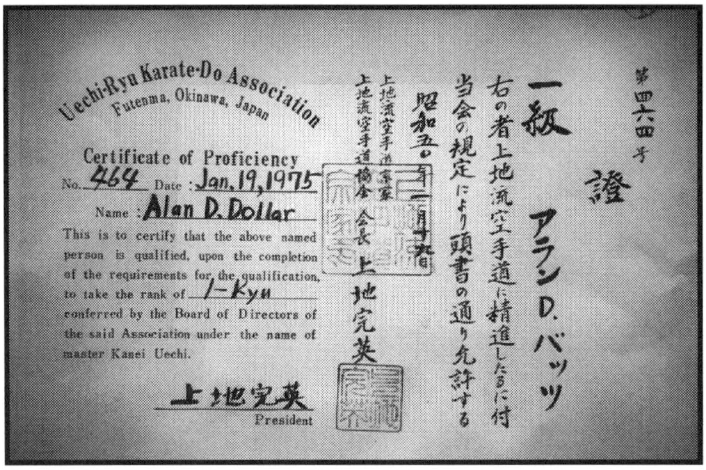

Uechi-Ryu Karate-Do Association
Futenma, Okinawa, Japan

Certificate of Proficiency

No. 464 Date : Jan. 19, 1975

Name : Alan D. Dollar

This is to certify that the above named person is qualified, upon the completion of the requirements for the qualification, to take the rank of 1-Kyu conferred by the Board of Directors of the said Association under the name of master Kanei Uechi.

上地完英
President

第四六四号

一級 證

アラン D. バッツ

右の者上地流空手道に精進したるに付
当会の規定により頭書の通り允許する

昭和五〇年一月十九日

上地流空手道宗家
上地流空手道協会 会長 上地完英

I never enjoyed sparring with him and often received injuries. The burning stare of Kiyohide Shinjo's eyes during sparring became my new standard of toughness and indestructibility.

I sparred extensively with Takamei Takayasu, who regularly placed second behind Kiyohide Shinjo in the annual Uechi ryu tournament. Mr. Takayasu now teaches Uechi ryu in France and Italy.

I completed all colored belt tests in the Kadena dojo and tested for black belt, *Shodan*, in the Futenma dojo before Kanei Uechi and the Uechi Ryu Karate Association on May 18, 1975.

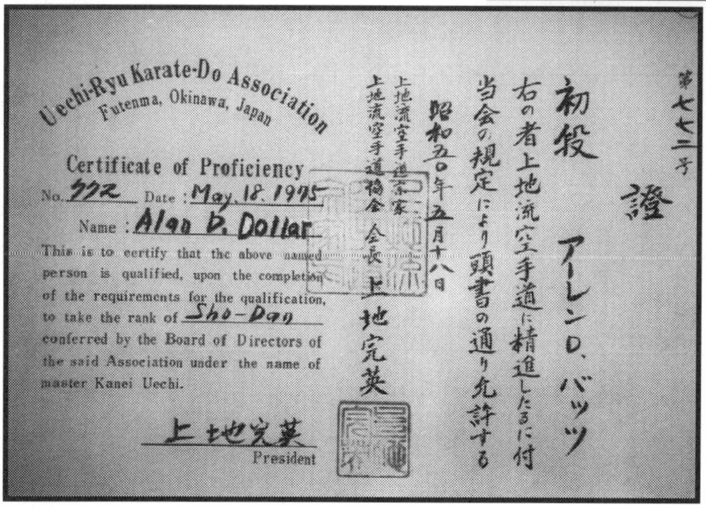

Uechi-Ryu Karate-Do Association
Futenma, Okinawa, Japan

Certificate of Proficiency

No. 772 Date: May. 18. 1975

Name: Alan D. Dollar

This is to certify that the above named person is qualified, upon the completion of the requirements for the qualification, to take the rank of Sho-Dan conferred by the Board of Directors of the said Association under the name of master Kanei Uechi.

上地完英
President

第七七二号

證

初段

アーレンD、バッツ

右の者上地流空手道に精進したるに付
当会の規定により頭書の通り允許する

昭和五〇年五月十八日

上地流空手道宗家
上地流空手道協会 会長 上地完英

I then began weapons training under Uechi ryu instructor Katsukiho Minowa, from the Naha dojo (Chapter IV). Kobudo instruction was not allowed until a black belt was earned in karate.

I continued kobudo training under Sensei Minowa until the end of my first tour in Okinawa. He had moved to Japan by the time I returned to Okinawa.

I remain a student of kobudo instructor Masakazu Kinjo. Sensei Kinjo began training under Sensei Minowa one year before I did. I also continue kobudo training under Yoshitsune Senaga and Shinyu Gushi and occasionally from Shinpo Matayoshi.

I visited Futenma dojo one day shortly after being promoted to Shodan and arranged to work out in Grand Master Kanei Uechi's class that day. I continued visiting whenever possible to receive further training from the Grand Master.

I naively thought that Sensei Shinjo might not find out I was visiting the Futenma dojo, but he did. I explained that I wanted to take the unique opportunity to train under Grand Master Uechi because of his history and prestigious position in Uechi ryu karate. The visits were approved because of the profound friendship between Kanei Uechi and Seiyu Shinjo

Both men had been taught directly by Kanbun Uechi yet they both taught in a very different manner. The soft approach of Kanei Uechi balanced the hard approach of Seiyu Shinjo. Together they epitomized Uechi ryu karate do.

I competed in the annual Uechi ryu tournament the same year I became a black belt. I placed fourteenth out of forty-five black belts representing all the Uechi ryu dojos of Okinawa.

The tournament was held in two stages. The first stage, kata competition, took place in the Futenma dojo. Sparring was held the following week at Kokusai University.

I had the opportunity to travel to Korea and Taiwan for short periods. While there I was able to train in styles from Kung fu to Tae Kwon Do.

Most Americans who trained in the dojos then were servicemen. I befriended three American civilians who had come to live in Okinawa to study karate. They were Peter Kellogg, from Kadena dojo and Arbie Kennefick and David Scott from the Futenma dojo. David Scott now heads an organization in England. Peter Kellogg and Arbie Kinnefick still live in Okinawa.

Leaving Okinawa was a depressing undertaking. The day I left Okinawa was the saddest day of my life. My sayonara party had been held the night before. At the end of the party Seiyu Shinjo and I stood outside in a downpour saying our good-byes. He leaned his forehead against my chest and we both cried. I felt like a son leaving his father.

I had grown up without much parental guidance or a dominant male figure. I always enjoyed the freedom from supervision but often found myself in trouble because of it.

Seiyu Shinjo was the strongest father figure in my life. He taught much more than karate. He taught people to be strong and to use that strength for good purposes. He was a ferocious karate man when in the dojo. When he was engaged in casual conversation a soft, warm personality came forth. He genuinely cared about people.

HAWAII TOUR OF DUTY AND A RETURN TO OKINAWA

Kaneohe Bay Hawaii was the first Marine base on which I was stationed. The intercept mission now changed to a tactical one. The rather easy life of living with the Army or Navy now gave way to the demanding daily training regimen of the Marines.

While stationed in Hawaii I trained under Gunnery Sergeant Richard Raymond, a Shorin ryu instructor on base. "Gunny" had spent a lot of time in Okinawa and was married to an Okinawan woman. I earned a Shodan in Shorin ryu but have not practiced the style since. I learned a lot from him about teaching Okinawan karate to westerners, especially children. I also taught Uechi ryu karate to Marines in his unit during afternoon physical training time.

Full contact karate was gaining popularity in America. The Professional Karate Association (PKA) was just forming. The full contact fights promoted by the organization were the forerunner of todays, media magnified, slugfests. The bloody combat bore no resemblance to traditional karate, from which it had started.

Gunny Raymond and I gathered a few other black belts and formed a full contact sparring team to represent the Marine Corps in knock-out matches around the island.

The matches were brutal displays of blood and guts, held in boxing rings or gym floors on various military bases around Oahu. The embryonic stages of American kick boxing closely resembled a street fight in a ring. It was reminiscent of the boxing matches held in the warehouse in Oakland several years earlier except with more blood. Rules were not well defined and the officials not very qualified.

The only protection we wore were the thin dipped foam hand pads common in karate practice today. My knuckles often tore through the gloves and cut my opponent's face. I experienced more facial contusions during that time than any era of training.

I fought my way to the title: Military Heavyweight Full Contact Champion of Hawaii in 1976. After three successful title defenses I volunteered for a special exercise that would be my ticket back to Okinawa.

At the completion of "Operation Bearing Thunder" in Korea, half of the intelligence detachment would continue on to Okinawa. The six month assignment in Okinawa was to assist the Army at the intercept sight located at Torri Station, five miles from the Kadena dojo. I lobbied until I was insured a position on the second phase of the operation.

On this, my second trip to Korea, I lived for a month in the field with Republic of Korea (ROK) Marines. They fashion themselves after the U.S. Marines and are very disciplined and conditioned. We would clear out an operations tent and hold mini karate tournaments: American Marines versus Korean Marines.

American Marines were always ready to fight but only a few of them really knew karate. Some were easy prey for the ROK Marines who were very tough and persistent. Fortunately I was much bigger than they were. This advantage with the close range methods of Uechi ryu karate proved quite effective.

I became a camp hero during that month and developed enormous respect for ROK Marines. Except the one who tried to shoot me.

During one of the evenings of sparring, one Korean became very angry after I had just won a match. I didn't understand the language but assumed he felt I had been too hard on the smaller man. He quickly chambered a round and took the safety off his rifle. Before he could make another move I had slipped under the tent flap and made a fast exit from the area.

Back in Okinawa for the second time, I immediately visited the Kadena dojo. The homecoming was overwhelming. Peter Kellogg, who started in the dojo three months before me, was still training diligently. Marty Dow, who had started just prior to my departure from Okinawa, was still active also. At the same time a senior American student of the Kadena dojo, John Ray, arrived unexpectedly from the Sinai desert. The reunion was electric. The group of Americans vowed their dedication to Uechi ryu karate and the Shinjo Kadena dojo.

I tested in Futenma and was promoted by the Uechi Ryu Association to second degree black belt, *Nidan*, on May 15, 1977. I had already made the decision to devote all my efforts to teaching karate after returning to Hawaii.

I presented my complete training experience to date and explained my devotion to Uechi ryu karate to Kanei Uechi and Seiyu Shinjo. I requested permission to teach Uechi ryu karate in Hawaii and later in America after my discharge. Kanei Uechi presented me with an instructor's certificate, *Jun Shihan*.

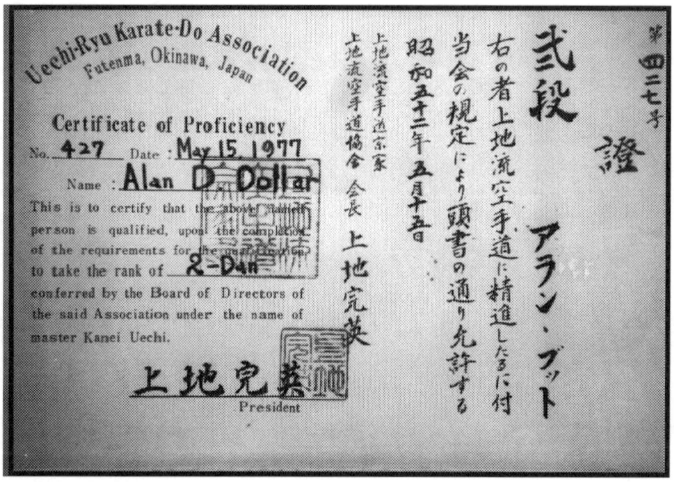

Uechi-Ryu Karate-Do Association
Futenma, Okinawa, Japan

Certificate of Proficiency

No. 427 Date : May 15, 1977

Name : Alan D. Dollar

This is to certify that the above named person is qualified, upon the completion of the requirements for the qualification to take the rank of 2-Dan conferred by the Board of Directors of the said Association under the name of master Kanei Uechi.

上地完英
President

第四二七号

證

弐段

アラン・ブット

右の者上地流空手道に精進したるに付
当会の規定により頭書の通り允許する
昭和五十二年五月十五日

上地流空手道宗家
上地流空手道協会 会長 上地完英

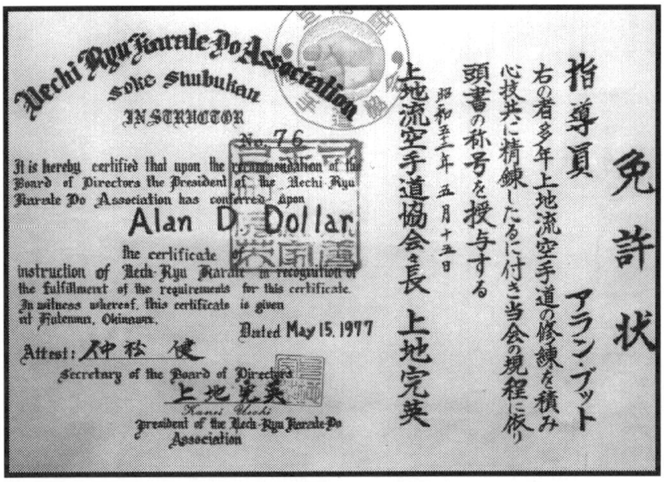

Uechi Ryu Karate Do Association
Soke Shubukan
INSTRUCTOR
No. 76

It is hereby certified that upon the recommendation of the Board of Directors the President of the Uechi-Ryu Karate Do Association has conferred upon

Alan D. Dollar

the certificate of instruction of Uechi-Ryu Karate in recognition of the fulfillment of the requirements for this certificate. In witness whereof, this certificate is given at Futenma, Okinawa.

Dated May 15, 1977

Attest: 仲松 健
Secretary of the Board of Directors

上地完英
Kanei Uechi
President of the Uechi-Ryu Karate Do Association

免許状

指導員 アラン・ブット

右の者多年上地流空手道の修錬を積み心技共に精錬したるに付き当会の規程に依り頭書の称号を授与する

昭和五二年五月十五日

上地流空手道協会々長 上地完英

The second parting from Okinawa was somewhat easier because it did not carry the finality of the first departure. It was understood I would be back to Okinawa.

I retired from full contact competition and devoted my time and energy to running a formal class of Uechi ryu karate. During subsequent detachments to Okinawa my students would train at Kadena dojo. Letters from Okinawa explained that Seiyu Shinjo was surprised, and quite pleased, at receiving students from Hawaii who already knew Sanchin and Kanshiwa katas.

硬軟自在
上地完文
上地完英

While on special assignment to Fort Devons, Massachusetts, I had the opportunity to train at the famous dojo of George Mattson, whom I had met in Okinawa.

後の先

RETURNING TO AMERICA

The return to civilian life and the cultural adjustment involved took longer than anticipated. Five years passed before the work schedule in my career allowed for the time to teach karate on a regular basis. During that five year period I maintained a regimen of kata, weightlifting, running and an occasional sparring match; sometimes planned, sometimes not. Weight training had reshaped my body into a muscular 225 pounds. Karate training enhanced the movement and application of that power.

Seiyu Shinjo died at an early age in 1981. All of his students, at home and abroad, were devastated. Peter Kellogg was the only member of the American group who was fortunate enough to be with Sensei Shinjo all the way to the end.

I converted my garage into a traditional Okinawan dojo and resumed teaching Uechi ryu karate again in 1982. I soon realized it was time to return to Okinawa for further training.

I could not imagine anyone replacing Seiyu Shinjo, except his son, nine time Okinawan Karate Champion, Kiyohide Shinjo. I enjoy his presence in the dojo much more as a Sensei than I did as a competitor.

During that visit I was promoted, by Kanei Uechi, to third degree black belt, *Sandan*, on November 4, 1982.

Uechi-Ryu
Karate Do

Uechiryu Karatedo Association
Certificate of Proficiency
RANK San-Dan
Name Alan Dollar
It is hereby certified that, upon the recommendation of the President of the Uechi Karate Organization concerned the Committee of Promotion Examinations in Okinawa has conferred the above-inscribed rank on the above mentioned person in recognition of the satisfactory fulfillment of the requirements for the rank.
Kanei Uechi
President of the Uechiryu Karatedo Association
証
アラン ドーラー
右は上地流空手道に精練したるに付き本会の昇段審査規程に依り頭書の段位を授与する
上地流空手道協会
会長 上地完英

The first Antioch Uechi Ryu Dojo

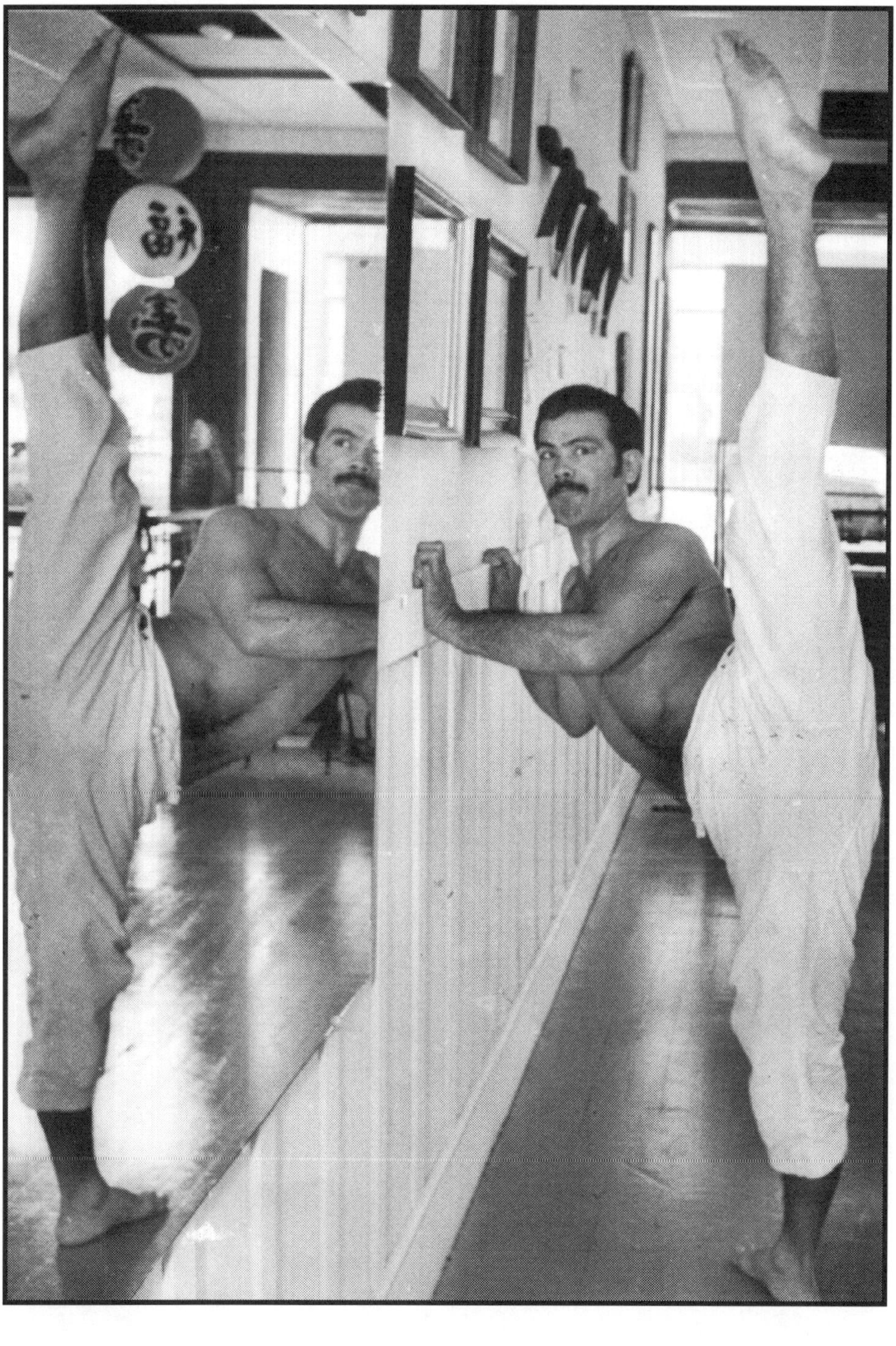

After returning to the United States, classes outgrew the garage facility. I leased a building and opened the first public Uechi ryu dojo in the San Francisco Bay Area. The humble dojo hosted visits from Tsutomu Nakahodo, Kiyohide Shinjo, Kanmei Uechi and Narahiro Shinjo.

First West Coast Uechi Ryu Tournament, 1982

I returned to Okinawa again in 1984 for further training. I was promoted, again in Futenma dojo by Kanei Uechi, to fourth degree black belt, *Yondan*, on November 11, 1984.

Sparring with Mark Brelsford

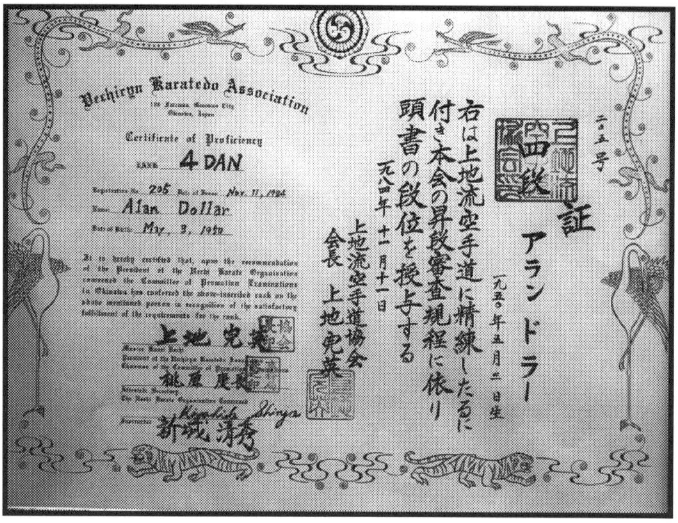

My commitment to teaching Uechi ryu karate grew. I began building a traditional dojo of Okinawan design. I continued working at my job, teaching karate and building the new dojo, commitments that required eighty hour work weeks for one year.

Soon after construction began I returned to Okinawa for further training and to announce the news of the new dojo. I tested for fifth degree black belt, *Godan* on November 13, 1987. I was also presented with Master Instructors Certificate number ninety-six, *Shihan.*

Kanei Uechi was very ill then. Kansei Uechi, Kanei's brother, died while I was in Okinawa..

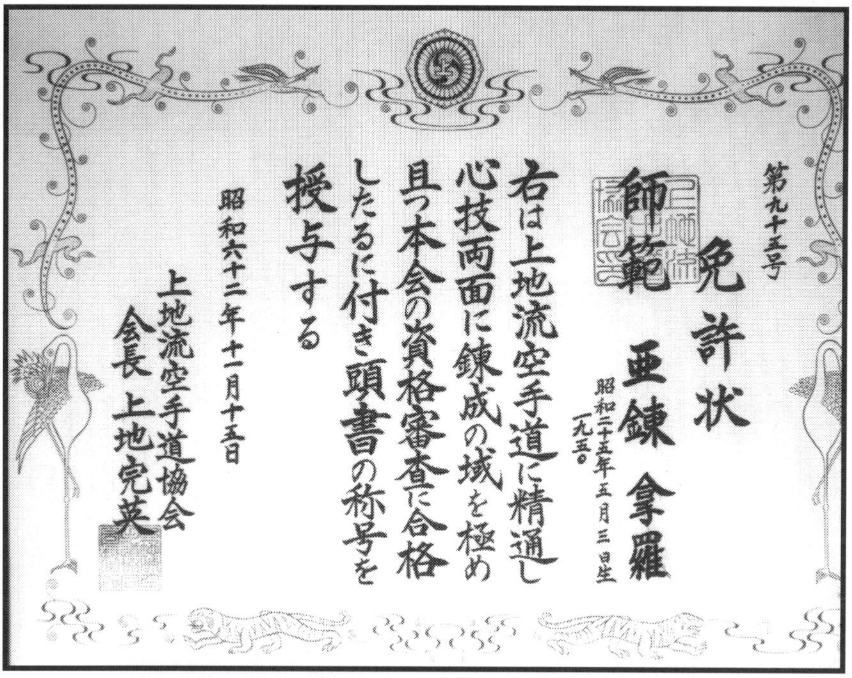

第九十五号

免許状

師範

亜錬 拿羅

昭和二十五年五月三日生 一九五〇

右は上地流空手道に精通し
心技両面に錬成の域を極め
且つ本会の資格審査に合格
したるに付き頭書の称号を
授与する

昭和六十二年十一月十五日

上地流空手道協会
会長 上地完英

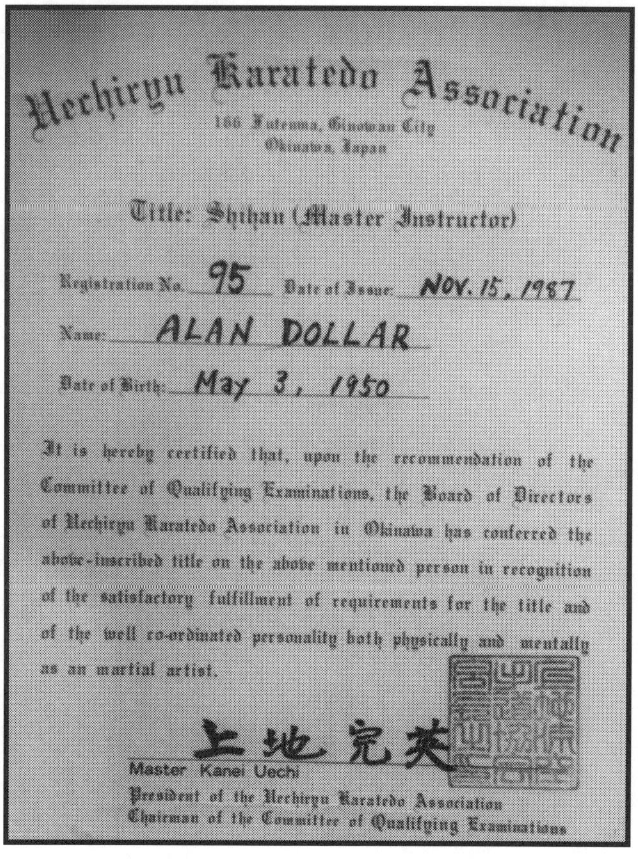

Uechiryu Karatedo Association

186 Futema, Ginowan City
Okinawa, Japan

Title: Shihan (Master Instructor)

Registration No. 95 Date of Issue: NOV. 15, 1987

Name: ALAN DOLLAR

Date of Birth: May 3, 1950

It is hereby certified that, upon the recommendation of the Committee of Qualifying Examinations, the Board of Directors of Uechiryu Karatedo Association in Okinawa has conferred the above-inscribed title on the above mentioned person in recognition of the satisfactory fulfillment of requirements for the title and of the well co-ordinated personality both physically and mentally as an martial artist.

上地完英
Master Kanei Uechi
President of the Uechiryu Karatedo Association
Chairman of the Committee of Qualifying Examinations

Antioch, Uechi Ryu Kenyukai Shububkan

The finished look of the new Antioch dojo was inspired by the remarkable appearance of Ric Martin's Largo, Florida, dojo

FORTIFYING THE COMMITMENT TO KARATE

By April, 1988, five black belts and I completed construction of the Uechi Ryu Karate Kenyukai Shubukan. It is truly one of the most unique karate dojos in the world. On May 11, 1988, I quit my job and became a professional karate instructor.

I feel very fortunate to be one of a handful of karate men to fulfill the dream of building my own facility, designed for and dedicated to, karate instruction. Ric Martin in Florida, Buzz Dirkin in New Hampshire and I are the only three Uechi ryu instructors in America to have accomplished this prodigious feat.

To up-date and enhance my knowledge of physical fitness training outside karate, I attended the Cooper Institute for Aerobics Research in 1992. I recommend this facility to any serious athlete or physical fitness instructor. Upon graduation I was certified as a physical fitness specialist and personal trainer.

I was promoted to sixth degree black belt *Renshi, Rokudan,* by Shinyu Gushi, James Thompson and Kiyohide Shinjo on August 7, 1992. The test was held in the Kenyukai Shubukan, Antioch California.

While residing in Okinawa twice and returning for training eight times, to this point, I achieved all colored and black belt tests from white belt through Godan in Okinawa. Each test was performed with many other candidates during regularly scheduled testing. Both Jun Shihan and Shihan licenses were issued by the unified Uechi Ryui Karate Do Association.

Uechiryu Karatedo Kenyukai
第四号
證
錬士六段
右は本会の称号段位審査
規程により頭書の通り允許する
平成四年八月七日
会長 新城清秀
RANK: 6 DAN
ALAN D. DOLLAR
KIYOHIDE SHINJO

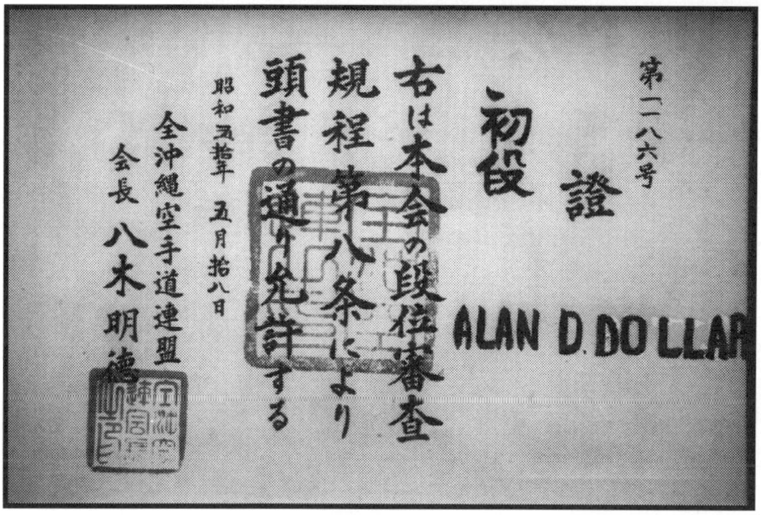
第一二八六号
證
初段
ALAN D. DOLLAR
右は本会の段位審査
規程第八条により
頭書の通り允許する
昭和五拾年 五月拾八日
全沖縄空手道連盟
会長 八木明徳

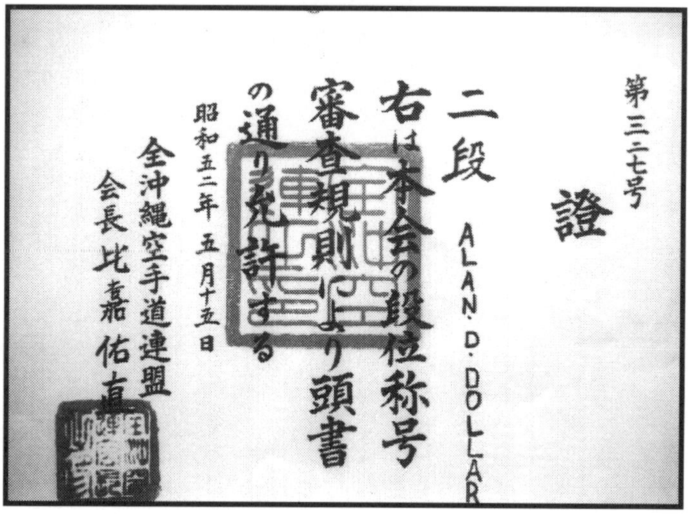
第三二七号
證
二段
ALAN·D·DOLLAR
右は本会の段位称号
審査規則により頭書
の通り允許する
昭和五二年 五月十五日
全沖縄空手道連盟
会長 比嘉佑直

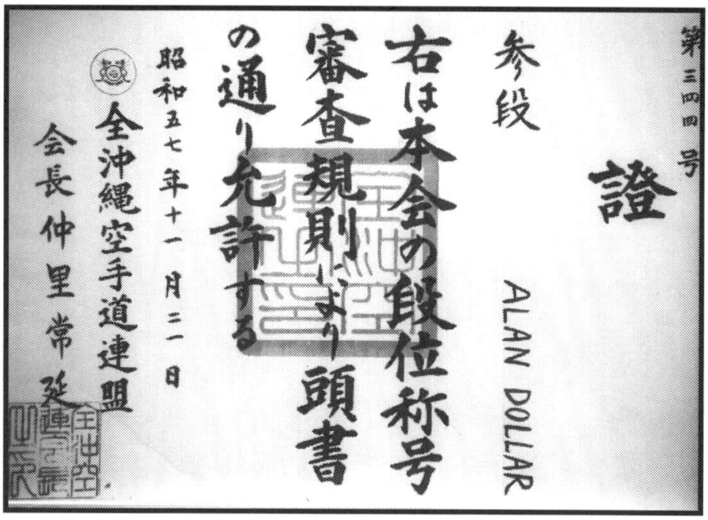
第三四四号

證

参段

ALAN DOLLAR

右は本会の段位称号審査規則により頭書の通り允許する

昭和五七年十一月二一日

全沖縄空手道連盟

会長仲里常延

Previously, when testing in Okinawa, all black belt ranks through Yondan were also certified by the All Okinawa Karate Association. A formal test is required for fifth degree black belt. On November 14, 1993, I tested and was promoted to Godan in that Association.

I have traveled extensively across America and to other countries over the last fourteen years for training in various traditional styles, and for tournament competition in kata, kobudo and kumite. I have taught Uechi ryu karate, kobudo, defense and physical fitness seminars across America, in Okinawa, Canada, Germany and continue to receive requests to teach in other countries.

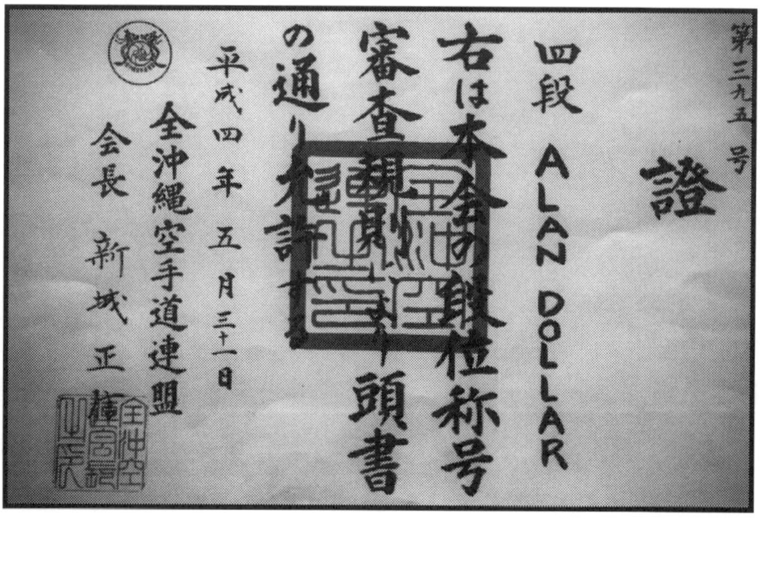
第三九五号

證

四段

ALAN DOLLAR

右は本会の段位称号審査規則により頭書の通り允許する

平成四年五月三十一日

全沖縄空手道連盟

会長 新城正[illegible]

第一八四号

證

五段　亜錬拿羅

右は本会の段位称号
審査規則により頭書
の通り允許する

平成五年十一月十四日

全沖縄空手道連盟
会長　翁長良光

I sponsored the first Uechi ryu tournament on the West Coast. The event became an international black belt tournament by the twelfth annual tournament in 1995.

The event had grown to be the largest Uechi ryu only karate tournament in the world. The series also holds the distinction of being the first American Uechi ryu tournament attended by Okinawan competitors. I retired the tournament series in 1995.

The Sparring Grand Champion in the sayonara year was Ikyua Higa from Okinawa. Mr. Higa went on to win the sparring championship in the World Pre-tournament held in Okinawa in August, 1995.

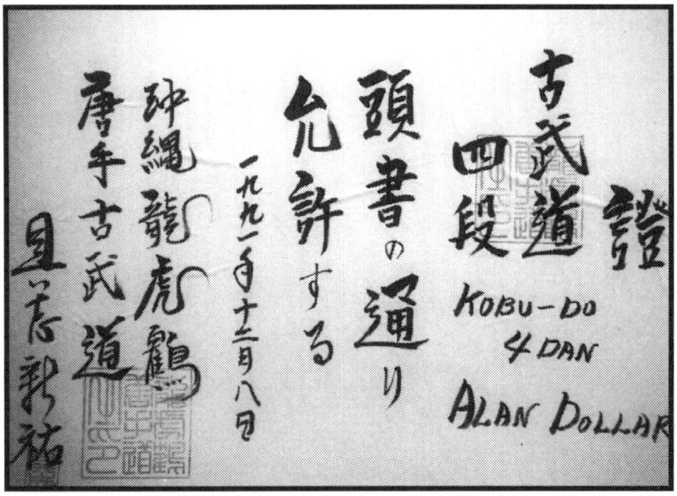

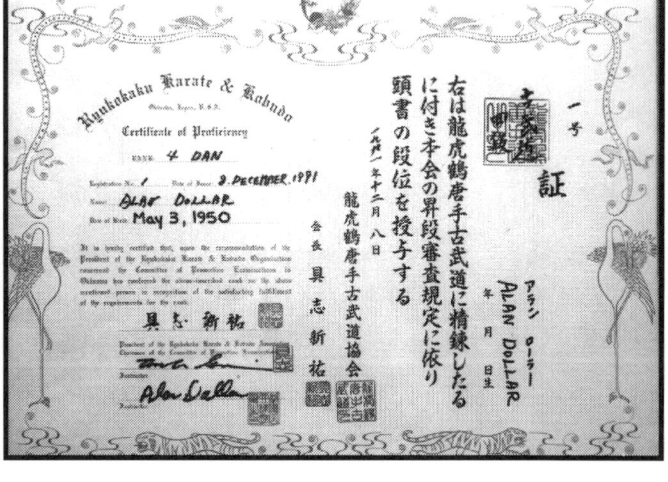

A special Uechi ryu note: Narahiro Shinjo, Kadena dojo, placed fourth in kata and Satoshi Kinjo, Kubagawa dojo, placed second in kobudo (sai) in that Okinawan Karate World Tournament.

I continue kobudo training in America under Shinyu Gushi (Chapter IV, Kobudo). I was promoted to *Yondan* on December 3, 1991, in Master Gushi's Ryu Ko Kaku Ken Association. I am scheduled to test for G*odan* in May, 1996.

To increase awareness of Uechi ryu karate world wide I have written magazine articles that have been published in five countries. I also produced a video series documenting the Uechi ryu style. It has been sold in fifteen countries and the majority of the United States. Future publications will explore Uechi ryu karate and kobudo in America.

All men possess an inherent desire to be strong, both physically and mentally. It has been man's historic role to defend the home, castle, farm and so forth. The desire to be courageous and strong enough to protect himself against violence is instinctive.

Past cultures faced adversities that required the cultivation of internal and physical strength. Todays world is more refined than it has ever been. Violence is still rampant and wars and conflicts still occur around the world yet the ability for man to survive by his own hand has diminished. The modern trend is to not get involved and avoid taking responsibility for yourself or your actions.

The technical society of today breeds masses, not warriors. One must seek training besides one's normal lifestyle to develop courage and combative strength. The martial arts have always been an excellent tool for this purpose.

Physical strength and mental fortitude are interdependent in the martial arts. Without developing mental strength and self-discipline, a physically strong person may easily be led down the wrong path. To gain mental strength, a strong, healthy body is necessary. Physical fitness breeds mental alertness.

The most imposing adversary to overcome in this quest is yourself. Balancing oneself and developing self-discipline are the underlying principles of karate practice. To overcome external adversity you must first learn to overcome internal adversity.

I am indebted to Okinawan Uechi ryu karate and the great people who have taught me for instilling this strength. Thank you for showing this aimless wanderer the correct path to follow!

Joe Lewis

Fumio Demura

Andre Tippet

Shintoku Takara

The Michigan summer camp of James Thompson.
Sensei Thompson is one of the world leaders of Uechi ryu karate

Washington D.C. Dojo— Sensei Marty Dow

Edmonton Canada Dojo— Sensei Neil Dunnigan

Kiyohide Shinjo tests Alice Dollar's Sanchin stance

Akira Tskyama

Karate demonstration at Shuri Castle

Alan Dollar's first taiko drum performance in Okinawa

Vice Governor of Okinawa, Mitsuko Tomon

Mr. and Mrs. Nakamatsu, Nobohiro Higa and Shinyu Gushi in Largo, Florida

Uechi Ryu Kenyukai Dojo in Vietsholsheim, Germany— Sensei Andreas Haberzetl. Sensei Haberzetl has propagated Uechi ryu karate in Germany.

Okinawan Karate World Championship

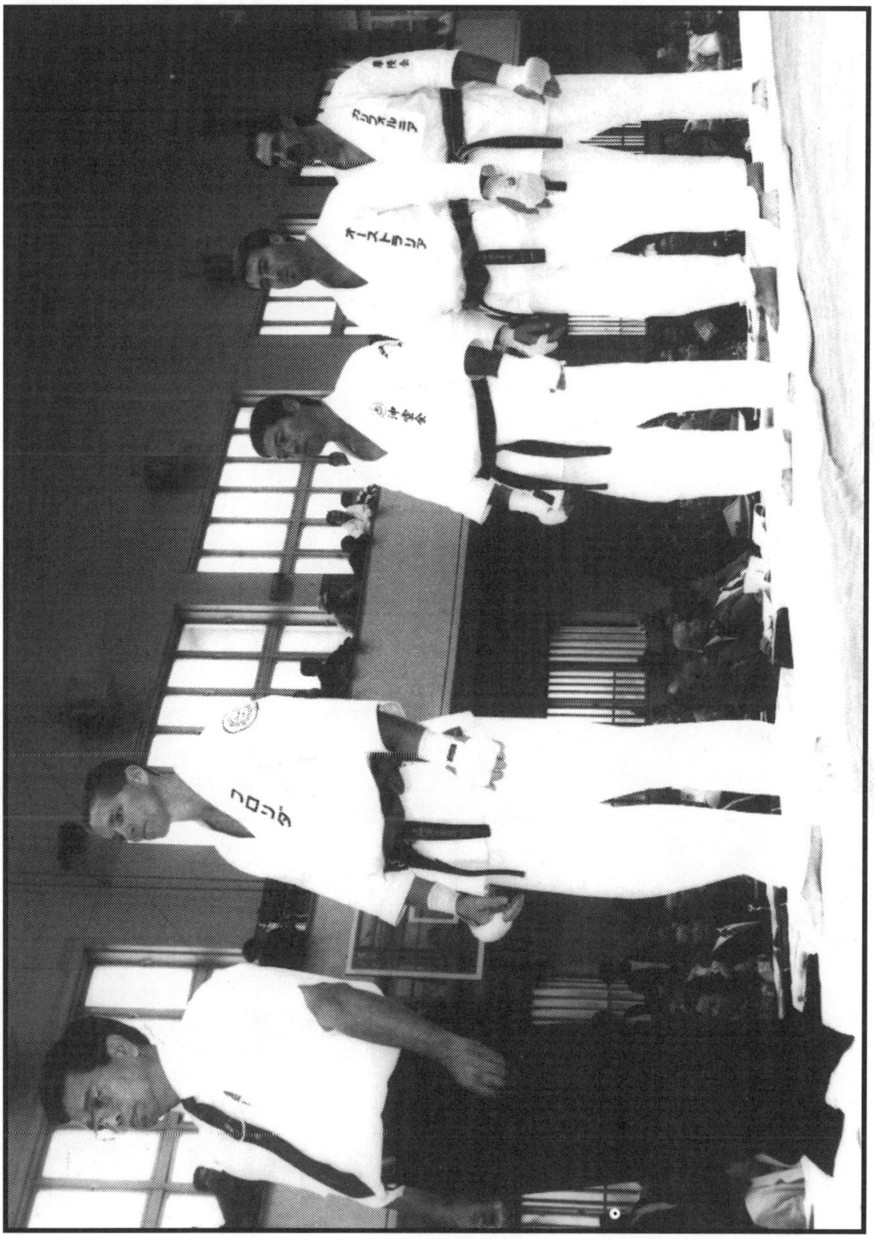

"Best Eight" Finalists, 1990

Nigel Mansell and the USA Team in Okinawa, December 1994

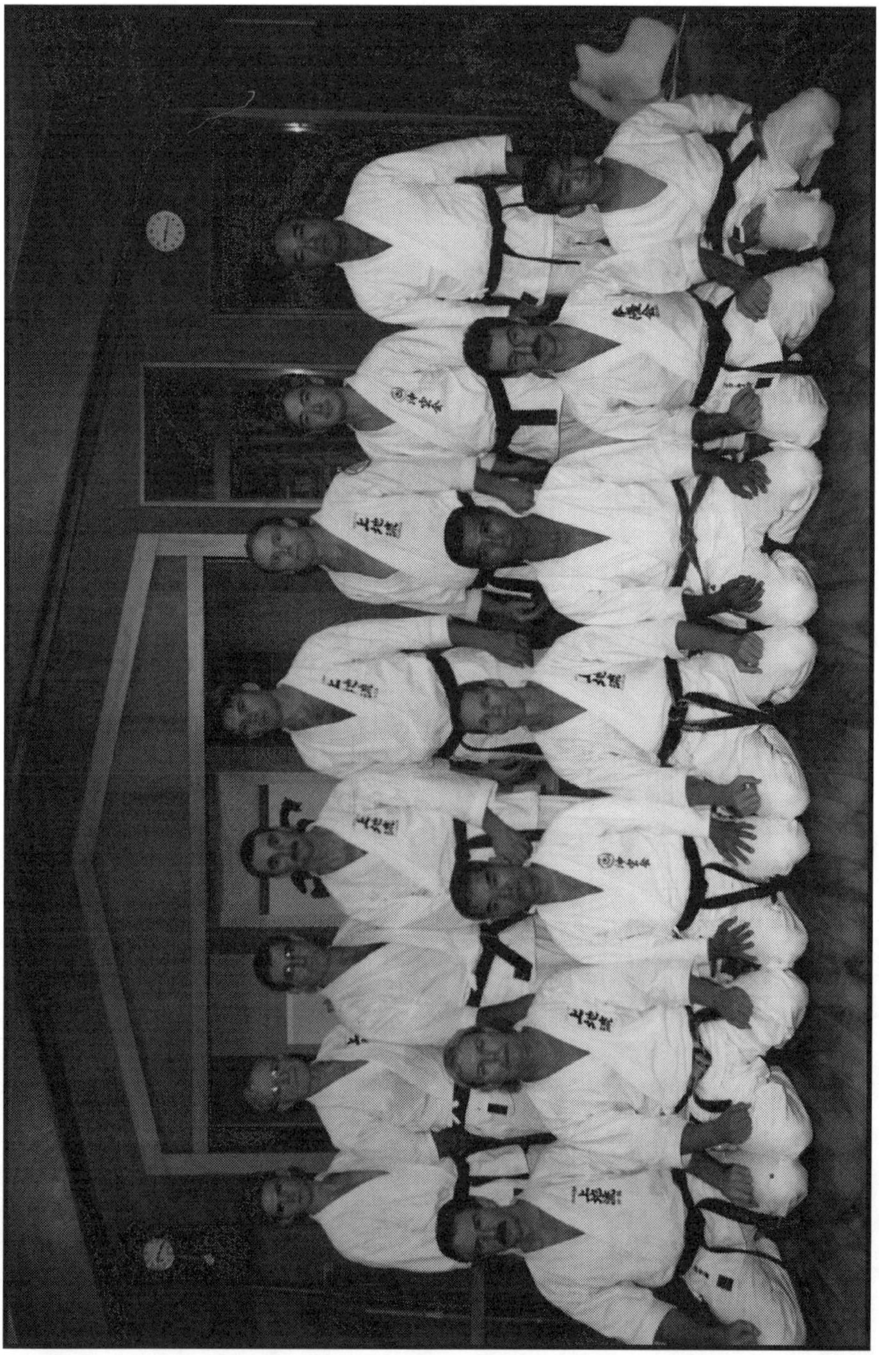

Kitanagusuku Dojo— Sensei Nakamatsu

Kadena Dojo— Sensei Shinjo

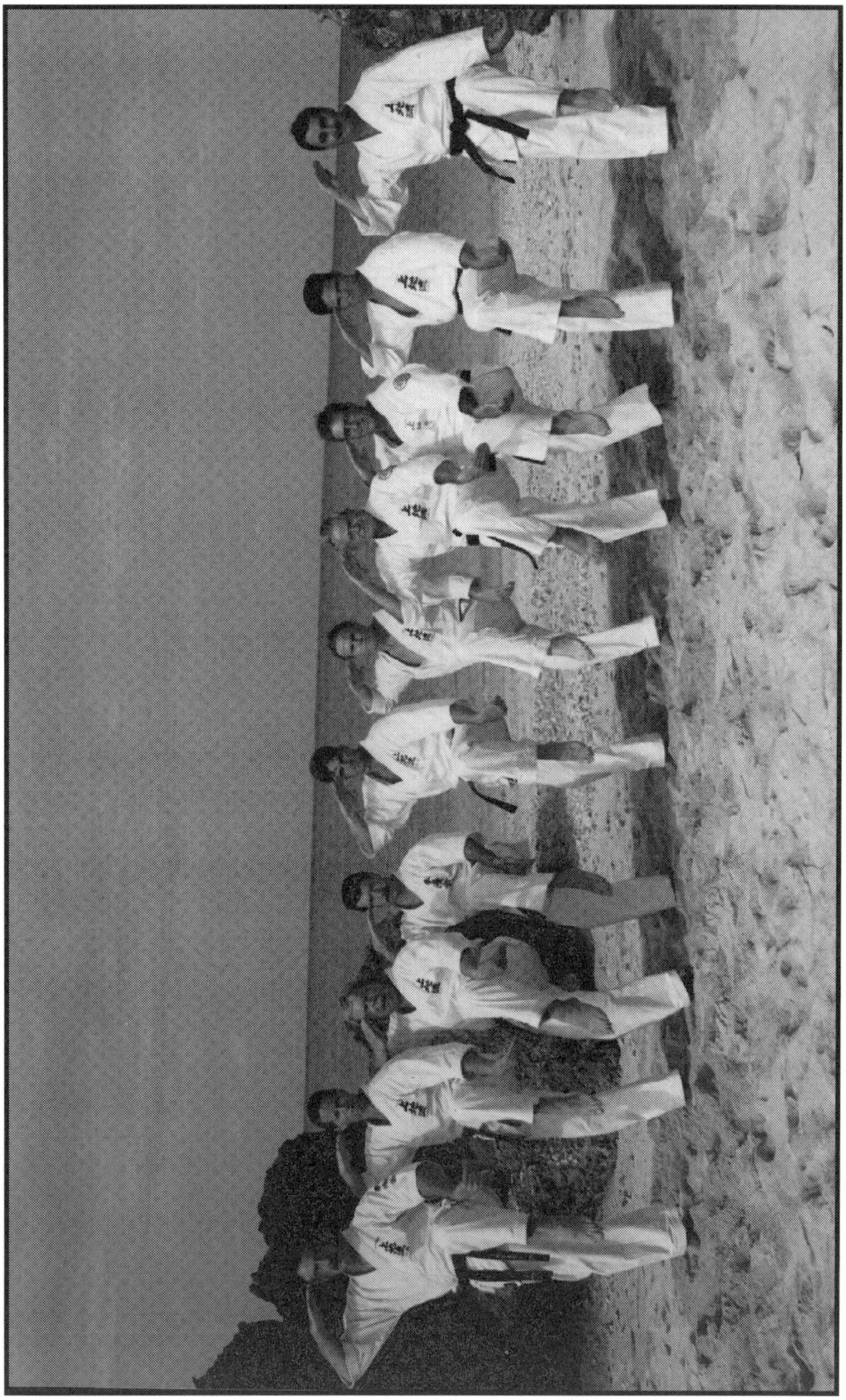

mr. Nigel Mansell

Rick Martin wins the Okinawan Karate World Championship, December 1994

The Zakimi Dojo of Master Seiko Toyama

Achieving 180° stretch for the first time, at forty-five years old, December 1995

UECHI RYU KARATE DO
KOSHUKAI TRAINING
1992

UECHI RYU KARATE DO
KOSHUKAI TRAINING
1993
OKINAWAN
CHAMPIONSHIP
TOURNAMENT

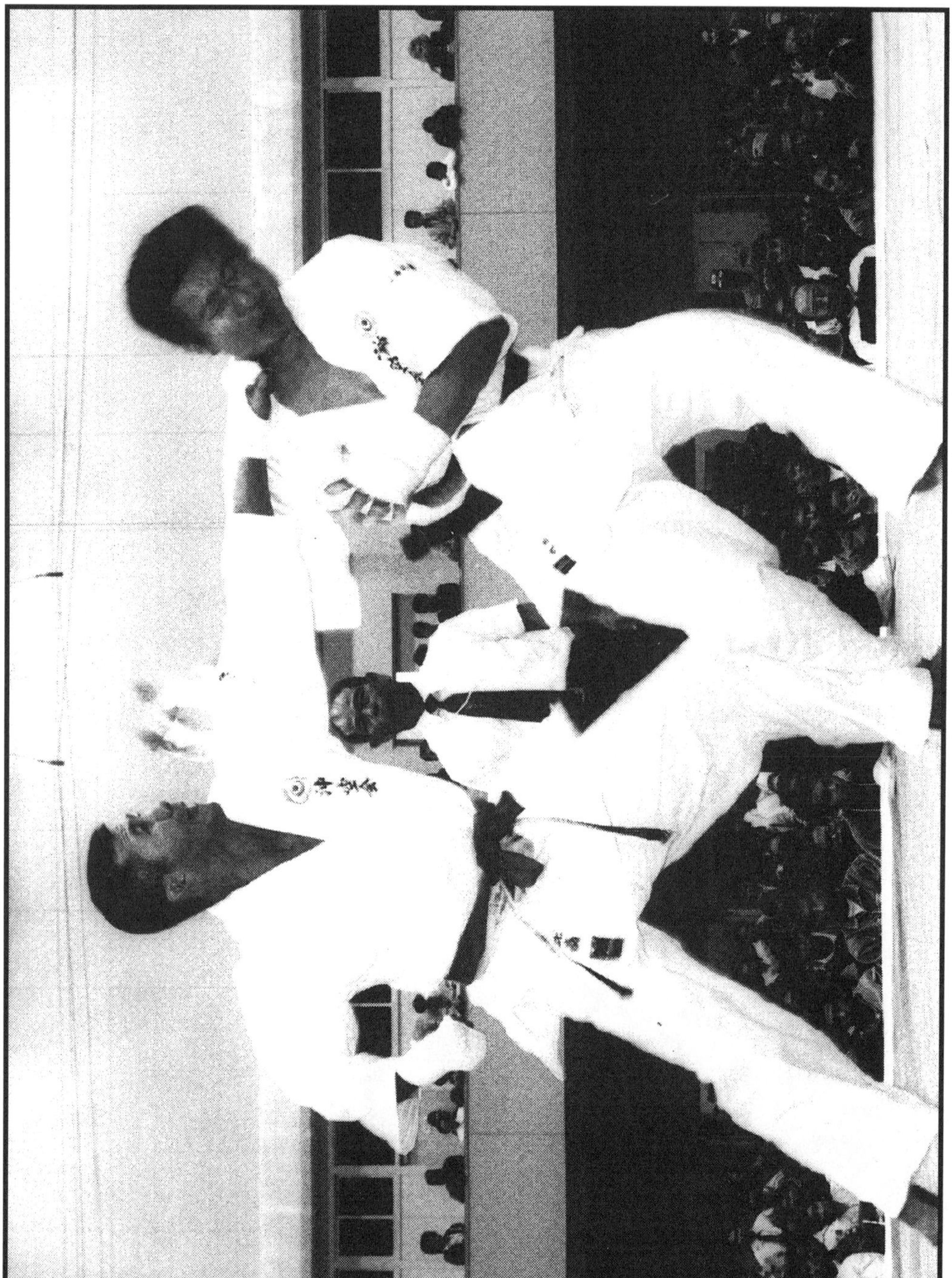

OKINAWAN KARATE
CHAMPIONSHIP TOURNAMENT
SATURDAY JUNE 3RD
LOS MEDANOS COLLEGE GYM
UECHI RYU KARATE DO
KOSHUKAI TRAINING

APPENDIX

Index

A

AB Tai 6
Akainko 258
akarenga 69, 287
All Japan Karate Team 98
anji 229, 240, 241
anko 14
Anko Itosu 68
Asato Uechi ryu dojo 93, 126
ashi kitae 275
ate 328
awamori 64

B

bashamuchya 182
bashofu 258
Big Tsunami 180
bingata 258
Bodhidharma 5
bojutsu 55
boseki 69
boshiken gamae 415
boshiken hasamu uchi 399, 400
boshiken tsuki age 400
bu 238
bubishi 25, 26, 273
bunkai 10, 14, 437
bushido 56
Butokuden 17

C

chi 7
chikara 25
chikate mani 10
Ch'ing dynasty 58
Chino no kenma 78, 93
chishi 279
Chojun Miyagi 68
choku dachi 387
Chou Tsu Ho or
    Chu Chi Wo 59, 61
ch'uan 5
chuan fa 58
chudan 309
chudan nukite 401
chudan shoken zuki 401
chudan tsuki 436
Chuko no hongi 78

D

Dai ni Seisan 96, 433
Dai Nippon Butoku Kai 26
Do 39
Doin 6, 7
Doinjutsu 6, 439
dojo 71
Dokyo 7

E

eisa 259
Eishun Ken 61

F

fudo dachi 387
Fukein Shoalin Temple 61
furi hiji zuki 398, 401
Futenma dojo 93

G

Gaiko 439
garmae 389
gedan 309, 357
gedan barai uke 415
gi 43, 96
gijin 71
ginza 160
go 379
Godan 44
goho 439
goju 26
Goju ryu 18
Gokenki 65, 67
Gosatu Bokuto 155

Grand Master 44
gyo 379

H

Hagakure 56
Hague 6
Haihan Chiken 250
hajki uke hiraken tsuki 436
han 249
han ten 393
Hanshi 44
hara-kiri 232
harai sukui uke 415
hasamu taoshi 415
Hei jo shin 3
Heiko dachi 387
hidari gomon. 247
Higaonna te 25
hiji tsuki 436
Himomaru Sangyo Kabushki Kaisha 69, 120
hirai sukui uke 401
hirate gamae 304, 398
hirate mawashi uke 400
hirate osae 321
hirate sukui uke 415
Hisaguwa Seizen 120
History of Chuzan 229, 231
Hito no michi 3
hiza ate 400
hiza ate uke 415
Hogen 10
hojoundo 436
Hokushin Jihen 59
hono odori 4

I

Ie-jima Island 67
ikyoryo 72, 124, 282, 377
Irekan 164
Isshin ryu 20

J

jiyu kumite 438
jodan 357
juho 439
jujutsu 39
jumbiundo 436
jutsu 39

K

kakushiken 65
kamekou baka 262
kami 278
kamikaze 124
kan-sen 247
Kanchin 96
kanji 10
Kanko ryu 26
Kanmei 79
Kanpo Yaku 64
Kansai (Osaka and Kobe), Japan. 68, 87
Kanshabo 432
Kanshabu 96
Kanshiwa 96
Kanshu 96
Kantoku and Tsuru Uechi 52
Kanzatobaru (Naha) dojo 91
kara 9
karate 38, 41, 75
Karate ni sente nashi 3
kasuri 258
kata 10, 39
Kempo 9 ,58
ken 249, 328
Ken Nakamatsu 100
kendo 18
Kenjinkai 69
kenpo 9
Kenritsu Butokukan 45
Kenyukai 107, 154
kiba dachi 398
Kigusuri 64
kihan 379
kiko 439
Kikoho 6

Kingai 25
Ko-kyu ho 396
kobayashi 17
kohai 77
Koho (Kogyo) Kojo 58
koho oshiro yori ashi 415
koken 65, 400
koku 231
Kokutae 133
Kokutae Dori 87
Kosuke Yonamine 100
kote kitae 160, 274
Koy no ship uchi 437
Koza dojo 100
Kugusku school 58
Kume Mura 44, 237
kumite 10, 39
kun 14
kung fu 5, 58
Kuroshio 227
Kuzushi 321
Kygyo ryu 58
Kyoshi 44
kyu tsuke 387
Kyushi 44
kyusho 332

L

Lao Tse 7
Liu Liu Kung 24

M

makiwara 38, 282
Mao Tse-tung 58
Matsubayshi 19
mawashi tsuki 436
Meiji 248
Meiji Era 44
Meisei Juku dojo 75
Menkyo Kaiden 62
Migushiku dojo 160
Miyako jofu 258
Miyamae Shogoko 123
monchu 262
morote boshiken tsuki age 400
morote boshiken zuki 394
morote gedan nuki 400
morote hajiki uke 415
morote Sanchin nukite 393
morote shoken kamae 400
muchi tengwa 414

N

Naha dojo 160
Naha te 9
Naiko 439
Nanko Tanrenho 439
Nansei no cho (Nansoe) 64
nekko dachi 433
Nihon Tetsudo Koyogyo 93
Nodake dojo 91
nuki 339
nukite 61, 65

O

Okikukai 108
Okinawa 231
Okinawa, History Of An Island People: 252
Oroku dojo 91
Osaka dojo 79
otosu hiji 338

P

Pangainoon chuan fa 32
Pangainoon Kempo Sho 64
Pangainoon Ryu Karate-jutsu Kenkyu-jo 33, 75
Pangainoon Ryu Kiyokai 101
paranku 259
prefecture 5, 51, 250

R

Renko 439
Renshi 44
Ri 379
Risen Gyogo 379
Rokudan 44
rokushakubo 396

Ru Ru Ko 24
ryu 440
Ryu Ryu Ko 24
Ryukyu 25
Ryukyu Islands 4
Ryukyu Jueneki 57
Ryukyu Tode Kenkyukai 25
Ryusen Tomoyose 87
Ryuyu Tomoyose 70

S

San Shi Liu 414
Sanchin dachi 400
Sanchin nukite 400
Sandairyu 67, 414
Sandee 73
sanju roku sei 237
Sanseiryu 67
sappu 321
sataya 266
Sayako Shinjo 87
Seichin 98
seiken tsuki 436
Seirui 96
Seisan 66
sekko-sen 247
seme te 437
sempei 77
Sen 379
seppuku 232
Shaolin Chuan fa 5
Shataku 71
Shataku dojo 120
shi sei 388
Shi-Go-Ki. 383
shime 397
Shinpa 18, 77
Shinsenjutsu 7
Shisan 398
shisha 261
Shito ryu 18
Sho En 240
Sho Hashi 238, 239
Sho Shi 238
Sho Shin 240, 241
Sho Taku, 240
Shobayashi 20
Shodan 44
Shohei ryu 108
shoken gedan zuki 400
shoken kosa no kamae 415
shoken sukui age uke 415
shomen geri 436
shomen hajiki 437
shomen nukite 437
shomen sokusen geri 400
shorin 17
Shotokan 18
Shoto 18
Shu 340
Shubu no seishin 78
Shuhabu 59
Shuri te 9, 38
Shusan Shaolin Temple 58
Shushiwa 59, 61
shuto 436
Soke Shubukan 98
sokutei 354
sokuto geri 436
Sosei Osho 61
Southern Shaolin Ken 61
sue goshi dachi 398, 401
suigetsu 336
Suparimpe 67
suri ashi 392

T

tai gitae 160, 273
Tai-gatame 396
Takinto 52
tan 281
tanden 388
Taoism 7
Taro Toguchi 53
tate hiji 400
tate hiji zuki 398
tate uchi 437
Tatsujin 152

te 4, 38
tenshin 393
tenshin kosoku geri 436
tenshin shoken tsuki 436
tenshin zensoku geri 436
tetsui 400
The Ryukyu Jueneki 8
ti or te 4
To 340
tode 9, 41, 75
toki 258
Tokusaburo Matsuda 57
Tomari te 34
Tonoho 6, 7, 439
Toona 24
tora 440
Toshiko 91
Toshiyuki Itokazu 99
tsuki 328
tsuru 440
tsuru dachi 398
tsuru no kamae 401

U

Uchi 328
Uechi gusuri 64
Uechi ryu 9, 38, 91
Uechi Ryu Karate Kenyukai Association 109
Uechi Ryu Karate-do Kiyokai 100
uke 436
uke te 437
ukwanshin udui 260
ura 436
uraken 401

W

Wabodan 69
Wado ryu 18
Wakayama Kogyo 123
wako 244
wamori 258
wari uke 400
watari uke 415
wauke 394
Wu Hsien Kuei 65

Y

yaku-so 258
yakusoku kumite dai ichi 438
yakusoku kumite dai ni 438
yakuza 379
yambara 233
yen 231
Yojojutsu 439
yoko uchi 437
Yomitan Uechi ryu dojo 169
yori ashi 401
yori ashi kotai 415
Yoshikawa 67

Z

Zakimi dojo 175
zan 232
Zen Nihon Karate-do Renmei. 99
Zen Okinawa Karate Championships 101
Zen Okinawa Karate Renmei 17, 44, 100
zenkutsu dachi 398, 400
zenshin yori ashi 399

PUBLICATIONS CONSULTED

Alexander, George W. *Okinawa: Island of Karate.* Lakeworth, Florida: Yamazato Publications, 1991.

Bishop, Mark. *Okinawan Karate: Teachers, Styles and Secret Techniques.* London: A & C Black (Publishers) Limited, 1989.

Demura, Fumio. *NUNCHAKU, Karate Weapon of Self-Defense.* Burbank, California: Ohara Publications, Inc., 1971.

Demura, Fumio, and Dan Ivan. *Advanced Nunchaku.* Burbank, California: Ohara Publications, Inc., 1976.

Demura, Fumio. *BO, Karate Weapon of Self-Defense.* Burbank, California: Ohara Publications, Inc., 1976.

Demura, Fumio. *TONFA, Karate Weapon of Self-Defense.* Burbank, California: Ohara Publications, Inc., 1982.

Demura, Fumio. *KAMA, Karate Weapon of Self-Defense.* Burbank, California: Ohara Publications, Inc., 1984.

Draeger, Donn F., and Robert W. Smith. *Comprehensive Asian Fighting Arts.* Tokyo, Japan:

Kodansha International Ltd., 1969.

Feifer, George. *Tennozan.* Ticknor & Fields, New York, 1992.

Funakoshi, Gichin. *Karate-Do, My Way of Life.* Japan: Kodansha International, 1975.

Griffith, Samuel B. *Sun Tzu, The Art of War.* Oxford University Press, 1963.

Inoue, Motokatsu. *Kama, Tekko, Tinbe and Surujin: Ancient Martial Arts of the Ryukyu Islands.* Tokyo, Japan: Seitohsha Co., Ltd., 1987.

Inoue, Motokatsu. *Bo, Sai, Tonfa and Nanchaku: Ancient Martial Arts of the Ryukyu Islands.* Tokyo, Japan: Seitohsha Co., Ltd., 1987.

McCarthy, Patrick. (translation and analysis). *The Bubishi: An Analytical Journey.*

Japan: Internation Ryukyu Karate Research Society, 1990.

Mills, Jon The Historic, *Cultural and Social Phenomenon of Okinawan Karate,* Cornell University Masters Thesis, 1985.

Nagamine, Shoshin. *The Essence of Okinawan Karate Do (Shorin-ryu).* Rutland, Vermont and Tokyo, Japan: Charles E. Tuttle Co., Inc., 1976.

Nakamatsu, Ken; baru, Keiko; Takamiyagi, Shigeru *Uechi Ryu Karate Do,* 1975.

Nakayama, Masatoshi. *Dynamic Karate.* Japan: Kodansha International, Ltd., 1966.

Reid, Howard, and Michael Croucher. *The Way of the Warrior: The Paradox of the Martial Arts.* New York: The Overlook Press, 1991.

Silvan, Jim. *Okinawan Karate: Its Teachers and Their Styles.* New York: Vantage Press Inc., 1993.

Photographs and illustrations were provided by:

Uechi Ryu Karate Do, Okinawa, 1975

Pages: 8, 11, 18, 41, 57, 65, 68, 70, 73, 74, 78, 79, 80, 82 bottom, 84, 90, 91, 92, 94, 96, 97, 98, 99, 107, 109, 111 bottom right, 124, 126, 129, 130, 193, 194 bottom, 207, 271, 272, 273 right, 277, 280 bottom left, 298, 299, 300, 325, 326, 350, 351, 352, 363, 379, 380, 434

Sieyu Shinjo and Kiyohide Shinjo, Kadena, Okinawa

Pages: 42, 48, 49, 50, 60, 85, 93, 95, 106, 111 top, 116, 117, 118, 123, 127, 128, 132, 134, 138, 139, 141, 142, 143, 144, 151, 158, 161, 165, 166, 167, 168, 186, 230, 270, 287 bottom left, 288 bottom, 324, 339, 367, 376, 447,

Nigel Mansell/John Townsend, Essex, England

Pages: 500, 502, 503, 504, 505, 506, 507

Alice Dollar, Antioch, California

Pages: 6, 13, 15, 19, 23, 31, 35, 243

Official photographer for the All Okinawa Karate Championship Tournament Series, Okinawa City, Okinawa

Pages: 111 bottom left, 112 top right, 347 bottom left, 494, 495, 496, 497, 501, 512

Okinawan Karate and Kobudo Graph, Okinawa Prefectural

Board of Education, 1995

Pages: 35 bottom, 40, 180, 234, 28 bottom left

National Archives, Pages: 253, 254 top

Don Barros, Pittsburg, California, Pages: 510, 522, 513

Norm Hagood, Tampa, Florida, Pages: 294,492

Kat Wade, Antioch, California, Page: 174

Bob Davidson, Antioch, California, Page: 2

Neil Dunnigan, Edmonton, Canada, Page: 486

Kenzo Nakasone, Naha, Okinawa, Back cover

Calligraphy provided by Michio Shinjo

All other photographs were taken by Alan Dollar

I would like to thank Shihan Peter Kellogg, the shima American, for the cultural education he has given me over the years. Sempi Kellogg has lived in Okinawa and trained in the Kadena Uechi ryu Dojo for twenty-two years.

Domo Arigato Goziamashita

Alan Dollar

To order this publication or to receive information about:

The world-wide Uechi Ryu Karate Kenyukai Association

Training and accommodations at the Antioch California Kenyukai Shubukan

Alan Dollar's Uechi Ryu Karate Training Video Series

Karate Seminars or Lectures

Future Publications

contact

Cherokee Communications

1001 Fitzuren Road

Antioch California

94509

(510) 778-4400

Fax (510)778-4468

email:

CherokeeCo @aol.com